Reflections of the West

A Cookbook

CREDITS

Hank Creekmore, Artist, Front Cover & Other Drawings
Lana Entsminger and Pam Shelton, Artists

This cookbook is a collection of our favorite recipes,
which are not necessarily original recipes.

Published by: Favorite Recipes® Press
P. O. Box 305142
Nashville, Tennessee 37230

Library of Congress Number: 91-34799
ISBN: 0-87197-318-9

Printed in the United States of America
First Printing: 1991   20,000 copies

SKYLINE CHAPTER TELEPHONE PIONEERS

The Telephone Pioneers of America is the largest volunteer association in the United States and in Canada. The Pioneers was established in 1911 by men and women who were dedicated pioneers of the telephone industry.

The Pioneer Triangle was adopted in 1911; its three sides are intended to symbolize the three principle objectives of the Telephone Pioneers: **Fellowship, Loyalty and Service.**

The base of the triangle stands for **Fellowship**, the reason for founding the Pioneer organization and the foundation stone on which Loyalty and Service rest.

Loyalty, represented by the left side of the triangle, marks the relationship of telephone people to each other as well as to the industry they serve. It is the link between Fellowship and Service.

Service, is the natural outgrowth of Fellowship and Loyalty and is signified by the right of the Triangle. Through Service, Pioneering contributes to the well-being and happiness of those it reaches within the organization, the industry and the community.

The motto of Fellowship, Loyalty, and Service, and the triangle design by which it is symbolized express the lasting companionship of those who have spent an important part of their lives as co-workers and friends, their allegiance to work and associates, and the ideal of ever-increasing usefulness.

On November 14, 1963 a Steering committee met to organize plans to formulate a new Telephone Pioneer Chapter. An application was drafted to create a chapter which would encompass a three state geographical area and include three existing councils of the Fredrick H. Reid Chapter, namely: Sawtooth Council (Idaho), Treasure State Council (Montana) and George Y. Wallace Council (Utah). The application was approved on February 25, 1964. The Chapter name "Skyline" was officially approved by chapter members during the first annual assembly held in Salt Lake City, Utah, June 1964. The Chapter reorganized in 1990 and now has 13 working councils and 8 clubs.

The Telephone Pioneers come together to "Answer the Call of Those in Need" and to "Improve the Quality of Life in our Communities."

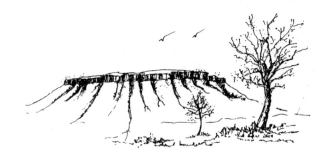

TELEPHONE PIONEER
MUSEUM AT LAGOON

In August of 1988 the Lagoon Corporation, which operates a large amusement park in Northern Utah, contacted the Telephone Pioneers and offered to provide space for a telephone museum in their Pioneer Village.

Until then the only telephone museums in Skyline Chapter area were located inside telephone company buildings where the public had very limited access. A special piece of America's history was restricted to telephone employees and retirees plus a few special groups, who made special arrangements to tour the museum. Fewer than one hundred people visited our museums during an average month. The Telephone Pioneers were pleased to have the opportunity to provide a museum where more people would see and enjoy the history of the telephone industry each year.

The Bonneville Council of the Telephone Pioneers began negotiation with officers of the Lagoon Amusement Park, in Farmington, Utah, to arrange for space to build a new Telephone Museum where it would be easily accessible to the public. Lagoon agreed to provide space in the Lagoon Pioneer Village as a location.

The Pioneer Village is an annex of the Lagoon Amusement Park which was created to preserve some of the history of the old west. The village houses reproduction of a nineteenth century town with preserved historic structures including log cabins, a one room school house and an old railroad station. Displays in the village include replicas of old homes, stores, and offices. The Telephone Museum was placed in a lovely old carriage house which once belonged to a former Utah governor. The Village also houses other museums including farming, mining, railroading, guns and horse drawn carriages. Thousands of school children from Utah and surrounding states visit the village each year.

Since the first transcontinental telephone line from New York to San Francisco was joined at Wendover, Utah in 1914, the history of the telephone is especially important to Utah.

In October, 1988 a committee was formed to organize the museum project. Volunteers were recruited from among the Telephone Pioneer organization, scout troops, youth and community groups. Weekly meetings were held to plan and to coordinate volunteer activities. Volunteer work days were incorporated with group picnics and overnight camp outs. Special outings were planned for older retired Pioneers in order to enlist help in identifying and dating many really old pieces of equipment. Over 2,052 volunteers were involved in the project. They donated 2,942 hours; raising funds, collecting artifacts and old photographs, cleaning and refurbishing equipment and researching telephone history. Most of the telephone antiques collected for the museum were donated by individual Telephone Pioneers and by U S West and AT&T. The value of items donated and purchased for display in the museum is in excess of $100,000.

On June 9, 1990 the Pioneer Village Telephone Museum was open to the public. It is estimated that over one million people will visit the museum during the first year of operation.

Thanks to Telephone Pioneers, an important piece of history is available for current and future generations to share.

CONTRIBUTOR LIST

Shirley Allen
Janel Anderson
Ric Anderson
Ray & Cheri Archibald
Georgene Baer
Ruth Baird
Betty Bartlett
Bertha Bateman
LaRae Bateman
Georgia Beam
Ellenor Berntson
EvaLue Bowen
Marsha Breen
Arline Brown
Marna C. Buffo
Alpha Burckardt
Karen D. Burk
Dorris Calton
Evelyn Cameron
Mary Lou Carlson
Florence L. Chamberlain
Bette Christensen
Doris Christensen
Marie Clark
Ann Coulam
Irene Crane
Hank Creekmore, Artist
Joy Cummings
Evelyn R. Damschen
Ruth Davis
Dixie Dennis
Wyn K. Doney
Marian Downs
Debbie Dudgeon
Jean Edwards
Lana Entsminger, Artist
Dorothy Ewer
Karren Fairbanks
Bernice Farner
Donna Farnes
Gary L. Ferrin
Elaine Fielding
June M. Fischer

Olga Fisher
Jean Ford
Judy Frazer
Gary & Ann Freeman
Chuck Friederich
Leona P. Geary
Karen Gee
Anna Godfrey
Gordon Goodwin
Ethel R. Grigg
Michelle Groothof
Donna Hager
Dena E. Hale
Florence Hall
Barbara Hamilton
Martha Hamilton
Joyce Harmon
Marguerite C. Harper
Norma Harrison
Barbara Hayes
Eleanor Helderman
E. Dale Henderson
Patty E. Henderson
Scott Hess
Pat Hess
Marion Hicken
Cathy Holm
Sarah H. Jensen
Hazel M. Johnson
Merla Jorgensen
Jan Keif
Irene Stewart Kemph
Jody Kenny
Sandy Kiser
Rose Kriegen
Enid Larsen
Hulda Larsen
Jeanne Larson
Linda Lay
Phyllis Lee
Virginia Lee
Kitty Lightfoot
Jan Lincoln

Lucille Linford
Darlene Loveall
Ruth Lovell
Waneta Lowman
Betty L. Mann
Deloris Marking
Jo Martin
Andree Maurice
Boots McMillan
Luella Merriman
Bob Millons
Mardi Millons
Ann Morrell
Corinne G. Morrison
Mary H. Morrison
Sherry Mosher
Shirley Moss
John & Louise Musgrave
Thelma A. Newbry
Nancy Nielsen
Emil & Doris Nygard
Linda P. Olsen
Marilyn Olsen
Mary Maureen Ozburn
Betty Raye Partridge
Helen Pearson
LuDean Pehrson
Louise Petersen
Dorothy Peterson
Ila Mae Peterson
Gary Pettinger
Sherlee A. Polglase
Becky Powell
Marilyn R. Privrasky
Patsy A. Randolph
Olna C. Rantz
Ione Raymond
Hope Reiste
Madeline Remmel
Annette Rich
Bobbi Rintala

Colleen Rogan
N. Leone Rogers
Terri Rogers
Sarah J. Schueler
Jackie Seamons
Pam Shelton, Artist
Peggy Shepherd
Selma Simper
Karla K. Slusser
Nancy Snow
Joy Staples
Susan Stemple
Gina Stinchfield
Robert L. Stommel
Mehl Ree Strate
Lyla L. Stuart
Erna Lou Sudbrock
Imogene Sweeney
Barbara Swenson
RaNee Taggart
Marjorie Thomas
Vi Thomson
Noreen Udall
Jan Velvick
Laurel A. Wadley
Angela Wagner
Marilyn Wagner
Carla Wallace
Carrol J. Walton
Cindy Warren
Marjorie Weeks
Arloa Weiss
Darla Wheeler
Ilene Wilson
Shirley Winn
Rita Winterberger
Doris Wolfe
Leona E. Wolfe
Nella A. Wollan
Barbara Woodward
Maxine Worsencroft

TABLE OF CONTENTS

NUTRITIONAL GUIDELINES

The editors have attempted to present these family recipes in a form that allows approximate nutritional values to be computed. Persons with dietary or health problems or whose diets require close monitoring should not rely solely on the nutritional information provided. They should consult their physicians or a registered dietitian for specific information.

Abbreviations for Nutritional Analysis

Cal — Calories	Dietary Fiber — Fiber	Sod — Sodium
Prot — Protein	T Fat — Total Fat	gr — gram
Carbo — Carbohydrates	Chol — Cholesterol	mg — milligrams

Nutritional information for these recipes is computed from information derived from many sources, including materials supplied by the United States Department of Agriculture, computer databanks and journals in which the information is assumed to be in the public domain. However, many specialty items, new products and processed foods may not be available from these sources or may vary from the average values used in these analyses. More information on new and/or specific products may be obtained by reading the nutrient labels. Unless otherwise specified, the nutritional analysis of these recipes is based on all measurements being level.

- **Artificial sweeteners** vary in use and strength so should be used "to taste," using the recipe ingredients as a guideline.
- **Artificial sweeteners** using aspartame (NutraSweet and Equal) should not be used as a sweetener in recipes involving prolonged heating which reduces the sweet taste. For further information on the use of these sweeteners, refer to package information.
- **Alcoholic ingredients** have been analyzed for the basic ingredients, although cooking causes the evaporation of alcohol thus decreasing caloric content.
- **Buttermilk, sour cream** and **yogurt** are the types available commercially.
- **Cake mixes** which are prepared using package directions include 3 eggs and ½ cup oil.
- **Chicken,** cooked for boning and chopping, has been roasted; this method yields the lowest caloric values.
- **Cottage cheese** is cream-style with 4.2% creaming mixture. Dry-curd cottage cheese has no creaming mixture.
- **Eggs** are all large.
- **Flour** is unsifted all-purpose flour.
- **Garnishes,** serving suggestions and other optional additions and variations are not included in the analysis.
- **Margarine** and **butter** are regular, not whipped or presoftened.
- **Milk** is whole milk, 3.5% butterfat. Lowfat milk is 1% butterfat. Evaporated milk is whole milk with 60% of the water removed.
- **Oil** is any type of vegetable cooking oil. Shortening is hydrogenated vegetable shortening.
- **Salt** and other ingredients to taste as noted in the ingredients have not been included in the nutritional analysis.
- If a choice of ingredients has been given, the nutritional analysis reflects the first option.

The Watering Hole

Beverages & Snacks

'89 H. Creekmore

BIG SKY COUNCIL

Great Falls, Montana

The Council is most proud to have developed a Clown Board for the Montana State School for the Deaf and Blind. Brightly painted clown faces invite the children to play with buttons, buzzers, lights, bells and telephones, with built-in rewards for correctly operating the buttons. The telephones also help develop conversational skills and encourage interchange between children and between the teachers and students.

The Council also participates in making and distributing Hug-A-Bears for small children who suffer trauma, loss or abuse; works in the local community to provide care packages of personal hygiene articles for the Mercy Home, serving mothers and children who flee from their homes without personal articles; tends trees and flowers in the Great Falls area; and helps the National Park Service to clear a trail in Glacier National Park for public access to St. Mary's Lake.

HOT CRANBERRY PUNCH

2 cups cranberry juice
2½ cups unsweetened
  pineapple juice
½ cup water

⅓ cup packed brown sugar
2 teaspoons allspice
2 cinnamon sticks
2 teaspoons whole cloves

Combine cranberry juice, pineapple juice and water in 10- to 12-cup percolator. Place brown sugar, allspice, cinnamon sticks and cloves in filter in percolator basket. Perk using manufacturer's instructions. Yield: 6 servings.

Approx Per Serving: Cal 154; T Fat <1 g; 1% Calories from Fat;
  Prot <1 g; Carbo 39 g; Fiber 1 g; Chol 0 mg; Sod 9 mg.

Sandy Kiser, Twin Falls, Idaho

RUSSIAN TEA

2 cups orange-flavored
  breakfast drink mix
¼ cup instant tea
1 cup sugar

1 envelope lemonade mix
2 teaspoons cinnamon
1 teaspoon cloves

Combine all ingredients in bowl; mix well. Store in airtight container. Stir 1 tablespoon mixture per serving into 1 cup hot water. Yield: 55 servings.

Approx Per Serving: Cal 36; T Fat <1 g; 0% Calories from Fat;
  Prot <1 g; Carbo 9 g; Fiber <1 g; Chol 0 mg; Sod 3 mg.

Martha Hamilton, Meridian, Idaho

WASSAIL

1 bottle of brandy
6 8-ounce bottles of lemon-
  lime soda
1 46-ounce can orange drink

1 gallon apple cider
8 cups cranberry juice
1 package cinnamon sticks

Combine all ingredients in large saucepan. Bring to a boil. Simmer until flavors are blended. Garnish with 3 orange slices. Yield: 36 servings.

Approx Per Serving: Cal 161; T Fat <1 g; 1% Calories from Fat;
  Prot <1 g; Carbo 36 g; Fiber <1 g; Chol 0 mg; Sod 13 mg.

Sandy Kiser, Twin Falls, Idaho

BROWN COW SODA

4 teaspoons chocolate sauce
2 scoops vanilla ice cream

¼ cup cold milk
1 cup (about) chilled root beer

Spoon chocolate sauce into tall chilled glass. Add ice cream. Pour in milk. Add enough root beer to finish filling glass. Yield: 1 serving.

Approx Per Serving: Cal 464; T Fat 17 g; 31% Calories from Fat; Prot 8 g; Carbo 75 g; Fiber 1 g; Chol 67 mg; Sod 195 mg.

Sherlee A. Polglase, Great Falls, Montana

FRUIT DRINK

2 8-ounce cans frozen orange juice concentrate, thawed
2 8-ounce cans frozen lemonade concentrate, thawed
1 46-ounce can pineapple juice

4 cups sugar
6 cups water
6 bananas, mashed
2 2-liter bottles of lemon-lime soda

Combine orange juice concentrate, lemonade concentrate, pineapple juice, sugar and water in large pitcher. Add bananas; mix well. Pour into freezer container. Freeze until firm. Remove from freezer. Let stand for 30 to 60 minutes. Place in punch bowl. Mash until slushy. Add lemon-lime soda. Yield: 30 servings.

Approx Per Serving: Cal 225; T Fat <1 g; 1% Calories from Fat; Prot 1 g; Carbo 57 g; Fiber 1 g; Chol 0 mg; Sod 9 mg.

Marna C. Buffo, Provo, Utah

COLLEGE MOCKTAIL

2 quarts pineapple juice
2 quarts apple juice
2 quarts orange juice

1 quart ginger ale
½ gallon orange sherbet

Combine all ingredients in punch bowl; mix well. Garnish with strawberries. Yield: 36 servings.

Approx Per Serving: Cal 152; T Fat 1 g; 7% Calories from Fat; Prot 1 g; Carbo 35 g; Fiber <1 g; Chol 4 mg; Sod 28 mg.

Nancy Nielsen, Hyrum, Utah

PIÑA COLADA

4 ounces master mix for piña
  coladas
1/2 teaspoon cream of coconut
1/2 teaspoon coconut snow

1 ounce pineapple juice
1¼ ounces white rum
  (optional)

Process crushed ice in blender until the consistency of snow. Add master mix, cream of coconut, coconut snow, pineapple juice and rum. Process until well blended. Yield: 1 serving.

Approx Per Serving: Cal 322; T Fat 21 g; 58% Calories from Fat;
  Prot 3 g; Carbo 14 g; Fiber <1 g; Chol 0 mg; Sod 58 mg.

Luella Merriman, Great Falls, Montana

HOLIDAY PUNCH

2 envelopes cherry drink mix
1 envelope unsweetened
  orange drink mix
1 envelope unsweetened
  raspberry drink mix
4 cups sugar

4 quarts water
1 12-ounce can frozen
  orange juice concentrate,
  thawed
1/2 gallon raspberry sherbet
2 quarts ginger ale

Combine cherry drink mix, orange drink mix and raspberry drink mix in large container. Add sugar, water and orange juice concentrate; mix well. Stir in sherbet. Add ginger ale just before serving. Yield: 25 servings.

Approx Per Serving: Cal 265; T Fat 1 g; 2% Calories from Fat;
  Prot 1 g; Carbo 66 g; Fiber <1 g; Chol 2 mg; Sod 25 mg.

Enid Larsen, Logan, Utah

WELLNESS DRINK

This is a great drink when you're not feeling well.

2 teaspoons honey
1 cup water

2 teaspoons apple cider
  vinegar

Combine all ingredients in glass; mix well. Yield: 1 serving.

Approx Per Serving: Cal 44; T Fat 0 g; 0% Calories from Fat;
  Prot <1 g; Carbo 12 g; Fiber 0 g; Chol 0 mg; Sod 1 mg.

Donna Hager, Billings, Montana

BRANDY SLUSH

2 cups water
2 cups sugar
4 black tea bags
7 cups water
1 12-ounce can frozen
   orange juice concentrate,
   thawed

1 12-ounce can frozen
   lemonade concentrate,
   thawed
3 cups brandy
1 2-liter bottle of lemon-
   lime soda

Bring 2 cups water, sugar and tea bags to a boil in saucepan. Let stand until cool. Remove tea bags. Combine tea with 7 cups water, concentrates and brandy in freezer container. Freeze until firm. Fill chilled glasses 2/3 full with slush. Add enough lemon-lime soda to fill glasses. Yield: 15 servings.

Approx Per Serving: Cal 341; T Fat <1 g; 0% Calories from Fat; Prot 1 g; Carbo 76 g; Fiber <1 g; Chol 0 mg; Sod 18 mg. Nutritional information includes entire amount of lemon-lime soda.

Lyla L. Stuart, Helena, Montana

SLUSH

8 cups water
2 cups sugar
3 bananas
1 12-ounce can frozen
   orange juice concentrate,
   thawed

1/2 cup lemon juice
1 48-ounce can pineapple
   juice
1 quart vodka or gin
1 2-liter bottle of lemon-
   lime soda

Bring water and sugar to a boil in saucepan. Cook until sugar dissolves, stirring frequently. Purée bananas in blender. Combine orange juice concentrate, lemon juice and pineapple juice in large freezer container. Add sugar water and puréed bananas; mix well. Stir in vodka. Freeze overnight. Remove from freezer. Let stand until slushy, stirring frequently. Spoon slush into glasses. Pour a small amount of lemon-lime soda over slush. Yield: 20 servings.

Approx Per Serving: Cal 301; T Fat <1 g; 1% Calories from Fat; Prot 1 g; Carbo 50 g; Fiber 1 g; Chol 0 mg; Sod 13 mg. Nutritional information includes entire amount of lemon-lime soda.

Hope Reiste, Great Falls, Montana

STRAWBERRY DAIQUIRIS

1 16-ounce package frozen sweetened strawberries, thawed
1 12-ounce can frozen pink lemonade concentrate, thawed

2 concentrate cans water
1½ concentrate cans rum
1 2-liter bottle of lemon-lime soda

Combine strawberries, lemonade concentrate, water and rum in freezer container; mix well. Freeze until partially firm; mixture will not freeze solid. Stir in lemon-lime soda just before serving. Yield: 16 servings.

Approx Per Serving: Cal 187; T Fat <1 g; 0% Calories from Fat; Prot <1 g; Carbo 30 g; Fiber 1 g; Chol 0 mg; Sod 15 mg.

Lyla L. Stuart, Helena, Montana

FROZEN STRAWBERRY DAIQUIRIS

1 12-ounce can frozen lemonade concentrate, thawed
1 6-ounce can frozen limeade concentrate, thawed
1 fifth of light rum

2 10-ounce packages frozen strawberries, thawed
1 lemonade concentrate can water
1 2-liter bottle of lemon-lime soda

Combine concentrates, rum, strawberries, water and lemon-lime soda in freezer container; mix well. Freeze until firm. Remove from freezer 1 hour before serving. Yield: 20 servings.

Approx Per Serving: Cal 177; T Fat <1 g; 0% Calories from Fat; Prot <1 g; Carbo 25 g; Fiber 1 g; Chol 0 mg; Sod 12 mg.

Arloa Weiss, Billings, Montana

Drink margaritas! The sugar gives you energy; the lime gives you strength; the tequila gives you an idea on what to do with the energy and strength.

DEVILED EGGS NOËL

This is my original recipe that I invented for a Mountain States Telephone Christmas party.

½ teaspoon dried minced onion
1½ capfuls brandy
6 hard-boiled eggs, peeled
3 tablespoons mayonnaise-type salad dressing

1¼ tablespoons Heinz 57 sauce
½ teaspoon dry mustard
Salt and pepper to taste
Paprika to taste

Reconstitute dried minced onion in brandy in bowl. Slice hard-boiled eggs into halves lengthwise. Remove yolks, reserving egg whites. Beat egg yolks, salad dressing, Heinz 57 sauce, mustard, salt and pepper in mixer bowl until smooth and creamy. Add reconstituted onion; mix well. Spoon egg yolk mixture into egg whites. Sprinkle with paprika. Garnish with parsley sprigs or olive slices. May substitute 1 heaping tablespoon minced onion for dried onion. Yield: 12 servings.

Approx Per Serving: Cal 59; T Fat 4 g; 64% Calories from Fat; Prot 3 g; Carbo 2 g; Fiber <1 g; Chol 107 mg; Sod 61 mg.

Gary Pettinger, Idaho Falls, Idaho

OLIVE-CHEESE SNACKS

¼ cup butter, softened
1 5-ounce jar bacon cheese spread
3 drops of bottled hot pepper sauce

¼ teaspoon Worcestershire sauce
¾ cup sifted flour
30 stuffed green olives

Cream butter and cheese spread in mixer bowl until light and fluffy. Add hot pepper sauce and Worcestershire sauce; mix well. Add flour; mix to form dough. Shape about 1 teaspoon dough around each olive. Place on ungreased baking sheet. Bake at 400 degrees for 12 to 15 minutes or until golden brown. May substitute margarine for butter if desired. Yield: 30 servings.

Approx Per Serving: Cal 44; T Fat 3 g; 66% Calories from Fat; Prot 1 g; Carbo 3 g; Fiber <1 g; Chol 7 mg; Sod 164 mg.

Ruth Lovell, Caldwell, Idaho

CHEESE BALL

16 ounces cream cheese, softened
2 tablespoons sour cream
Garlic salt to taste
2 tablespoons Beau Monde seasoning
1/2 cup chopped green onions
1/2 cup chopped pecans

Beat cream cheese and sour cream in mixer bowl until smooth. Add garlic salt and Beau Monde seasoning; mix well. Chill until firm. Shape into ball using plastic wrap. Roll in green onions and pecans. Yield: 32 servings.

Approx Per Serving: Cal 64; T Fat 6 g; 87% Calories from Fat; Prot 1 g; Carbo 1 g; Fiber <1 g; Chol 16 mg; Sod 43 mg. Nutritional information does not include Beau Monde seasoning.

Nancy Snow, Ogden, Utah

CRAB MEAT MOLD

1 10-ounce can cream of mushroom soup
1 tablespoon unflavored gelatin
3 tablespoons cold water
8 ounces cream cheese, softened
1 7-ounce can crab meat, drained
1 small onion, grated
1 cup chopped celery
1 cup mayonnaise

Heat soup over low heat, stirring frequently. Dissolve gelatin in water. Add with cream cheese to soup. Cook over low heat until cream cheese is melted, stirring frequently. Remove from heat. Add crab meat, onion, celery and mayonnaise; mix well. Spoon into small oiled mold. Chill overnight. Dip bottom of mold in warm water. Invert and unmold onto serving platter. Serve with rye bread or crackers. May serve as a spread in bowl if desired. Yield: 64 servings.

Approx Per Serving: Cal 46; T Fat 4 g; 83% Calories from Fat; Prot 1 g; Carbo 1 g; Fiber <1 g; Chol 9 mg; Sod 78 mg.

Thelma A. Newbry, Pocatello, Idaho

All people smile in the same language.

CRAB MEAT AND CREAM CHEESE BALL

8 ounces cream cheese,
  softened
1/2 small onion, minced
1/4 cup mayonnaise
1 1/2 teaspoons lemon juice
1/2 teaspoon garlic salt

1 1/2 teaspoons
  Worcestershire sauce
1/2 cup chili sauce
6 ounces fresh crab meat,
  shredded

Beat cream cheese, onion, mayonnaise, lemon juice, garlic salt and Worcestershire sauce in bowl. Shape to fit in center of shallow dish. Chill, covered with plastic wrap, overnight. Cover mixture with chili sauce. Cover entire surface with shredded crab meat. Place in center of large platter and surround with assorted crackers. May substitute frozen for fresh crab meat if desired. Yield: 16 servings.

Approx Per Serving: Cal 96; T Fat 8 g; 73% Calories from Fat;
  Prot 4 g; Carbo 3 g; Fiber <1 g; Chol 28 mg; Sod 274 mg.

Andree Maurice, Boise, Idaho

SMOKED SALMON BALL

11 ounces cream cheese,
  softened
2 tablespoons dried onion
  flakes
1 tablespoon lemon juice
1/4 teaspoon prepared
  horseradish

1 tablespoon chopped parsley
1/4 teaspoon garlic powder
1/2 teaspoon liquid smoke
1   7-ounce can salmon,
  drained
1/2 cup chopped parsley
1/2 cup chopped pecans

Beat cream cheese until smooth. Add onion flakes, lemon juice, horseradish, 1 tablespoon parsley, garlic powder and liquid smoke in bowl; mix well. Stir in salmon. Shape into 1 large or 2 small balls. Roll in 1/2 cup parsley and pecans. Yield: 34 servings.

Approx Per Serving: Cal 54; T Fat 5 g; 79% Calories from Fat;
  Prot 2 g; Carbo 1 g; Fiber <1 g; Chol 13 mg; Sod 64 mg.

Thelma A. Newbry, Pocatello, Idaho

BOGNA CALDA

1 cup butter, softened
1/2 cup oil
4 to 8 cloves of garlic, puréed

2 2-ounce cans anchovy
filets, chopped

Combine butter, oil, garlic and anchovy filets in saucepan. Heat over low heat for 10 minutes; do not boil or brown. Serve hot with assorted chilled fresh vegetables such as celery, carrots, cauliflower, green pepper strips and cabbage leaves. Yield: 25 servings.

Approx Per Serving: Cal 111; T Fat 12 g; 95% Calories from Fat;
Prot 1 g; Carbo <1 g; Fiber <1 g; Chol 23 mg; Sod 67 mg.

Marna C. Buffo, Provo, Utah

SOMBRERO DIP

1 1/2 pounds lean ground beef
1 large onion, chopped
Chili powder to taste
Salt to taste
2 16-ounce cans kidney
beans
3 tablespoons chili powder

1/2 cup catsup
2 tablespoons Tabasco sauce
2 cups shredded sharp
Cheddar cheese
2 bunches green onions,
finely chopped
2 cups sliced green olives

Brown ground beef with onion, chili powder to taste and salt in skillet, stirring frequently; drain. Drain 1 can kidney beans. Combined drained beans with remaining undrained beans, 3 tablespoons chili powder, catsup and Tabasco sauce in blender container. Process for 2 to 3 minutes or until well blended. Layer ground beef mixture, bean mixture, Cheddar cheese, green onions and green olives in electric skillet. Cook for 15 to 20 minutes or until heated through. Serve warm with tortilla chips. Yield: 25 servings.

Approx Per Serving: Cal 154; T Fat 10 g; 55% Calories from Fat;
Prot 10 g; Carbo 8 g; Fiber 4 g; Chol 27 mg; Sod 704 mg.

Susan Stemple, Great Falls, Montana

TACO DIP

1 17-ounce can refried beans
1 8-ounce can avocado dip
1 8-ounce can sweet onion
  dip
1 cup sour cream
1 bunch green onions,
  chopped

1 4-ounce can olives,
  chopped
1 4-ounce can green chilies,
  chopped
3 tomatoes, chopped
2 cups shredded Cheddar
  cheese

Layer refried beans, avocado dip, onion dip, sour cream, green onions, olives, green chilies, tomatoes and shredded Cheddar cheese in 9x12-inch dish. Serve with favorite chips. Yield: 50 servings.

Approx Per Serving: Cal 93; T Fat 8 g; 73% Calories from Fat;
  Prot 2 g; Carbo 4 g; Fiber 1 g; Chol 11 mg; Sod 122 mg.

Norma Harrison, St. George, Utah

SEVEN-LAYER MEXICAN TACO DIP

2 cups sour cream
1/2 cup mayonnaise
1 envelope taco seasoning
  mix
3 avocados
Lemon juice to taste
1 17-ounce can refried beans
1 tablespoon lemon juice

1 cup taco sauce
Garlic salt to taste
3 tomatoes, peeled, chopped
1 bunch green onions,
  chopped
1 4-ounce can black olives,
  chopped
1 cup shredded cheese

Combine sour cream, mayonnaise and taco seasoning mix in bowl; mix well. Peel and slice avocados; sprinkle with lemon juice to taste. Spread refried beans on serving plate; sprinkle with 1 tablespoon lemon juice. Spread taco sauce over beans; sprinkle with garlic salt. Layer avocados, sour cream mixture, tomatoes, green onions and black olives over top. Sprinkle with shredded cheese. Yield: 20 servings.

Approx Per Serving: Cal 213; T Fat 17 g; 70% Calories from Fat;
  Prot 5 g; Carbo 12 g; Fiber 6 g; Chol 20 mg; Sod 467 mg.

Sandy Kiser, Twin Falls, Idaho

SPECIAL TACO DIP

1 17-ounce can refried beans
3 cups sour cream
8 ounces cream cheese,
  softened
1 medium avocado, chopped
1 green onion, chopped
Worcestershire sauce to taste

1 cup shredded Cheddar
  cheese
1 medium tomato, chopped
1 medium green bell pepper,
  chopped
1 4-ounce can olives,
  chopped

Line bowl with refried beans. Process sour cream, cream cheese, avocado, green onion and Worcestershire sauce in blender until well mixed. Spread on refried beans. Layer Cheddar cheese, tomato, green pepper and olives over top. Yield: 20 servings.

Approx Per Serving: Cal 190; T Fat 16 g; 74% Calories from Fat;
  Prot 5 g; Carbo 8 g; Fiber 3 g; Chol 34 mg; Sod 234 mg.

Andree Maurice, Boise, Idaho

SPINACH DIP

1 10-ounce package frozen
  chopped spinach, thawed,
  drained
1 8-ounce can water
  chestnuts, drained,
  chopped
Chopped green onions to
  taste

1 envelope vegetable soup
  mix
2 cups sour cream
1 cup mayonnaise
Minced garlic to taste
1 loaf French bread

Combine spinach, water chestnuts, green onions, vegetable soup mix, sour cream, mayonnaise and garlic in bowl; mix well. Chill in refrigerator. Scoop out center of French bread to form shell; cut center into bite-sized pieces. Spoon dip into bread shell. Place on serving platter with bread pieces for dipping. Yield: 20 servings.

Approx Per Serving: Cal 222; T Fat 16 g; 62% Calories from Fat;
  Prot 4 g; Carbo 17 g; Fiber 1 g; Chol 17 mg; Sod 430 mg.

Sandy Kiser, Twin Falls, Idaho

DIP FOR RAW VEGETABLES

1 cup sour cream
1 cup mayonnaise
1/2 cup finely chopped pecans
1 teaspoon prepared
    horseradish

1 1/2 teaspoons grated onion
1 teaspoon dry mustard
1/2 teaspoon Worcestershire
    sauce
1/2 teaspoon lemon pepper

Combine all ingredients in bowl; mix well. Chill for several hours. Serve with assorted fresh vegetables. Yield: 32 servings.

Approx Per Serving: Cal 78; T Fat 8 g; 93% Calories from Fat;
    Prot <1 g; Carbo 1 g; Fiber <1 g; Chol 7 mg; Sod 44 mg.

Ilene Wilson, Logan, Utah

CRITTERS

3 12-ounce packages small
    oyster crackers
1 1/2 cups oil
1 teaspoon lemon pepper
1 1/2 tablespoons dillweed

Garlic powder to taste
Salt and pepper to taste
1 1-ounce package original
    ranch salad dressing mix

Place crackers in large baking pan. Mix remaining ingredients in bowl. Pour over crackers; toss to coat. Bake at 225 degrees for 2 hours, stirring every 15 minutes. Yield: 45 servings.

Approx Per Serving: Cal 162; T Fat 10 g; 55% Calories from Fat;
    Prot 2 g; Carbo 16 g; Fiber 1 g; Chol 0 mg; Sod 328 mg.

Martha Hamilton, Meridian, Idaho

HAROLD'S CHOCOLATE BALLS

2 8-ounce bars chocolate
    almond candy, grated
12 ounces whipped topping

1/2 16-ounce package vanilla
    wafers

Melt chocolate in double boiler; remove from heat. Stir in whipped topping. Spoon into bowl. Chill until partially set. Process wafers in food processor until fine crumbs. Drop chocolate mixture by spoonfuls into crumbs; shape into balls. Yield: 48 servings.

Approx Per Serving: Cal 93; T Fat 6 g; 53% Calories from Fat;
    Prot 1 g; Carbo 10 g; Fiber <1 g; Chol 5 mg; Sod 27 mg.

Lucille Linford, Pocatello, Idaho

ORANGE BALLS

4 cups confectioners' sugar
1 12-ounce can orange juice
   concentrate
1/2 cup margarine, softened

1 12-ounce package vanilla
   wafers, crushed
1 cup chopped pecans
4 cups coconut

Beat first 3 ingredients in mixer bowl until smooth. Add vanilla wafer crumbs and pecans; mix well. Chill for 1 hour. Shape into balls; roll in coconut. Yield: 80 servings.

Approx Per Serving: Cal 90; T Fat 4 g; 40% Calories from Fat; Prot 1 g; Carbo 13 g; Fiber 1 g; Chol 3 mg; Sod 30 mg.

Lucille Linford, Pocatello, Idaho

HEAT WAVE CHOCOLATE MACAROONS

1½ cups quick-cooking oats
1 cup flaked coconut
1/4 cup chopped walnuts
3/4 cup sugar

1/4 cup milk
1/4 cup margarine
3 tablespoons baking cocoa

Combine oats, coconut and walnuts in bowl. Combine remaining ingredients in 2-quart saucepan. Cook over medium heat for 5 minutes, stirring occasionally. Stir in oat mixture. Drop by spoonfuls onto waxed paper-lined tray. Chill in refrigerator. Yield: 24 servings.

Approx Per Serving: Cal 86; T Fat 4 g; 42% Calories from Fat; Prot 1 g; Carbo 12 g; Fiber 1 g; Chol <1 mg; Sod 25 mg.

Betty Bartlett, Mendon, Utah

COCONUT PEAKS

1/4 cup margarine, melted
2 cups confectioners' sugar
3 cups flaked coconut

1/4 cup half and half
1 cup chocolate chips
2 teaspoons oil

Mix first 4 ingredients in bowl. Drop by teaspoonfuls onto waxed paper-lined tray. Chill until set. Shape into peaks. Melt chocolate chips with oil in double boiler. Dip candy bottoms in chocolate. Let stand until firm. Yield: 40 servings.

Approx Per Serving: Cal 84; T Fat 5 g; 49% Calories from Fat; Prot <1 g; Carbo 11 g; Fiber 1 g; Chol 1 mg; Sod 16 mg.

Jean Edwards, Clancy, Montana

BEEF JERKY

1½ pounds flank steak
1 teaspoon liquid smoke
1 teaspoon MSG
1 teaspoon onion powder

¼ cup soy sauce
¼ cup Worcestershire sauce
Barbecue salt to taste

Trim fat from steak. Freeze steak until partially frozen. Cut into ⅛-inch thick slices. Combine liquid smoke, MSG, onion powder, soy sauce, Worcestershire sauce and barbecue salt in shallow dish. Add steak slices. Marinate in refrigerator overnight, turning occasionally to coat. Drain on paper towels; pat dry. Place baking sheet or foil underneath oven rack. Arrange steak slices in single layer on oven rack. Bake at 125 degrees with oven door slightly ajar for 8 to 12 hours or to desired degree of doneness. Yield: 8 servings.

Approx Per Serving: Cal 123; T Fat 5 g; 37% Calories from Fat;
   Prot 17 g; Carbo 2 g; Fiber <1 g; Chol 48 mg; Sod 1193 mg.

Nancy Nielsen, Hyrum, Utah

BEEF SAUSAGE STICK

5 pounds ground beef
5 tablespoons Tender-Quick
¼ teaspoon celery salt
2½ teaspoons peppercorns

2½ teaspoons garlic powder
2¼ teaspoons mustard seed
1 teaspoon hickory salt

Combine ground beef, Tender-Quick, celery salt, peppercorns, garlic powder, mustard seed and hickory salt in bowl; mix well. Chill, covered, for 24 hours. Place in sausage stuffer tube. Bake or dehydrate at 150 degrees for 8 to 10 hours. May substitute 6 parts water and 1 part liquid smoke for hickory salt and wipe mixture on each stick before baking. Yield: 25 servings.

Approx Per Serving: Cal 185; T Fat 13 g; 63% Calories from Fat;
   Prot 17 g; Carbo <1 g; Fiber <1 g; Chol 59 mg; Sod 159 mg.
   Nutritional information does not include Tender-Quick.

Terri Rogers, Great Falls, Montana

CHICKEN SALAD CROISSANTS

3/4 cup diced, cooked chicken
1/4 cup chopped celery
1/4 cup drained pineapple
   tidbits
1 cup mayonnaise
1 tablespoon lemon juice
1 tablespoon onion flakes

1/2 teaspoon seasoning salt
1/4 teaspoon lemon pepper
2 tablespoons chopped
   cashews
2 large croissants, split
2 cups alfalfa sprouts

Toss chicken, celery and pineapple in bowl. Combine mayonnaise, lemon juice, onion flakes, seasoning salt and lemon pepper in bowl. Stir into chicken mixture. Add cashews; mix well. Mound chicken salad onto croissants. Top with alfalfa sprouts. May substitute walnuts for cashews. Yield: 4 servings.

Approx Per Serving: Cal 604; T Fat 54 g; 79% Calories from Fat;
   Prot 12 g; Carbo 20 g; Fiber 2 g; Chol 62 mg; Sod 836 mg.

Lyla L. Stuart, Helena, Montana

STUFFED HARD ROLLS

1 pound ground beef
1 small onion, chopped
Salt and pepper to taste

6 semihard rolls
1   10-ounce can tomato soup
12 cheese strips

Brown ground beef with onion in skillet, stirring frequently. Add salt and pepper; mix well. Cut top crust from rolls; scoop out centers. Crumble roll centers into bowl. Add ground beef mixture and soup; mix well. Stuff into roll shells. Replace tops. Crisscross 2 cheese strips on top of each roll. Place in shallow baking pan. Bake at 350 degrees for 20 to 25 minutes. Yield: 6 servings.

Approx Per Serving: Cal 489; T Fat 31 g; 57% Calories from Fat;
   Prot 30 g; Carbo 23 g; Fiber 1 g; Chol 103 mg; Sod 1338 mg.

Lucille Linford, Pocatello, Idaho

*The largest room in the world is the room
for self-improvement.*

PIZZA MUFFINS

6 English muffins, split,
  toasted
6 tablespoons tomato sauce

¾ cup shredded cheese
Oregano, salt and pepper to
  taste

Spread split toasted English muffins with tomato sauce. Top with cheese. Sprinkle with oregano, salt and pepper. Broil until cheese starts to bubble. Serve hot. Yield: 12 servings.

Approx Per Serving: Cal 99; T Fat 3 g; 26% Calories from Fat;
  Prot 4 g; Carbo 14 g; Fiber 1 g; Chol 7 mg; Sod 337 mg.

Lucille Linford, Pocatello, Idaho

CHICKEN-IN-A-BISCUIT

3 5-ounce cans chicken
1 cup finely chopped celery
¼ cup finely chopped onion
¼ cup finely chopped olives

18 boiled eggs, coarsely
  chopped
¾ cup (or more) salad
  dressing

Combine first 5 ingredients in large bowl; mix well. Stir in enough salad dressing to moisten. May spread filling between homemade biscuits or miniature cream puffs. Yield: 48 servings.

Approx Per Serving: Cal 62; T Fat 4 g; 60% Calories from Fat;
  Prot 5 g; Carbo 1 g; Fiber <1 g; Chol 88 mg; Sod 89 mg.

Shirley Winn, Richmond, Utah

CORNED BEEF BARBECUE SANDWICHES

2 12-ounce cans corned beef
1 cup catsup
¾ cup water
3 tablespoons Worcestershire
  sauce

1 tablespoon chili powder
2 tablespoons cider vinegar
¼ teaspoon cayenne pepper
10 whole wheat buns
10 sweet pickles

Combine first 7 ingredients in 12-inch electric skillet. Bring to a simmer, stirring to break up corned beef. Simmer for about 15 minutes. Spoon filling between buns. Add 1 pickle to each sandwich. Yield: 10 servings.

Approx Per Serving: Cal 314; T Fat 12 g; 35% Calories from Fat;
  Prot 23 g; Carbo 29 g; Fiber 3 g; Chol 61 mg; Sod 1345 mg.

Patsy A. Randolph, Rigby, Idaho

Grazing the North Forty

Salads

'89 H. Creekmore

BONNEVILLE COUNCIL

Salt Lake City, Utah

Members of the Bonneville Council pitch in every Sunday to serve breakfast to the homeless. Every Sunday at 6:00 A.M., Jake Lyons parks a trailer in its customary spot under the entrance ramp to Interstate 15 and Jennie Dudley begins to cook and serve some 700 hot meals to the homeless of Salt Lake City. With the help of Lyons, Betty Comstock and other Skyline Chapter members, she has done it every Sunday for years, ever since she discovered that the city's soup kitchens were closed on Sundays.

The first kitchen was Jennie's horse trailer, which was very inconvenient and was soon outgrown. A benefactor then donated a 35-foot camping trailer and about 280 Skyline members participated to renovate and outfit the trailer. Area merchants donated materials for new plumbing, sinks and cabinets for storage. Utah Technical College provided the tools and labor to rig the camper to hold butane tanks. The kitchen relies on the goodness of the community and the good Lord to provide the food and supplies, and somehow, that faith seems always to be rewarded with what is needed.

BLUEBERRY SALAD

2 3-ounce packages
  blackberry gelatin
2 cups boiling water
1 8-ounce can crushed
  pineapple
1 16-ounce can blueberries

8 ounces cream cheese,
  softened
2 cups sour cream
1/2 cup confectioners' sugar
1/2 teaspoon vanilla extract
1 1/2 cups chopped pecans

Dissolve gelatin in boiling water in bowl. Drain pineapple and blueberries, reserving juice. Add enough cold water to reserved juice to measure 1 cup. Stir into gelatin. Add pineapple and blueberries. Chill until set. Blend cream cheese, sour cream, confectioners' sugar and vanilla in bowl. Spread over congealed layer. Sprinkle pecans over top. May substitute black cherry gelatin for blackberry. Yield: 12 servings.

Approx Per Serving: Cal 367; T Fat 25 g; 58% Calories from Fat;
  Prot 5 g; Carbo 34 g; Fiber 2 g; Chol 38 mg; Sod 123 mg.

Terri Rogers, Great Falls, Montana

EASY FRUIT SALAD

This salad goes well with everything and is super for potlucks.

16 ounces cottage cheese
1 3-ounce package orange
  gelatin
1 11-ounce can mandarin
  oranges
1 12-ounce can pineapple
  tidbits

8 ounces whipped topping
1 cup miniature
  marshmallows
1/2 cup chopped pecans

Combine cottage cheese and dry gelatin in bowl; mix well. Drain oranges and pineapple well. Add to cottage cheese mixture. Fold in whipped topping, marshmallows and pecans. Chill for 1 hour. May substitute maraschino cherries for pecans. Yield: 8 servings.

Approx Per Serving: Cal 317; T Fat 15 g; 40% Calories from Fat;
  Prot 9 g; Carbo 39 g; Fiber 2 g; Chol 8 mg; Sod 280 mg.

Evelyn R. Damschen, Anaconda, Montana

FRUIT AND PUDDING SALAD

2 8-ounce cans mandarin
  oranges
1 12-ounce can pineapple
  chunks
1 8-ounce can sliced peaches
1 8-ounce can pears

1 4-ounce package tapioca
  pudding mix
1 4-ounce package vanilla
  pudding and pie filling
  mix
3 bananas

Drain canned fruit, reserving juices. Add enough water to reserved juices to measure 4 cups. Combine juices and pudding mixes in saucepan; mix well. Cook pudding using package directions. Let stand until cool, stirring occasionally. Slice bananas. Add to pudding; stir gently until coated. Add drained fruit; mix well. Chill, covered, until serving time. Yield: 12 servings.

Approx Per Serving: Cal 169; T Fat <1 g; 2% Calories from Fat;
  Prot 1 g; Carbo 44 g; Fiber 2 g; Chol 0 mg; Sod 131 mg.

Luella Merriman, Great Falls, Montana

CONGEALED FRUIT SALAD

1 6-ounce package apricot
  gelatin
2 cups boiling water
2 cups cold water
1 20-ounce can crushed
  pineapple, drained
2 bananas, chopped
1 cup miniature
  marshmallows

2 tablespoons butter,
  softened
2 tablespoons flour
1/2 cup pineapple juice
1/2 cup sugar
1 egg, beaten
1 envelope whipped topping
  mix, prepared

Dissolve gelatin in boiling water in bowl. Add cold water. Chill until partially set. Add pineapple, bananas and marshmallows; mix well. Pour into 9x13-inch dish. Chill until firm. Blend butter and flour in small saucepan. Stir in pineapple juice gradually. Add sugar and egg; mix well. Cook until thickened, stirring constantly. Let stand until cool. Fold in prepared whipped topping. Spread over congealed layer. May substitute peach gelatin for apricot. Yield: 18 servings.

Approx Per Serving: Cal 141; T Fat 3 g; 20% Calories from Fat;
  Prot 2 g; Carbo 27 g; Fiber 1 g; Chol 17 mg; Sod 56 mg.

Elaine Fielding, Orem, Utah

DELICIOUS LIME FRUIT SALAD

1²/₃ cups pear juice
1 3-ounce package lime
   gelatin
6 ounces cream cheese,
   softened
1 28-ounce can chopped
   pears, drained

1 12-ounce can crushed
   pineapple, drained
¹/₂ cup chopped pecans
1 cup whipping cream,
   whipped

Heat pear juice almost to the boiling point. Dissolve gelatin in hot juice. Pour hot mixture gradually over cream cheese in mixer bowl; beat until smooth. Chill until partially set. Add pears, pineapple and pecans. Fold in whipped cream. Pour into 9x12-inch dish. Chill until firm. Yield: 15 servings.

Approx Per Serving: Cal 200; T Fat 13 g; 54% Calories from Fat;
Prot 2 g; Carbo 22 g; Fiber 1 g; Chol 34 mg; Sod 61 mg.

Karen D. Burk, Helena, Montana

LEMON GELATIN SALAD

1 6-ounce package lemon
   gelatin
1 16-ounce can crushed
   pineapple
2 bananas, sliced
12 ounces miniature
   marshmallows

2 eggs, beaten
3 tablespoons flour
¹/₂ cup sugar
1 cup whipping cream
Sugar to taste

Prepare gelatin using package directions. Chill until partially set. Drain pineapple, reserving juice. Add pineapple and bananas to gelatin; mix well. Pour into 9x13-inch dish. Sprinkle marshmallows over top; press into gelatin slightly. Chill in refrigerator. Bring reserved pineapple juice to a boil in saucepan. Beat eggs with flour and ¹/₂ cup sugar. Stir a small amount of hot juice into egg mixture; stir egg mixture into hot juice. Cook until thickened, stirring constantly. Let stand until completely cooled. Whip cream in mixer bowl; sweeten as desired. Fold into cooled mixture. Spread over marshmallows. Chill until serving time. Yield: 15 servings.

Approx Per Serving: Cal 248; T Fat 7 g; 23% Calories from Fat;
Prot 3 g; Carbo 46 g; Fiber 1 g; Chol 50 mg; Sod 72 mg.

Luella Merriman, Great Falls, Montana

LIME AND COTTAGE CHEESE SALAD

18 large marshmallows
1½ cups boiling water
1 3-ounce package lime
  gelatin
1 cup cottage cheese

1 cup crushed pineapple,
  drained
1 cup whipped cream
½ cup chopped walnuts

Dissolve marshmallows in boiling water in 2-quart bowl. Add gelatin; stir until dissolved. Chill until partially set. Fold in cottage cheese, pineapple, whipped cream and walnuts. Chill until firm. Serve plain or with favorite dressing. Yield: 10 servings.

Approx Per Serving: Cal 186; T Fat 9 g; 42% Calories from Fat;
  Prot 5 g; Carbo 23 g; Fiber 1 g; Chol 19 mg; Sod 129 mg.

Nella A. Wollan, Plentywood, Montana

APRICOT PRETZEL SALAD

2 cups crushed pretzels
½ cup sugar
¼ cup melted margarine
8 ounces cream cheese,
  softened
½ cup sugar

8 ounces whipped topping
1 6-ounce package apricot
  gelatin
2½ cups boiling water
1 8-ounce can crushed
  pineapple, drained

Combine pretzels, ½ cup sugar and margarine in 9x13-inch baking dish; mix well. Press over bottom of dish to form crust. Bake at 350 degrees for 6 minutes. Let stand until cool. Blend cream cheese with ½ cup sugar in small bowl. Fold in whipped topping. Spread over cooled crust. Chill in refrigerator. Dissolve gelatin in boiling water in bowl. Chill until partially set. Mix in pineapple. Spoon over cream cheese layer. Chill until set. Garnish with additional whipped topping. Yield: 15 servings.

Approx Per Serving: Cal 291; T Fat 13 g; 39% Calories from Fat;
  Prot 4 g; Carbo 41 g; Fiber 1 g; Chol 17 mg; Sod 365 mg.

Anna Godfrey, Smithfield, Utah

FANCY STRAWBERRY GELATIN SALAD

1 6-ounce package
   strawberry gelatin
1 cup boiling water
1 16-ounce can cranberry
   sauce
2 cups mashed bananas

1 8-ounce can juice-pack
   crushed pineapple
4 cups fresh strawberries,
   crushed
2 cups sour cream

Dissolve gelatin in boiling water in bowl. Add cranberry sauce, bananas, undrained pineapple and strawberries; mix well. Pour half the mixture into 9x13-inch dish. Chill for 1 hour or until firm. Spread sour cream over congealed layer. Spoon remaining gelatin mixture over sour cream layer. Chill until firm. May substitute 4 cups frozen strawberries for fresh. Yield: 12 servings.

Approx Per Serving: Cal 253; T Fat 8 g; 29% Calories from Fat;
   Prot 3 g; Carbo 44 g; Fiber 3 g; Chol 17 mg; Sod 78 mg.

Barbara Hamilton, Boise, Idaho

MOLDED WHITE SALAD

1 3-ounce package lemon
   gelatin
10 large marshmallows
2 cups boiling water
8 ounces cream cheese,
   softened

1 cup drained crushed
   pineapple
1/2 cup whipping cream,
   whipped

Dissolve gelatin and marshmallows in boiling water in mixer bowl. Add cream cheese; beat until smooth. Chill until partially set. Beat until light. Fold in pineapple and whipped cream. Pour into gelatin mold. Chill until set. Unmold onto serving plate. Yield: 10 servings.

Approx Per Serving: Cal 187; T Fat 12 g; 58% Calories from Fat;
   Prot 3 g; Carbo 18 g; Fiber <1 g; Chol 41 mg; Sod 105 mg.

Arline Brown, Missoula, Montana

CHINESE CHICKEN SALAD

3 tablespoons rice vinegar
1 tablespoon sesame seed oil
1 tablespoon vegetable oil
1 teaspoon salt
1/2 teaspoon pepper
2 tablespoons sugar
1 head lettuce
1/2 cup sliced mushrooms
4 green onions, chopped

1/2 cup sliced radishes
1 large chicken breast, cooked, shredded
3 tablespoons toasted sesame seed
1/2 cup toasted slivered almonds
2 to 4 cups oil for deep frying
2 1/2 ounces Maifun rice sticks

Mix first 6 ingredients in small bowl. Cut lettuce into bite-sized pieces. Combine with next 6 ingredients in salad bowl; toss to mix. Heat 2 to 4 cups oil in wok or deep saucepan to 400 degrees or until a small piece of rice stick puffs up and floats to surface immediately on being dropped into hot oil. Deep-fry rice sticks a small amount at a time; drain. Add puffed rice sticks and dressing to salad; toss lightly. Serve immediately. Yield: 6 servings.

Approx Per Serving: Cal 229; T Fat 16 g; 57% Calories from Fat;
Prot 10 g; Carbo 16 g; Fiber 3 g; Chol 12 mg; Sod 553 mg.
Nutritional information does not include oil for deep frying.

Ray and Cheri Archibald, Oakley, Idaho

RAMEN CHICKEN SALAD

1/2 cup oil
3 tablespoons vinegar
1 tablespoon sugar
1 teaspoon salt
1/2 teaspoon pepper
1/2 teaspoon MSG
1/2 head cabbage, chopped
2 green onions, chopped

2 cups chopped cooked chicken
2 tablespoons sesame seed, toasted
2 tablespoons slivered almonds, toasted
1 package chicken-flavored ramen noodles

Combine first 6 ingredients in small bowl or jar; mix well and set aside. Combine cabbage, green onions, chicken, sesame seed and almonds in bowl. Crumble noodles over salad; sprinkle seasoning packet from noodles over top. Add dressing; toss to mix. Chill, covered, overnight. Yield: 10 servings.

Approx Per Serving: Cal 201; T Fat 16 g; 69% Calories from Fat;
Prot 10 g; Carbo 6 g; Fiber 1 g; Chol 25 mg; Sod 539 mg.

Barbara Woodward, Wellsville, Utah

FRUITED CHICKEN SALAD

4 cups chopped cooked
  chicken
1 15-ounce can pineapple
  chunks, drained
1 11-ounce can mandarin
  oranges, drained
1 cup chopped celery
1/2 green bell pepper,
  chopped

2 tablespoons grated onion
1/2 cup sliced ripe olives
1/2 cup cashews
1/2 cup mayonnaise
1/2 cup plain yogurt
1 tablespoon prepared
  mustard
Lemon juice to taste

Combine chicken, pineapple, oranges, celery, green pepper, onion, olives and cashews in bowl. Blend mayonnaise, yogurt, mustard and lemon juice in small bowl. Add to chicken mixture; toss to mix. Chill until serving time. Spoon onto lettuce-lined plates. Garnish with chow mein noodles. Yield: 6 servings.

Approx Per Serving: Cal 494; T Fat 32 g; 56% Calories from Fat;
  Prot 31 g; Carbo 26 g; Fiber 3 g; Chol 95 mg; Sod 396 mg.

Marjorie Thomas, Boise, Idaho

CHICKEN AND FRUIT SALAD

3 cups chopped cooked
  chicken
Segments of 1 peeled orange,
  chopped
1 banana, sliced

20 to 25 grapes, cut into halves
1 cup chopped celery
1 apple, chopped
1/2 cup slivered almonds
3/4 cup mayonnaise

Combine chicken, orange, banana, grapes, celery, apple, almonds and mayonnaise in bowl; mix lightly. Chill until serving time. May add pineapple, strawberries or other fruit as desired. Yield: 8 servings.

Approx Per Serving: Cal 336; T Fat 25 g; 67% Calories from Fat;
  Prot 18 g; Carbo 13 g; Fiber 2 g; Chol 59 mg; Sod 176 mg.

Joy Staples, Twin Falls, Idaho

JAPANESE PUFFED RICE SALAD

4 to 8 ounces cooked
  chicken, shredded
1 head lettuce, shredded
4 green onions, chopped
2 tablespoons slivered
  almonds
2 to 4 tablespoons sesame
  seed, toasted
1/4 cup vegetable oil
3 tablespoons rice vinegar

1 tablespoon sesame oil
2 tablespoons sugar
1 teaspoon salt
1 teaspoon MSG
1/2 teaspoon pepper
20 won ton skins
Oil for deep frying
4 or 5 bunches Maifun rice
  sticks, deep-fried

Combine first 5 ingredients in salad bowl. Combine vegetable oil, rice vinegar, sesame oil, sugar, salt, MSG and pepper in small bowl or jar; mix well. Add to salad; toss lightly. Chill in refrigerator. Cut won ton skins into 1/2-inch strips. Deep-fry in hot oil until light golden brown; drain. Add won tons and rice sticks to salad just before serving. May omit chicken. Yield: 6 servings.

Approx Per Serving: Cal 284; T Fat 21 g; 63% Calories from Fat;
  Prot 15 g; Carbo 12 g; Fiber 2 g; Chol 34 mg; Sod 1249 mg.
  Nutritional information does not include won ton skins
  or rice sticks and oil for deep frying.

Patty E. Henderson, Boise, Idaho

SHRIMP AND RICE-A-RONI SALAD

1 7-ounce package chicken-
  flavored Rice-A-Roni
1 8-ounce can shrimp,
  drained
1 5-ounce can water
  chestnuts, drained, finely
  chopped

1 cup finely chopped green
  bell pepper
1 cup finely chopped celery
3 medium green onions,
  finely chopped
1 cup mayonnaise
1/2 teaspoon curry powder

Cook Rice-A-Roni using package directions. Let stand until cool. Combine with shrimp, water chestnuts, green pepper, celery and green onions in bowl. Blend mayonnaise with curry powder. Add to rice mixture; mix lightly. Chill until serving time. Yield: 8 servings.

Approx Per Serving: Cal 420; T Fat 25 g; 54% Calories from Fat;
  Prot 10 g; Carbo 38 g; Fiber 1 g; Chol 65 mg; Sod 790 mg.

Phyllis Lee, Great Falls, Montana

SHRIMP MOLD

1 10-ounce can tomato soup
8 ounces cream cheese,
  softened
2 envelopes unflavored
  gelatin
2 tablespoons cold water
2 cups cooked salad shrimp
1 cup chopped celery
1 medium onion, chopped

½ cup chopped green bell
  pepper
1 tablespoon Worcestershire
  sauce
1 cup mayonnaise
2 tablespoons horseradish,
  drained
Salt and pepper to taste
Tabasco sauce to taste

Heat soup in saucepan. Add cream cheese. Heat until cream cheese melts, stirring constantly. Soften gelatin in cold water. Add to hot soup mixture; stir until dissolved. Add remaining ingredients; mix well. Pour into well greased 1-quart mold or 6x10-inch dish. Chill until firm. Unmold onto serving plate or cut into squares. May substitute two 6-ounce cans lobster or crab meat for shrimp. Yield: 8 servings.

Approx Per Serving: Cal 378; T Fat 33 g; 77% Calories from Fat;
  Prot 12 g; Carbo 10 g; Fiber 1 g; Chol 103 mg; Sod 578 mg.

Madeline Remmel, Great Falls, Montana

AVOCADO SEA RING SALAD

2 3-ounce packages lemon
  gelatin
1 cup boiling water
2 cups cold water
3 tablespoons vinegar
3 tablespoons pickle relish
5 drops of Tabasco sauce
¾ teaspoon salt
¼ teaspoon garlic salt

1 teaspoon crushed basil
2 tablespoons chopped green
  bell pepper
2 tablespoons chopped onion
2 tablespoons chopped
  pimento
1 large avocado
2 hard-boiled eggs, sliced
1 cup cooked shrimp

Dissolve gelatin in boiling water in bowl. Add next 10 ingredients; mix well. Chill until partially set. Cut avocado lengthwise into halves; discard seed and skin. Cut into slices. Fold avocado, eggs and shrimp into gelatin. Spoon into 1½-quart ring mold. Chill until firm. Unmold onto serving plate. Yield: 10 servings.

Approx Per Serving: Cal 135; T Fat 5 g; 29% Calories from Fat;
  Prot 6 g; Carbo 19 g; Fiber 2 g; Chol 65 mg; Sod 336 mg.

Ruth Lovell, Caldwell, Idaho

CALIFORNIA BEAN SALAD

1 16-ounce can green beans
1 16-ounce can kidney beans
1 16-ounce can garbanzo
   beans
1 16-ounce can pitted black
   olives
½ green bell pepper,
   chopped

1 small red onion, sliced
½ cup vegetable oil
½ cup wine vinegar
¼ cup Burgundy
½ cup sugar
¼ teaspoon basil
¼ teaspoon garlic powder

Drain beans and olives well; place in large bowl. Combine green pepper, onion, oil, vinegar, wine, sugar, basil and garlic powder in blender container. Process until well mixed. Pour over bean mixture. Let stand for 3 hours to overnight. Yield: 15 servings.

Approx Per Serving: Cal 227; T Fat 15 g; 55% Calories from Fat;
Prot 5 g; Carbo 23 g; Fiber 6 g; Chol 0 mg; Sod 412 mg.

Martha Hamilton, Meridian, Idaho

BROCCOLI AND TOMATO SALAD

2 pounds fresh broccoli
1 large tomato, peeled,
   chopped
1 small onion, chopped

1 cup mayonnaise
Salt and pepper to taste
Curry powder or garlic salt
   to taste

Cut flowerets from broccoli; chop stems. Cook in a small amount of water in saucepan until tender-crisp; drain and rinse with cold water. Combine broccoli, tomato and onion in salad bowl. Blend mayonnaise with salt, pepper and curry powder or garlic salt in small bowl. Add to vegetables; toss lightly. Chill until serving time. Yield: 8 servings.

Approx Per Serving: Cal 236; T Fat 22 g; 80% Calories from Fat;
Prot 4 g; Carbo 8 g; Fiber 4 g; Chol 16 g; Sod 189 mg.

Merla Jorgensen, Pocatello, Idaho

BROCCOLI AND RAISIN SALAD

2 bunches fresh broccoli,
  finely chopped
1 small red onion, chopped
1 cup raisins
1 cup dry-roasted sunflower
  seed

8 ounces bacon, crisp-fried,
  crumbled
1 cup mayonnaise
1/2 cup sugar
2 tablespoons vinegar

Combine broccoli, onion, raisins, sunflower seed and bacon in salad bowl. Blend mayonnaise, sugar and vinegar in small bowl. Pour over broccoli mixture; toss lightly to mix. Yield: 12 servings.

Approx Per Serving: Cal 401; T Fat 30 g; 65% Calories from Fat;
  Prot 11 g; Carbo 26 g; Fiber 4 g; Chol 27 mg; Sod 424 mg.

Arloa Weiss, Billings, Montana

CABBAGE SALAD

1/4 cup sesame seed
1 head cabbage, chopped
1 bunch green onions,
  chopped
2 packages ramen noodles
1   3-ounce package sliced
  almonds

1 cup vegetable oil
1/4 cup vinegar
1/4 cup sugar
2 teaspoons salt
1 teaspoon pepper
2 teaspoons MSG

Sprinkle sesame seed on baking sheet. Toast at 350 degrees for 20 minutes or until golden brown. Let stand until cool. Combine cabbage and green onions in salad bowl. Crumble noodles; add to cabbage mixture. Reserve a portion of almonds for garnish. Add remaining almonds and toasted sesame seed to cabbage mixture. Combine oil, vinegar, sugar, salt, pepper and MSG in bowl; mix well. Add to cabbage mixture; toss until coated. Chill until serving time. Yield: 20 servings.

Approx Per Serving: Cal 167; T Fat 15 g; 77% Calories from Fat;
  Prot 2 g; Carbo 8 g; Fiber 1 g; Chol 0 mg; Sod 729 mg.

Helen Pearson, Idaho Falls, Idaho

CHINESE CABBAGE SALAD

1 large head Chinese
  cabbage, shredded
5 green onions, chopped
2 packages plain ramen
  noodles, crushed
1 2-ounce package slivered
  almonds

1/2 cup sesame seed
1/2 cup butter
1/2 cup oil
1/2 cup sugar
1 teaspoon soy sauce
1/4 cup vinegar
1/2 teaspoon salt

Combine cabbage and green onions in salad bowl. Sauté noodles, almonds and sesame seed in butter in skillet until golden brown; drain on paper towels. Let stand until cool. Add to cabbage mixture. Combine oil, sugar, soy sauce, vinegar and salt in bowl or jar; mix well. Add dressing when ready to eat. Yield: 15 servings.

Approx Per Serving: Cal 228; T Fat 19 g; 73% Calories from Fat;
    Prot 3 g; Carbo 13 g; Fiber 1 g; Chol 17 mg; Sod 260 mg.

Janel Anderson, Helena, Montana

ZIPPY CARROTS

5 cups sliced carrots
1 medium sweet onion, sliced
1 medium green bell pepper,
  cut into rings
1 10-ounce can tomato soup
1/2 cup vegetable oil
3/4 cup sugar

3/4 cup vinegar
1 teaspoon prepared mustard
1 teaspoon salt
1/2 teaspoon pepper
1 teaspoon Worcestershire
  sauce

Cook carrots in a small amount of water in saucepan for 10 minutes or until tender-crisp; drain and chill. Combine carrots, onion and green pepper in bowl. Combine soup, oil, sugar, vinegar, mustard, salt, pepper and Worcestershire sauce in bowl; beat with wire whisk until well blended. Pour over vegetables; stir gently. Chill, covered, for 12 hours. Drain vegetables. Garnish edge of salad bowl with lettuce leaves and parsley sprigs. Yield: 10 servings.

Approx Per Serving: Cal 208; T Fat 12 g; 48% Calories from Fat;
    Prot 1 g; Carbo 27 g; Fiber 2 g; Chol 0 mg; Sod 442 mg.

Mary H. Morrison, Missoula, Montana

CAULIFLOWER SALAD

1 head cauliflower
Salt to taste
1 cup sour cream
1 cup mayonnaise

1 bunch small green onions,
  chopped
Chives, garlic salt and onion
  salt to taste

Soak cauliflower in warm salted water to cover for 1 1/2 hours; drain well. Combine sour cream and mayonnaise in bowl; blend well. Add green onions, chives, garlic salt and onion salt; mix well. Slice cauliflower to desired thickness; place in bowl. Add dressing; mix to coat. Chill, covered, overnight. Yield: 15 servings.

Approx Per Serving: Cal 145; T Fat 15 g; 90% Calories from Fat;
  Prot 1 g; Carbo 3 g; Fiber 1 g; Chol 16 mg; Sod 95 mg.

Peggy Shepherd, Helena, Montana

PEA AND CAULIFLOWER SALAD

2   10-ounce packages frozen
  peas
1/2 teaspoon salt
1 head cauliflower, chopped

1 cup mayonnaise
2 tablespoons dried minced
  onion

Cook peas with salt in a small amount of boiling water in saucepan for 3 minutes; drain and rinse with cold water. Drain well. Combine with cauliflower, mayonnaise and onion in bowl; mix gently. Chill for several hours. Yield: 20 servings.

Approx Per Serving: Cal 106; T Fat 9 g; 73% Calories from Fat;
  Prot 2 g; Carbo 5 g; Fiber 2 g; Chol 7 mg; Sod 151 mg.

Mardi Millons, Helena, Montana

*People who don't value praise rarely do
anything worthy of it.*

MOLDED SOUR CREAM AND CUCUMBER SALAD

1 6-ounce package lime
  gelatin
2 cups boiling water
3 cups sour cream
1 large green bell pepper
2 large cucumbers, peeled,
  seeded

1/2 cup minced fresh parsley
1/4 cup chopped green onions
1 teaspoon salt
1/4 teaspoon white pepper
2 tablespoons horseradish
2 teaspoons celery seed

Dissolve gelatin in boiling water in large bowl. Let stand until cool. Blend in sour cream. Chop green pepper and cucumbers finely. Add to gelatin mixture. Stir in parsley, green onions, salt, white pepper, horseradish and celery seed; mix well. Pour into gelatin mold. Chill until firm. Unmold onto plate lined with red lettuce leaves. Yield: 15 servings.

Approx Per Serving: Cal 149; T Fat 10 g; 57% Calories from Fat;
    Prot 3 g; Carbo 14 g; Fiber 1 g; Chol 20 mg; Sod 207 mg.

Hazel M. Johnson, Murray, Utah

CUCUMBERS IN SOUR CREAM

2 medium cucumbers, peeled
1 medium onion, sliced
11/4 teaspoons salt
1 cup sour cream

2 tablespoons vinegar
1/4 teaspoon sugar
1/8 teaspoon paprika
1 tablespoon parsley flakes

Score cucumbers lengthwise with fork; cut into thin slices. Combine cucumber and onion slices in bowl. Sprinkle with salt. Let stand for 10 minutes. Drain and press out excess liquid. Combine sour cream, vinegar, sugar, paprika and parsley flakes in small bowl; mix well. Add to cucumber mixture; mix gently with fork. Chill until serving time. Yield: 10 servings.

Approx Per Serving: Cal 63; T Fat 5 g; 67% Calories from Fat;
    Prot 1 g; Carbo 4 g; Fiber 1 g; Chol 10 mg; Sod 280 mg.

Shirley Moss, Boise, Idaho

MANDARIN SALAD

8 cups torn salad greens
2 or 3 green onions, chopped
1 cup grape halves
1 11-ounce can mandarin
    oranges, drained
1/2 cup chopped pecans
2 or 3 ribs celery, sliced
    diagonally

2 tablespoons sesame seed
3 tablespoons sugar
1/2 cup vegetable oil
1 teaspoon salt
2 tablespoons vinegar
Pepper to taste

Combine salad greens, green onions, grapes, oranges, pecans and celery in salad bowl. Toast sesame seed on baking sheet at 350 degrees for 5 minutes. Combine with sugar, oil, salt, vinegar and pepper in small bowl; mix well. Pour over salad; toss lightly. Yield: 8 servings.

Approx Per Serving: Cal 254; T Fat 20 g; 68% Calories from Fat; Prot 2 g; Carbo 19 g; Fiber 3 g; Chol 0 mg; Sod 289 mg.

Sarah H. Jensen, Richfield, Utah

MARINATED VEGGIE SALAD

3/4 cup cider vinegar
1/2 cup vegetable oil
1 teaspoon salt
1 cup sugar
1 tablespoon water
1 teaspoon pepper
1 20-ounce can French-style
    green beans, drained
1 16-ounce package frozen
    tiny peas

1 16-ounce can Shoe Peg
    corn, drained
1 2-ounce jar chopped
    pimento, drained
1 cup chopped celery
1 green bell pepper, chopped
1 medium onion, chopped
1 8-ounce can sliced water
    chestnuts, drained

Combine vinegar, oil, salt, sugar, water and pepper in saucepan. Bring to a boil, stirring until sugar dissolves. Let stand until cool. Combine vegetables in bowl. Add cooled vinegar mixture; mix gently. Chill, covered, for 12 hours, stirring occasionally. Do not cook peas or substitute for Shoe Peg corn. Yield: 10 servings.

Approx Per Serving: Cal 280; T Fat 12 g; 35% Calories from Fat; Prot 5 g; Carbo 43 g; Fiber 5 g; Chol 0 mg; Sod 526 mg.

June M. Fischer, Preston, Idaho

POPULAR POTATO SALAD

3 pounds red potatoes
Salt and freshly ground
  pepper to taste
5 green onions
1 cup frozen tiny peas,
  thawed

1 cup chopped celery
1/4 cup chopped fresh parsley
1 3-ounce jar bacon bits
3/4 cup mayonnaise
1 teaspoon Dijon mustard

Scrub potatoes; cut into halves. Cook potatoes in boiling water for 15 to 20 minutes or until tender; drain and cool. Cut into cubes; place in bowl. Season with salt and pepper. Chop green onions and one-third of the tops finely. Add green onions, peas, celery, parsley and bacon to potatoes. Blend mayonnaise and mustard in small bowl. Add to potato mixture; mix well. Chill, covered, for several hours. Yield: 8 servings.

Approx Per Serving: Cal 400; T Fat 20 g; 44% Calories from Fat;
  Prot 6 g; Carbo 50 g; Fiber 8 g; Chol 12 mg; Sod 466 mg.

Bertha Bateman, Logan, Utah

SPINACH AND MUSHROOM SALAD

2 bunches spinach, torn
1 head lettuce, torn
1 purple onion, sliced
12 ounces fresh mushrooms,
  sliced
3/4 cup shredded Swiss
  cheese
1 cup cottage cheese
8 ounces bacon, crisp-fried,
  crumbled

1/3 cup white vinegar
3/4 cup vegetable oil
1/3 cup sugar
2 1/4 teaspoons dried minced
  onion
3/4 teaspoon salt
1/3 teaspoon prepared
  mustard
2 1/4 teaspoons poppy seed

Combine spinach, lettuce, sliced onion, mushrooms, cheeses and bacon in salad bowl; toss to mix. Combine vinegar, oil, sugar, dried onion, salt, mustard and poppy seed in small bowl; mix well. Add to spinach mixture just before serving; toss lightly. Yield: 8 servings.

Approx Per Serving: Cal 506; T Fat 39 g; 67% Calories from Fat;
  Prot 22 g; Carbo 21 g; Fiber 6 g; Chol 38 mg; Sod 920 mg.

Betty Bartlett, Mendon, Utah

Cattle Drives

Meats

'89 H. CREEKMORE

BRIDGERLAND COUNCIL

Logan and Brigham City, Utah

This photograph was taken on June 29, 1991, at the Jensen Living Historical Farm in Wellsville, Utah. The Bridgerland Council, dressed in the clothes of the 1917 era portrayed by the farm, built an open-wire line to the farmhouse. The Council worked hard to dig the holes and set the poles by hand, but a good time was had by all.

OLD TIMER'S ROAST

1 4-pound beef roast
Salt and pepper to taste
2 onions, sliced

2 cloves of garlic, chopped
3 bay leaves
1 12-ounce can beer

Rub all sides of roast with salt and pepper. Place in roasting pan. Arrange onions, garlic and bay leaves around roast. Pour beer into pan. Roast, covered, in slow oven for several hours or until done to taste. Discard bay leaves. May use cooking juices for gravy. Yield: 8 servings.

Approx Per Serving: Cal 331; T Fat 13 g; 38% Calories from Fat; Prot 43 g; Carbo 5 g; Fiber 1 g; Chol 128 mg; Sod 73 mg.

Terri Rogers, Great Falls, Montana

GREEN PEPPER STEAK

1 pound beef chuck or round
  steak
1/4 cup soy sauce
1 clove of garlic, minced
1 1/2 teaspoons grated fresh
  ginger or 1/2 teaspoon
  ground ginger
1/4 cup oil

1 cup thinly sliced green
  onions
1 cup 1-inch squares red or
  green bell pepper
2 stalks celery, thinly sliced
1 tablespoon cornstarch
1 cup water
2 tomatoes, cut into wedges

Trim fat from beef. Cut cross grain with very sharp knife into 1/8-inch thick strips. Combine soy sauce, garlic and ginger in bowl; mix well. Add beef. Marinate for several minutes. Heat oil in large skillet or wok over high heat. Add beef. Stir-fry until brown. Add green onions, bell pepper and celery. Stir-fry for 10 minutes or until tender-crisp. Stir in mixture of cornstarch and water. Cook until thickened, stirring constantly. Add tomatoes. Cook until heated through. May cover beef and simmer for 30 to 40 minutes if it is not of desired tenderness after browning. May reduce recipe by half, adding water as needed, or double recipe, using 1 3/4 cups water and 1 1/2 tablespoons cornstarch. Yield: 4 servings.

Approx Per Serving: Cal 316; T Fat 20 g; 58% Calories from Fat; Prot 24 g; Carbo 10 g; Fiber 2 g; Chol 64 mg; Sod 1088 mg.

Sarah J. Schueler, Baker, Montana

BURGER BUNDLES

1 6-ounce package
   stove-top stuffing mix
1 pound ground beef
1/3 cup evaporated milk
1 tablespoon catsup

1 10-ounce can cream of
   mushroom soup
2 teaspoons Worcestershire
   sauce

Prepare stuffing mix using package directions. Mix ground beef with evaporated milk in bowl. Divide into 4 portions. Press into 6-inch circles on waxed paper. Spoon stuffing into centers of circles. Shape circles into balls, molding to enclose filling. Place in 1 1/2-quart baking dish. Combine catsup, soup and Worcestershire sauce in saucepan. Heat until bubbly, mixing well. Pour over meatballs. Bake at 350 degrees for 45 to 50 minutes or until done to taste. Yield: 4 servings.

Approx Per Serving: Cal 498; T Fat 25 g; 45% Calories from Fat; Prot 29 g; Carbo 40 g; Fiber <1 g; Chol 81 mg; Sod 1461 mg.

Lucille Linford, Pocatello, Idaho

BERT'S FAMOUS AWARD-WINNING CHILI

*This chili sold for $50.00 a quart when Bert prepared it for a
U S West "Men Only" auction fund raiser.*

2 pounds extra-lean ground
   beef
2 medium onions, finely
   chopped
4 cloves of garlic, minced
1 16-ounce jar plain
   spaghetti sauce
1 3/4 cups clear beef broth

1 tablespoon Worcestershire
   sauce
1 tablespoon cumin
1/4 cup chili powder
1/4 teaspoon cayenne pepper
1 tablespoon baking cocoa
2 16-ounce cans kidney beans
2 16-ounce cans chili beans

Brown ground beef in large saucepan over medium heat, stirring until crumbly; drain. Add remaining ingredients; mix well. Bring to a boil; reduce heat. Simmer, covered, for 1 to 1 1/2 hours or until done to taste, stirring occasionally. Serve with shredded sharp Cheddar cheese and chopped green onions, Mexican Corn Bread (page 101) and tossed salad. Yield: 8 servings.

Approx Per Serving: Cal 514; T Fat 21 g; 35% Calories from Fat; Prot 36 g; Carbo 49 g; Fiber 20 g; Chol 74 mg; Sod 1364 mg.

Mary Lou Carlson, Helena, Montana

CABBAGE CHILI

1 large onion, chopped
1 pound ground beef
2 cups stewed tomatoes
2 medium potatoes, chopped

¼ large head cabbage,
  shredded
Salt and pepper to taste

Sauté onion and ground beef in saucepan until cooked through but not brown; drain. Add tomatoes, potatoes, cabbage, salt, pepper and enough water to cover. Simmer until cabbage is tender. May omit potatoes if desired. Yield: 4 servings.

Approx Per Serving: Cal 381; T Fat 17 g; 38% Calories from Fat;
  Prot 25 g; Carbo 35 g; Fiber 5 g; Chol 74 mg; Sod 272 mg.

Joy Cummings, Sandy, Utah

TACOS AND BURRITOS

1 pound ground beef
½ medium onion, chopped
1 envelope taco seasoning
  mix
½ 16-ounce can refried
  beans

6 ounces medium Cheddar
  cheese, shredded
8 flour tortillas
4 taco shells

Cook ground beef with onion in saucepan just until cooked through; drain. Prepare taco seasoning mix with water using package directions. Stir into ground beef mixture. Simmer until moisture is absorbed but mixture is not dry. Reserve ⅓ of the beef mixture for tacos. Add beans and cheese to remaining beef mixture; mix until cheese melts. Spoon onto centers of tortillas. Fold tortillas to enclose filling, tucking in ends. Stack in serving dish. Spoon reserved beef mixture into taco shells. Arrange on serving plate. Serve with toppings such as chopped tomato, chopped lettuce or spinach, sour cream, black or green olives, taco sauce or salsa, chopped onion or additional shredded cheese. Yield: 4 servings of 1 taco and 2 burritos.

Approx Per Serving: Cal 777; T Fat 39 g; 44% Calories from Fat;
  Prot 43 g; Carbo 69 g; Fiber 9 g; Chol 119 mg; Sod 1772 mg.
  Nutritional information does not include toppings.

Gary Pettinger, Idaho Falls, Idaho

RAMONA'S REVENGE

4 Lynn Wilson's refrigerator
  tamales
1 10-ounce can tomato soup
1 12-ounce can kidney beans
1 16-ounce can chili with
  beans
1 12-ounce can whole
  kernel corn

1 4-ounce can sliced olives
1 pound ground beef
1 large onion, chopped
1 cup shredded Cheddar
  cheese

Layer tamales, soup, undrained beans, chili, corn and olives in large baking dish. Brown ground beef with onion in skillet, stirring frequently; drain. Spoon over layers. Top with cheese. Bake at 350 degrees for 30 minutes or until bubbly. May use jalapeño olives for a spicier taste. Yield: 6 servings.

Approx Per Serving: Cal 588; T Fat 35 g; 51% Calories from Fat;
  Prot 32 g; Carbo 45 g; Fiber 9 g; Chol 82 mg; Sod 1748 mg.

Marilyn Wagner, Riverdale, Utah

BEAN SPROUT CASSEROLE

1 pound ground beef
1 cup finely chopped celery
1 onion, chopped
1 10-ounce can cream of
  chicken soup
1 10-ounce can cream of
  mushroom soup

1 soup can water
1 16-ounce can bean sprouts
1 8-ounce can water
  chestnuts
3/4 cup uncooked rice

Brown ground beef in skillet, stirring until crumbly; drain. Add celery, onion, soups, water, bean sprouts, water chestnuts and rice; mix well. Spoon into 9x13-inch baking dish. Bake at 350 degrees for 2 hours or until rice is tender. Yield: 10 servings.

Approx Per Serving: Cal 222; T Fat 10 g; 42% Calories from Fat;
  Prot 12 g; Carbo 21 g; Fiber 2 g; Chol 32 mg; Sod 497 mg.

Ila Mae Peterson, Richfield, Utah

CABBAGE CASSEROLE

1 pound ground round
1 small head cabbage,
coarsely chopped

1 medium onion, chopped
1   10-ounce can tomato soup

Brown ground round in skillet, stirring until crumbly; drain. Spread 1/3 of the cabbage in 2-quart baking dish. Layer ground round, onion and remaining cabbage 1/2 at a time in prepared dish. Spoon soup over layers; do not mix. Bake, covered, at 350 degrees for 1 hour. Yield: 4 servings.

Approx Per Serving: Cal 308; T Fat 17 g; 50% Calories from Fat;
Prot 24 g; Carbo 16 g; Fiber 3 g; Chol 74 mg; Sod 570 mg.

Laurel A. Wadley, Sandy, Utah

SPICY HAMBURGER AND NOODLE CASSEROLE

10 ounces uncooked flat
noodles
Salt to taste
1 1/2 pounds ground beef
2 green bell peppers,
chopped
2 onions, chopped
1   10-ounce can tomato soup

2 cups tomato juice
1   8-ounce can mushrooms
1   4-ounce bottle of stuffed
green olives, drained,
sliced
1 teaspoon chili powder
1 cup shredded Cheddar
cheese

Cook noodles in salted water in saucepan until tender; drain but do not rinse. Brown ground beef with green peppers and onions in skillet, stirring frequently; drain. Combine with soup, tomato juice, mushrooms, olives, chili powder and noodles in bowl; mix gently. Spoon into 9x13-inch baking dish. Bake at 275 degrees for 45 minutes. Sprinkle with cheese. Bake for 15 minutes longer. Yield: 12 servings.

Approx Per Serving: Cal 296; T Fat 14 g; 43% Calories from Fat;
Prot 18 g; Carbo 26 g; Fiber 2 g; Chol 47 mg; Sod 716 mg.

Hulda Larsen, Logan, Utah

SAUERKRAUT HOT DISH

2 large onions, chopped
1 pound ground beef
1 16-ounce can sauerkraut
3 tablespoons brown sugar
1 16-ounce can French-style
   green beans

1 10-ounce can cream of
   chicken soup
1 16-ounce package frozen
   Tater Tots

Sauté onions in nonstick skillet; remove with slotted spoon. Brown ground beef in skillet, stirring until crumbly; drain. Stir in onions. Alternate layers of ground beef mixture, sauerkraut, brown sugar and green beans in 2-quart baking dish until all ingredients are used. Spoon soup over layers. Top with Tater Tots. Bake at 350 degrees for 1 hour. Yield: 8 servings.

Approx Per Serving: Cal 328; T Fat 16 g; 44% Calories from Fat;
   Prot 15 g; Carbo 33 g; Fiber 4 g; Chol 40 mg; Sod 1254 mg.

Barbara Swenson, Belt, Montana

SHIPWRECK

1 pound ground beef
Salt and pepper to taste
2 medium potatoes, sliced
1 small onion, sliced

1 16-ounce can pork and
   beans
1 10-ounce can tomato soup

Brown ground beef in skillet, stirring until crumbly; drain. Season with salt and pepper. Spread potatoes and onion in 2-quart baking dish. Sprinkle with salt and pepper. Layer pork and beans and browned ground beef over potatoes and onions. Spoon soup over layers. Bake at 350 degrees for 1 hour. Yield: 4 servings.

Approx Per Serving: Cal 525; T Fat 19 g; 32% Calories from Fat;
   Prot 31 g; Carbo 61 g; Fiber 9 g; Chol 82 mg; Sod 947 mg.

Terri Rogers, Great Falls, Montana

A budget is an attempt to live below your yearnings.

WESTERN CASSEROLE

1½ pounds lean ground beef
1 large onion, chopped
1 green bell pepper, chopped
½ cup packed brown sugar
1   15-ounce can tomato sauce

3 cups cooked sliced carrots
2   15-ounce cans butter
   beans
6 slices bacon, cut into
   quarters

Brown ground beef in skillet, stirring until crumbly. Add onion and green pepper. Sauté until vegetables are tender; drain. Combine brown sugar and tomato sauce in 3-quart baking dish, stirring to mix well. Add ground beef mixture, carrots and undrained butter beans; mix well. Arrange bacon over top. Bake at 350 degrees for 1½ hours. Flavor improves if casserole is made ahead. Yield: 8 servings.

Approx Per Serving: Cal 408; T Fat 15 g; 33% Calories from Fat;
   Prot 25 g; Carbo 45 g; Fiber 12 g; Chol 60 mg; Sod 749 mg.

Betty L. Mann, Provo, Utah

TWO-TONE MEAT LOAF

1 pound ground beef
3 tablespoons finely
   chopped onion
2 tablespoons chopped parsley
1 cup soft bread crumbs
1 cup evaporated milk
¾ teaspoon salt
½ teaspoon pepper
1 pound ground veal

1 cup chopped celery
1 cup chopped carrots
1 tablespoon chopped onion
1 cup soft bead crumbs
¾ cup evaporated milk
¾ teaspoon salt
⅛ teaspoon pepper
1   8-ounce can spicy tomato
   sauce

Combine ground beef, 3 tablespoons onion, parsley, 1 cup bread crumbs, 1 cup evaporated milk, ¾ teaspoon salt and ½ teaspoon pepper in bowl; mix well. Press into baking pan. Combine ground veal, celery, carrots, 1 tablespoon onion, 1 cup bread crumbs, ¾ cup evaporated milk, ¾ teaspoon salt and ⅛ teaspoon pepper in bowl; mix well. Spread evenly over ground beef mixture. Bake at 350 degrees for 1 hour or until brown. Pour tomato sauce over top. May substitute sausage for veal or mushroom sauce for tomato sauce if preferred. Yield: 8 servings.

Approx Per Serving: Cal 305; T Fat 15 g; 43% Calories from Fat;
   Prot 30 g; Carbo 14 g; Fiber 1 g; Chol 111 mg; Sod 755 mg.

Darlene Loveall, Sandy, Utah

LASAGNA

1½ pounds lean ground beef
½ cup chopped onion
⅛ teaspoon garlic powder
¼ cup vegetable oil
2 8-ounce cans tomato sauce
1 6-ounce can tomato paste
1 cup (or more) water
Salt to taste
¼ teaspoon pepper
1 teaspoon oregano
⅛ teaspoon allspice
⅛ teaspoon nutmeg
1 8-ounce package lasagna
   noodles
8 ounces cottage cheese
8 ounces mozzarella cheese,
   shredded
¼ cup grated Parmesan cheese

Brown ground beef with onion and garlic powder in oil in skillet, stirring until ground beef is crumbly; drain. Add tomato sauce and tomato paste. Rinse cans with water; add to meat sauce mixture. Stir in next 5 ingredients. Simmer for 1 hour. Cook noodles using package directions. Spread a small amount of meat sauce in 9x13-inch baking dish. Layer noodles, cottage cheese, mozzarella cheese and remaining meat sauce ½ at a time in prepared dish. Sprinkle with Parmesan cheese. Bake at 375 degrees for 20 to 25 minutes or until bubbly. Yield: 6 servings.

Approx Per Serving: Cal 664; T Fat 37 g; 50% Calories from Fat;
    Prot 42 g; Carbo 42 g; Fiber 3 g; Chol 112 mg; Sod 900 mg.

Marjorie Weeks, Cascade, Idaho

MOCK LASAGNA CASSEROLE

1 pound ground beef
2 8-ounce cans tomato sauce
½ cup water
½ teaspoon basil
½ teaspoon garlic salt
½ teaspoon pepper
1½ cups uncooked elbow
   macaroni
1½ cups cream-style cottage
   cheese
6 ounces process American
   cheese, shredded

Brown ground beef in skillet, stirring until crumbly; drain. Add tomato sauce, water, basil, garlic salt and pepper; mix well. Simmer, covered, for 15 minutes, stirring occasionally. Cook macaroni using package directions; drain. Layer macaroni, cottage cheese, shredded cheese and meat sauce ½ at a time in 2-quart baking dish. Bake at 375 degrees for 30 minutes. Yield: 6 servings.

Approx Per Serving: Cal 388; T Fat 22 g; 51% Calories from Fat;
    Prot 30 g; Carbo 18 g; Fiber 2 g; Chol 84 mg; Sod 1289 mg.

Elaine Fielding, Orem, Utah

LASAGNA PIE

1 pound ground beef
1 large onion, chopped
1 small green bell pepper, chopped
1 8-count can biscuits
16 ounces cottage cheese
8 ounces mozzarella cheese, shredded

8 ounces Cheddar cheese, shredded
1 16-ounce jar spaghetti sauce
1 cup baking mix
1/2 cup milk

Brown ground beef with onion and green pepper in skillet over medium heat, stirring frequently until ground beef is crumbly and well done; drain. Press biscuits to flatten. Line deep-dish pie plate with biscuits. Alternate layers of ground beef mixture, cottage cheese, mixture of mozzarella and Cheddar cheeses and spaghetti sauce in prepared dish until all ingredients are used, ending with cheeses. Combine baking mix and milk in bowl; mix well. Spread over layers. Bake at 375 degrees for 35 minutes or until crusty brown. Serve immediately. Yield: 6 servings.

Approx Per Serving: Cal 774; T Fat 44 g; 52% Calories from Fat; Prot 46 g; Carbo 46 g; Fiber 2 g; Chol 134 mg; Sod 1706 mg.

Joy Cummings, Sandy, Utah

FRENCH MEAT PIE

I remember my grandmother making this
French-Canadian Toutseur, or French meat pie.

1 large onion, thinly sliced
2 tablespoons oil
1 pound ground beef
1 pound ground pork
Salt and pepper to taste

1 teaspoon allspice
2 cups mashed cooked potatoes
1 recipe 2-crust pie pastry

Sauté onion in oil in skillet; remove with slotted spoon. Add ground beef and ground pork. Cook until light brown, stirring until crumbly; drain. Add salt, pepper and allspice. Fold in potatoes and onion. Spoon into pastry-lined 9-inch pie plate. Top with remaining pastry. Trim edge and cut vents. Bake at 425 degrees for 15 minutes or until golden brown. Yield: 6 servings.

Approx Per Serving: Cal 699; T Fat 38 g; 50% Calories from Fat; Prot 34 g; Carbo 38 g; Fiber 3 g; Chol 97 mg; Sod 659 mg.

Rita Winterberger, Huson, Montana

SHEPHERD'S PIE

This is a good way to use leftover mashed potatoes.

1 pound ground beef
1 large onion, chopped
1/2 green bell pepper,
  chopped
Salt and pepper to taste

1 deep-dish pie shell
1 16-ounce can whole
  kernel corn
2 cups mashed cooked
  potatoes

Cook ground beef with onion, green pepper, salt and pepper in skillet until well done but not overcooked, stirring frequently. Spoon into pie shell. Layer undrained corn and potatoes over ground beef mixture. Bake in preheated 350-degree oven for 30 to 35 minutes or until brown. Serve hot with salad and French bread. Yield: 6 servings.

Approx Per Serving: Cal 429; T Fat 22 g; 45% Calories from Fat;
    Prot 20 g; Carbo 42 g; Fiber 3 g; Chol 51 mg; Sod 615 mg.

Joy Cummings, Sandy, Utah

WORKING MOM'S HAMBURGER SOUP

1 pound ground beef
1 10-ounce can vegetable
  soup
1 10-ounce can bean and
  bacon soup
2 soup cans water

1 8-ounce can tomato sauce
1/2 teaspoon chili powder
1/2 teaspoon sugar
1/2 teaspoon onion powder
Salt and pepper to taste

Brown ground beef in saucepan, stirring until crumbly; drain. Add soups, water, tomato sauce, chili powder, sugar, onion powder, salt and pepper; mix well. Simmer for 15 minutes. Yield: 6 servings.

Approx Per Serving: Cal 255; T Fat 14 g; 47% Calories from Fat;
    Prot 18 g; Carbo 16 g; Fiber 2 g; Chol 50 mg; Sod 924 mg.

Marion Hicken, Logan, Utah

A little experience often upsets a lot of theory.

HAMBURGER SOUP

1 pound ground beef
2 quarts hot water
4 carrots, chopped
1 turnip, chopped
1 cup shredded cabbage
1 cup chopped celery
1 large onion, chopped
1 tablespoon Worcestershire
  sauce

1 10-ounce can tomato soup
1 10-ounce package frozen
  peas
4 beef bouillon cubes
1 teaspoon savory salt
1/8 teaspoon curry powder
Oregano and basil to taste
Salt and pepper to taste
1/4 cup uncooked macaroni

Brown ground beef in saucepan, stirring until crumbly; drain. Add water, carrots, turnip, cabbage, celery, onion, Worcestershire sauce, soup, peas, bouillon cubes, savory salt, curry powder, oregano, basil, salt and pepper; mix well. Simmer for 2 hours. Add macaroni. Simmer for 30 minutes longer. Yield: 8 servings.

Approx Per Serving: Cal 208; T Fat 9 g; 38% Calories from Fat; Prot 15 g; Carbo 19 g; Fiber 4 g; Chol 37 mg; Sod 1074 mg.

Joy Staples, Twin Falls, Idaho

TACO SOUP

1 1/2 pounds ground beef
1 onion, chopped
2 16-ounce cans pinto beans

2 16-ounce cans tomatoes
3 cups water
1 envelope taco sauce mix

Brown ground beef in saucepan, stirring until crumbly; drain. Add onion, beans, tomatoes, water and taco sauce mix; mix well. Simmer until of desired consistency. Garnish servings with sour cream if desired. Yield: 8 servings.

Approx Per Serving: Cal 377; T Fat 13 g; 31% Calories from Fat; Prot 27 g; Carbo 39 g; Fiber 15 g; Chol 56 mg; Sod 672 mg.

Maxine Worsencroft, Twin Falls, Idaho

*Be careful of your thoughts; they may become
words at any moment.*

LAMB CURRY

My mother won a cooking contest with this recipe 25 years ago.
It is attractive served in a rice ring.

1½ pounds lamb shoulder, diced	¼ teaspoon ginger
1 cup chopped onion	1 teaspoon salt
2 tablespoons oil	¼ teaspoon pepper
3 tablespoons flour	1 tablespoon mint apple jelly
2 teaspoons curry powder	1½ cups onion soup
	4 cups cooked rice

Brown lamb with onion in oil in skillet. Combine flour, curry powder, ginger, salt, pepper and jelly in bowl; mix until smooth. Add to skillet; mix well. Stir in soup. Simmer for 1½ hours. Serve over rice. Yield: 6 servings.

Approx Per Serving: Cal 361; T Fat 11 g; 27% Calories from Fat;
Prot 22 g; Carbo 42 g; Fiber 1 g; Chol 59 mg; Sod 665 mg.

Karla K. Slusser, Boise, Idaho

HAIGAGAN KABOBS

This dish was served in San Francisco's famous Omar Khayyam Restaurant years ago. For best results, don't add water, don't cover, don't turn bundles and don't try to hurry the cooking.

2 pounds lamb shoulder	1 eggplant, peeled
2 green bell peppers	1 large potato, peeled
2 tomatoes	Salt and pepper to taste
1 onion	

Cut lamb into 4 pieces. Cut green peppers and tomatoes into halves. Cut onion, eggplant and potato into quarters. Divide lamb and vegetables between 4 sheets of baking parchment. Sprinkle with salt and pepper. Wrap bundles tightly; place in baking pan. Bake at 375 degrees for 3½ hours. Serve kabobs with cooking juices in parchment. May substitute foil for baking parchment. Yield: 4 servings.

Approx Per Serving: Cal 337; T Fat 11 g; 31% Calories from Fat;
Prot 39 g; Carbo 19 g; Fiber 4 g; Chol 118 mg; Sod 101 mg.

Florence L. Chamberlain, Caldwell, Idaho

STUFFED PEPPERS

8 green bell pepper shells
1 recipe corn bread, crumbled
2 16-ounce cans stewed
  tomatoes

1 16-ounce can corn, drained
1 16-ounce can peas, drained
1 1-pound canned ham, cubed
8 slices bacon

Parboil peppers in salted water for 5 minutes. Rinse with cold water; drain. Mix corn bread, tomatoes, corn, peas and ham in bowl. Spoon into peppers; place in baking pan. Top with bacon. Bake at 350 degrees for 45 minutes. Yield: 8 servings.

Approx Per Serving: Cal 397; T Fat 14 g; 31% Calories from Fat;
  Prot 21 g; Carbo 49 g; Fiber 8 g; Chol 50 mg; Sod 1445 mg.

Dorris Calton, Ogden, Utah

PORK CHOP BAKE

6 pork chops
2 10-ounce cans sauerkraut
1 onion, chopped
1 tablespoon brown sugar

1 10-ounce can cream of
  chicken soup
2 cups mashed cooked
  potatoes

Brown pork chops in skillet. Sauté sauerkraut and onion with brown sugar in skillet. Spoon into baking dish. Top with pork chops. Spread soup over chops. Bake at 350 degrees for 1 hour or until tender. Spoon mashed potatoes around edge. Broil until edges of potatoes are brown. Yield: 6 servings.

Approx Per Serving: Cal 275; T Fat 10 g; 32% Calories from Fat;
  Prot 24 g; Carbo 24 g; Fiber 3 g; Chol 66 mg; Sod 1258 mg.

Barbara Swenson, Belt, Montana

PORK CHOP CASSEROLE

8 pork chops
1 16-ounce bottle of
  Russian salad dressing

1 envelope onion soup mix
1 8-ounce jar apricot jam

Brown pork chops in skillet. Place in baking dish. Spoon mixture of next 3 ingredients over pork chops. Bake at 350 degrees for 1 hour. Serve with Rice Casserole (page 147). Yield: 8 servings.

Approx Per Serving: Cal 502; T Fat 36 g; 63% Calories from Fat;
  Prot 21 g; Carbo 26 g; Fiber <1 g; Chol 98 mg; Sod 622 mg.

Dorothy Ewer, Logan, Utah

TOMMY'S ITALIAN SAUSAGE LASAGNA

1 pound Italian sausage
1 clove of garlic, minced
1 16-ounce can tomatoes
2 6-ounce cans tomato paste
1 cup water
1 tablespoon whole basil
1½ teaspoons salt
1 10-ounce package lasagna
   noodles

2 eggs
3 cups ricotta cheese
½ cup grated Parmesan
   cheese
2 tablespoons parsley flakes
1 teaspoon salt
½ teaspoon pepper
1 16-ounce package thinly
   sliced mozzarella cheese

Brown sausage in skillet; drain. Add garlic, tomatoes, tomato paste, water, basil and 1½ teaspoons salt; mix well. Simmer, covered, for 15 minutes, stirring frequently. Cook noodles using package directions; drain and rinse. Beat eggs in bowl. Add ricotta cheese, Parmesan cheese, parsley flakes, 1 teaspoon salt and pepper; mix well. Layer noodles, meat sauce, ricotta cheese mixture and mozzarella cheese ½ at a time in 9x13-inch baking dish. Bake at 375 degrees for 30 minutes. Let stand for 10 minutes before serving. Serve with garlic bread and green salad. Yield: 8 servings.

Approx Per Serving: Cal 642; T Fat 36 g; 51% Calories from Fat;
    Prot 37 g; Carbo 42 g; Fiber 2 g; Chol 169 mg; Sod 1534 mg.

Dorris Calton, Ogden, Utah

SPAGHETTI SAUCE WITH
ITALIAN SAUSAGE

1 pound Italian sausage
1 large onion, chopped
2 cloves of garlic, minced
2 tablespoons minced parsley
1 cup hot water (optional)
1 4-ounce can mushrooms
1 16-ounce can tomato sauce

1 16-ounce can stewed
   tomatoes
2 tablespoons red wine
1 teaspoon MSG
2 bay leaves
¼ teaspoon rosemary
½ teaspoon oregano

Brown sausage in skillet; drain. Combine remaining ingredients in saucepan; mix well. Add sausage. Simmer for 2 to 2½ hours or until of desired consistency, adding additional water if needed. Remove bay leaves. Yield: 8 servings.

Approx Per Serving: Cal 128; T Fat 7 g; 49% Calories from Fat;
    Prot 7 g; Carbo 9 g; Fiber 2 g; Chol 21 mg; Sod 1278 mg.

Terri Rogers, Great Falls, Montana

Tenderfoot Treats

Poultry & Seafood

'89 H. CREEKMORE

COLOR COUNTRY COUNCIL

Cedar City and St. George, Utah

The Council's largest yearly service project is to prepare and serve the Recognition Dinner for the Utah Summer Games. An average of about 2000 people have been served each year for the last seven years. The Council donates over 700 hours of time and labor to make the dinner the success that it is.

BAKED CHICKEN BREASTS

8 8-ounce chicken breast
filets
8 1-ounce slices Swiss cheese
1/4 cup water

1 10-ounce can cream of
chicken soup
1/3 cup melted butter
2 cups seasoned stuffing mix

Rinse chicken and pat dry. Arrange in shallow 2 or 3-quart baking dish. Place 1 slice cheese on each piece of chicken. Spoon mixture of water and soup over top. Drizzle with butter; sprinkle with stuffing mix. Bake at 350 degrees for 1 hour or until tender. May substitute process cheese for Swiss cheese or seasoned crumbs for stuffing mix. Yield: 8 servings.

Approx Per Serving: Cal 458; T Fat 20 g; 41% Calories from Fat;
Prot 51 g; Carbo 16 g; Fiber <1 g; Chol 147 mg; Sod 759 mg.

Florence Hall, Logan, Utah

CHICKEN BARBECUED IN FOIL

3 tablespoons butter
1 tablespoon brown sugar
3/4 cup chopped onion
1 teaspoon vinegar
2 tablespoons
Worcestershire sauce

1 teaspoon prepared mustard
1/4 cup lemon juice
1/2 cup catsup
1 2 1/2 to 3-pound chicken,
cut into halves
Salt and pepper to taste

Combine butter, brown sugar, onion, vinegar, Worcestershire sauce, mustard, lemon juice and catsup in saucepan; mix well. Bring to a boil; reduce heat. Simmer for 15 minutes. Rinse chicken and pat dry. Rub with salt and pepper. Place each chicken half on large piece of heavy-duty foil. Spoon half the sauce over chicken. Fold foil to enclose chicken, sealing tightly. Place in baking pan. Bake at 350 degrees for 1 hour or at 200 degrees for 2 hours. Open foil. Broil until brown. Serve with sauce. Yield: 4 servings.

Approx Per Serving: Cal 469; T Fat 22 g; 42% Calories from Fat;
Prot 51 g; Carbo 17 g; Fiber 1 g; Chol 175 mg; Sod 666 mg.

Jeanne Larson, Burley, Idaho

CHICKEN AND BEER BAKE

6 chicken breasts, skinned
Salt and pepper to taste
4 to 5 tablespoons flour
1/4 cup oil
2 10-ounce cans cream of
  chicken soup
1 tablespoon soy sauce
1/2 cup beer
1/2 cup slivered almonds
1 4-ounce can sliced
  mushrooms

Rinse chicken and pat dry. Sprinkle with salt and pepper. Coat with flour. Brown on both sides in oil in skillet. Place in 9x13-inch baking dish. Combine soup, soy sauce, beer, almonds and mushrooms in bowl; mix well. Spoon over chicken. Bake at 350 degrees for 1 hour. Yield: 6 servings.

Approx Per Serving: Cal 342; T Fat 21 g; 57% Calories from Fat;
    Prot 21 g; Carbo 16 g; Fiber 2 g; Chol 44 mg; Sod 1038 mg.

Deloris Marking, Billings, Montana

CHICKEN AND BROCCOLI CASSEROLE

1 chicken, cut up
2 10-ounce packages frozen
  broccoli
2 10-ounce cans cream of
  chicken soup
1 cup mayonnaise
1/2 cup milk
1 teaspoon curry powder
1 cup shredded Cheddar
  cheese

Rinse chicken and pat dry. Cook in water to cover in saucepan until tender. Drain and bone chicken. Cook broccoli using package directions; drain. Combine soup, mayonnaise, milk and curry powder in bowl; mix well. Alternate layers of chicken, broccoli and soup mixture in baking dish. Top with cheese. Bake at 350 degrees for 45 minutes. Yield: 8 servings.

Approx Per Serving: Cal 510; T Fat 38 g; 66% Calories from Fat;
    Prot 33 g; Carbo 11 g; Fiber 2 g; Chol 115 mg; Sod 897 mg.

Gary and Ann Freeman, Burley, Idaho

BUTTERMILK CHICKEN

1 chicken, cut up
1 cup buttermilk
1½ cups flour
Salt and pepper to taste

1   10-ounce can cream of
    chicken soup
1 soup can buttermilk

Rinse chicken and pat dry. Dip in 1 cup buttermilk; coat with mixture of flour, salt and pepper. Arrange in greased baking pan. Bake in preheated 425-degree oven for 30 minutes. Combine soup and soup can of buttermilk in bowl; mix well. Spoon over chicken. Bake for 20 to 30 minutes longer or until done to taste. May double sauce mixture and serve over rice. Yield: 6 servings.

Approx Per Serving: Cal 409; T Fat 12 g; 28% Calories from Fat;
Prot 40 g; Carbo 32 g; Fiber 1 g; Chol 108 mg; Sod 562 mg.

Cathy Holm, Pocatello, Idaho

CHICKEN CASSEROLE

1 chicken
1   8-ounce can sliced water
    chestnuts
2   10-ounce cans cream of
    chicken soup

½ cup butter
1   14-ounce can chicken
    broth
1   6-ounce package dressing
    croutons

Rinse chicken well. Cook in water to cover in saucepan until tender. Drain and bone chicken; place in 9x13-inch baking dish. Layer water chestnuts and soup over chicken. Heat butter and chicken broth in saucepan until butter melts. Add croutons; toss until moistened. Sprinkle over layers. Bake, covered with foil, at 350 degrees for 25 minutes or until bubbly. Yield: 8 servings.

Approx Per Serving: Cal 430; T Fat 23 g; 49% Calories from Fat;
Prot 31 g; Carbo 24 g; Fiber 1 g; Chol 113 mg; Sod 1170 mg.

Mehl Ree Strate, Orem, Utah

IMPERIAL CHICKEN

1 chicken, cut up
1 cup fine dry bread crumbs
1/4 cup grated Parmesan
  cheese
2 tablespoons chopped
  parsley

1 clove of garlic, finely
  minced, or garlic powder
  to taste
1 teaspoon salt
1/4 teaspoon pepper
1/3 cup melted butter

Rinse chicken and pat dry. Combine bread crumbs, cheese, parsley, garlic, salt and pepper in bowl; mix well. Dip chicken in butter in bowl; coat with crumb mixture. Arrange in 9x13-inch baking dish; drizzle with remaining butter. Bake at 375 degrees for 45 minutes. May turn during baking time to brown both sides if desired. Yield: 6 servings.

Approx Per Serving: Cal 386; T Fat 20 g; 48% Calories from Fat; Prot 37 g; Carbo 13 g; Fiber 1 g; Chol 132 mg; Sod 724 mg.

Evelyn R. Damschen, Anaconda, Montana

CHICKEN ITALIANO

6 chicken breast filets
1/2 cup freshly grated
  Parmesan cheese
2 tablespoons minced fresh
  parsley

1 teaspoon oregano
1 clove of garlic, minced
1/2 teaspoon freshly ground
  pepper
6 tablespoons melted butter

Rinse chicken and pat dry. Combine Parmesan cheese, parsley, oregano, garlic and pepper in bowl; mix well. Dip chicken in butter in bowl; coat with cheese mixture. Arrange in 9x13-inch baking dish. Drizzle with remaining butter. Bake at 375 degrees for 25 minutes or until tender. Yield: 6 servings.

Approx Per Serving: Cal 204; T Fat 14 g; 64% Calories from Fat; Prot 18 g; Carbo 1 g; Fiber <1 g; Chol 73 mg; Sod 264 mg.

Sherlee A. Polglase, Great Falls, Montana

*Patience is the ability to "idle your motor" when
you feel like "stripping your gears."*

PARMESAN CHICKEN

4 chicken breast filets
¾ cup cornflake crumbs
¾ cup grated Parmesan
  cheese

¾ cup (1 ounce) ranch
  dressing mix
½ cup melted margarine

Rinse chicken and pat dry. Cut each filet into halves. Combine cornflake crumbs, cheese and salad dressing mix in bowl; mix well. Dip chicken in melted margarine in bowl; coat with crumb mixture. Arrange on rack in 9x13-inch baking pan. Sprinkle with remaining crumb mixture. Bake, covered, at 350 degrees for 20 minutes. Bake, uncovered, for 20 to 25 minutes or until done to taste. Yield: 4 servings.

Approx Per Serving: Cal 409; T Fat 28 g; 62% Calories from Fat;
  Prot 22 g; Carbo 16 g; Fiber <1 g; Chol 48 mg; Sod 1239 mg.

N. Leone Rogers, Salt Lake City, Utah

CHICKEN ROLLS

5 large chicken breasts
8 ounces cream cheese,
  softened
1 4-ounce can mushrooms,
  drained
½ teaspoon pepper
2 8-count cans crescent rolls

¼ cup melted margarine
1½ cups finely crushed
  seasoned stuffing mix
¼ cup flour
1 10-ounce can cream of
  chicken soup

Rinse chicken well. Cook in water to cover in saucepan until tender. Drain, reserving 2 cups chicken broth. Bone and chop chicken. Combine cream cheese, mushrooms and pepper in bowl; mix well. Mix in chicken. Separate roll dough into triangles. Spoon chicken onto triangles. Roll to enclose filling. Dip rolls in melted margarine in bowl; coat with stuffing mix. Arrange on baking sheet. Bake at 350 degrees until brown. Blend flour with enough reserved chicken broth to make a smooth paste in saucepan. Add remaining broth and soup; mix well. Cook until thickened, stirring constantly. Serve with chicken rolls. Yield: 8 servings.

Approx Per Serving: Cal 492; T Fat 30 g; 54% Calories from Fat;
  Prot 18 g; Carbo 39 g; Fiber <1 g; Chol 57 mg; Sod 1150 mg.

LuDean Pehrson, Logan, Utah

ANNA BELLE'S ENCHILADAS

4 cups chopped cooked
  chicken
1 cup shredded Monterey
  Jack cheese ·
1/2 cup (or more) chopped
  onion

3 12-ounce cans enchilada
   sauce
12 corn tortillas
1 1/2 cups shredded Monterey
   Jack cheese
1/2 cup chopped black olives

Combine chicken, 1 cup cheese and onion in bowl; mix well. Heat 1 can enchilada sauce in skillet. Soften tortillas in hot sauce. Spoon chicken mixture onto tortillas; roll to enclose filling. Arrange in baking pan. Heat remaining enchilada sauce in saucepan. Pour over enchiladas. Sprinkle with 1 1/2 cups cheese and olives. Bake at 350 degrees for 30 minutes. May substitute turkey for chicken or Cheddar cheese for Monterey Jack cheese. Yield: 6 servings.

Approx Per Serving: Cal 600; T Fat 29 g; 42% Calories from Fat;
  Prot 45 g; Carbo 43 g; Fiber 8 g; Chol 129 mg; Sod 1438 mg.

Terri Rogers, Great Falls, Montana

CHICKEN AND CHILIES ENCHILADAS

1 2 1/2-pound chicken
2 10-ounce cans cream of
   chicken soup
1 4-ounce can chopped
   green chilies

2 cups sour cream
12 flour tortillas
2 cups shredded mild
   Cheddar cheese

Rinse chicken well. Cook in water to cover in saucepan until tender. Drain and bone chicken. Combine soup, green chilies and sour cream in bowl; mix well. Place chicken on tortillas. Spoon some of the soup mixture over chicken. Roll tortillas to enclose filling; arrange in 9x13-inch baking dish. Spoon remaining soup mixture over top; sprinkle with cheese. Bake at 350 degrees for 1 hour. Yield: 6 servings.

Approx Per Serving: Cal 799; T Fat 46 g; 51% Calories from Fat;
  Prot 47 g; Carbo 51 g; Fiber 2 g; Chol 165 mg; Sod 1367 mg.

Mehl Ree Strate, Orem, Utah

CHICKEN ENCHILADAS

2 cups chopped cooked
  chicken
1 onion, chopped
2 cups shredded Cheddar
  cheese
8 flour tortillas
2 tablespoons flour

1 tablespoon melted
  shortening
2¹/₂ cups water
1 tablespoon chili powder
Minced garlic to taste
Salt and pepper to taste

Layer chicken, onion and half the cheese on tortillas. Fold tortillas over and roll to enclose filling. Arrange in baking pan. Sprinkle with remaining cheese. Blend flour with shortening in saucepan. Add water, chili powder, garlic, salt and pepper; mix well. Cook until thickened, stirring constantly. Pour over enchiladas. Bake at 550 degrees for 10 to 15 minutes or until bubbly and brown. Yield: 8 servings.

Approx Per Serving: Cal 316; T Fat 17 g; 46% Calories from Fat;
  Prot 20 g; Carbo 23 g; Fiber 2 g; Chol 61 mg; Sod 349 mg.

Jody Kenny, Ogden, Utah

CHICKEN ENCHILADA CASSEROLE

1 medium onion, chopped
2 tablespoons margarine
1 10-ounce can cream of
  chicken soup
1 10-ounce can cream of
  mushroom soup
1 4-ounce can chopped
  green chilies
1 cup chicken broth

3 jalapeño peppers, chopped
1 8-count package small
  corn tortillas, cut into
  quarters
3 pounds chicken breasts,
  cooked, shredded
1 pound Cheddar cheese,
  shredded
¹/₄ cup slivered almonds

Sauté onion in margarine in skillet until brown. Combine soups, green chilies, chicken broth and jalapeño peppers in bowl; mix well. Add onion; mix well. Spoon ¹/₃ of the mixture into greased and floured 9x13-inch baking dish. Layer tortillas, chicken, remaining soup mixture and cheese ¹/₂ at a time in prepared dish. Top with almonds. Bake at 350 degrees for 30 minutes. Yield: 6 servings.

Approx Per Serving: Cal 957; T Fat 48 g; 45% Calories from Fat;
  Prot 97 g; Carbo 33 g; Fiber 5 g; Chol 277 mg; Sod 1571 mg.

Joyce Harmon, Brigham City, Utah

CHICKEN TACO CASSEROLE

1 cup chopped onion
2 tablespoons oil
2 tablespoons taco
  seasoning, or to taste
1³/₄ teaspoons chili powder
¹/₄ teaspoon salt
¹/₄ teaspoon pepper
1¹/₂ cups sour cream

3 10-ounce cans cream of
   mushroom soup
3 cups chopped cooked
  chicken
6 to 8 flour tortillas
2 tablespoons oil
1 cup shredded Monterey
  Jack cheese

Sauté onion in 2 tablespoons oil in skillet until tender but not brown. Add taco seasoning, chili powder, salt, pepper, sour cream and soup; mix well. Cook until heated through, stirring constantly. Add chicken. Brush tortillas with 2 tablespoons oil; tear into pieces. Layer tortillas and chicken mixture ¹/₂ at a time in greased 9x13-inch baking dish. Top with shredded cheese. Bake at 350 degrees until bubbly. Yield: 8 servings.

Approx Per Serving: Cal 546; T Fat 35 g; 57% Calories from Fat;
    Prot 25 g; Carbo 35 g; Fiber 2 g; Chol 80 mg; Sod 1642 mg.

Barbara Hayes, Ogden, Utah

CHICKEN TORTILLA CASSEROLE

5 or 6 chicken breasts
12 corn tortillas
1 4-ounce can whole chili
   peppers
¹/₂ cup milk
1 10-ounce can cream of
   mushroom soup

1 10-ounce can cream of
   chicken soup
1 medium onion, chopped or
  finely grated
Salt and pepper to taste
1 pound Tillamook cheese,
  shredded

Rinse chicken and pat dry; wrap in foil. Bake at 400 degrees for 1 hour. Bone chicken. Cut tortillas and chili peppers into 1-inch strips. Combine milk, soups, onion, salt and pepper in bowl; mix well. Layer soup mixture, tortillas, chicken, chili peppers and cheese ¹/₃ at a time in buttered large baking pan. Chill in refrigerator for 24 hours. Bake at 300 degrees for 1 hour. May substitute chicken broth for chicken soup. Yield: 10 servings.

Approx Per Serving: Cal 375; T Fat 21 g; 50% Calories from Fat;
    Prot 25 g; Carbo 23 g; Fiber 3 g; Chol 74 mg; Sod 766 mg.

Terri Rogers, Great Falls, Montana

SOPA DE SECA

1 small onion, chopped
1 clove of garlic, minced
1 10-ounce can cream of
    mushroom soup
1 10-ounce can cream of
    chicken soup
1 14-ounce can chicken
    broth

1 4-ounce can (or more)
    chopped green chilies
6 chicken breasts, cooked,
    chopped
12 ounces Cheddar cheese,
    shredded
1 10-count package corn
    tortillas, cut into quarters

Combine onion, garlic, soups, chicken broth, green chilies, chicken and half the cheese in bowl; mix well. Spread 1/3 of the mixture in greased 9x13-inch baking dish. Layer tortillas and remaining chicken mixture 1/2 at a time in prepared dish. Top with remaining cheese. Bake at 350 degrees for 40 minutes or until bubbly. Yield: 10 servings.

Approx Per Serving: Cal 314; T Fat 17 g; 48% Calories from Fat;
    Prot 22 g; Carbo 20 g; Fiber 3 g; Chol 61 mg; Sod 816 mg.

Marsha Breen, Great Falls, Montana

CHICKEN TACO RICE

1 pound chicken breast filets
2 tablespoons oil
1 14-ounce can chicken
    broth
1 8-ounce can tomato sauce
1 envelope taco seasoning
    mix
1 12-ounce can corn, drained

1 medium red or green bell
    pepper, cut into strips
1 1/2 cups uncooked instant
    rice
1/2 cup shredded Cheddar
    cheese
2 cups tortilla chips
1/2 cup sour cream

Rinse chicken and pat dry; slice into strips. Stir-fry in hot oil in skillet until light brown. Add chicken broth, tomato sauce and taco seasoning mix. Bring to a boil; reduce heat. Simmer, covered, for 5 minutes. Stir in corn and bell pepper. Bring to a boil. Stir in rice. Cover and remove from heat. Let stand for 5 minutes. Fluff with fork. Serve with cheese, tortilla chips and sour cream. May use combination of red and green bell peppers. Yield: 4 servings.

Approx Per Serving: Cal 691; T Fat 28 g; 36% Calories from Fat;
    Prot 35 g; Carbo 77 g; Fiber 5 g; Chol 77 mg; Sod 2027 mg.

Arloa Weiss, Billings, Montana

CHICKEN POTPIE

2 cups chopped cooked
  chicken
2 10-ounce cans cream of
  potato soup
1/2 cup milk

1 16-ounce can mixed
  vegetables, drained
1 package all-ready
  refrigerator pie pastry

Combine chicken, soup, milk and vegetables in bowl; mix gently. Spoon into pastry-lined 9-inch deep-dish pie plate. Top with remaining pastry. Flute and trim edge; cut vents. Bake at 375 degrees for 40 minutes or until brown. Yield: 6 servings.

Approx Per Serving: Cal 375; T Fat 20 g; 48% Calories from Fat;
  Prot 21 g; Carbo 28 g; Fiber 4 g; Chol 52 mg; Sod 1087 mg.

Cindy Warren, Kaysville, Utah

LIGHT AND ZESTY CHICKEN AND RICE

4 chicken breasts
1/3 cup Italian salad dressing
2/3 cup uncooked rice
1 16-ounce package frozen
  mixed broccoli, carrots and
  water chestnuts

1 3-ounce can French-fried
  onions
13/4 cups chicken broth
1/2 teaspoon Italian seasoning

Rinse chicken and pat dry. Arrange in 8x12-inch baking dish. Pour salad dressing over top. Bake at 400 degrees for 20 minutes. Sprinkle rice, mixed vegetables and 1/2 can French-fried onions around and under chicken. Pour chicken broth over top; sprinkle with Italian seasoning. Bake for 25 minutes. Top with remaining onions. Bake for 2 to 3 minutes longer. Let stand for 5 minutes. Yield: 4 servings.

Approx Per Serving: Cal 415; T Fat 17 g; 36% Calories from Fat;
  Prot 22 g; Carbo 47 g; Fiber 4 g; Chol 45 mg; Sod 551 mg.

Waneta Lowman, Pocatello, Idaho

CHICKEN SCAMPI

2 pounds chicken filets
1/4 cup finely grated onion
1 tablespoon minced garlic
1/2 cup butter
1/4 cup olive oil

Juice of 1 lemon
1/4 cup minced fresh parsley
1 teaspoon salt
1/2 teaspoon pepper
1 tomato, chopped

Rinse chicken and pat dry. Cut into 1/2-inch pieces. Sauté onion and garlic in butter and oil in skillet. Add chicken, lemon juice, parsley, salt and pepper. Cook for 5 to 8 minutes or until chicken is cooked through, stirring constantly. Add tomato. Cook until heated through. Serve over noodles or rice. Yield: 8 servings.

Approx Per Serving: Cal 262; T Fat 19 g; 67% Calories from Fat;
Prot 20 g; Carbo 2 g; Fiber <1 g; Chol 80 mg; Sod 420 mg.

Arloa Weiss, Billings, Montana

SUNDAY CHICKEN

1 10-ounce can cream of
   chicken soup
1 10-ounce can cream of
   mushroom soup
1 soup can water

1 1/4 cups uncooked rice
1 envelope onion soup mix
8 chicken breasts
1 teaspoon MSG

Combine cream of chicken soup, cream of mushroom soup, water and rice in bowl; mix well. Spread in 10x15-inch baking pan. Sprinkle with 1/4 envelope dry soup mix. Rinse chicken and pat dry. Arrange over rice mixture. Sprinkle with remaining soup mix and MSG. Bake, covered with foil, at 325 degrees for 2 hours. May add canned mushrooms if desired. Yield: 8 servings.

Approx Per Serving: Cal 246; T Fat 6 g; 21% Calories from Fat;
Prot 18 g; Carbo 29 g; Fiber <1 g; Chol 40 mg; Sod 1222 mg.

RaNee Taggart, Smithfield, Utah

SWEET AND SOUR CHICKEN

20 chicken wings
1 16-ounce bottle of
   Russian salad dressing

1 envelope onion soup mix
1 10-ounce jar apricot
   preserves

Rinse chicken and pat dry. Arrange in rectangular baking dish. Combine salad dressing, soup mix and preserves in bowl; mix well. Rinse salad dressing bottle with a small amount of water and add to sauce. Pour over chicken; cover loosely with foil. Bake at 350 degrees for 1½ hours. Let stand for 10 to 15 minutes for thicker sauce. Serve sauce over rice, potatoes or noodles. May substitute cut up chicken for wings. Yield: 5 servings.

Approx Per Serving: Cal 714; T Fat 51 g; 62% Calories from Fat;
    Prot 19 g; Carbo 50 g; Fiber 1 g; Chol 110 mg; Sod 968 mg.
    Nutritional information includes entire amount of sauce.

Luella Merriman, Great Falls, Montana

TURKEY CASSEROLE

¾ cup chopped onion
1 cup chopped celery
½ cup butter
2 10-ounce cans cream of
   chicken soup
1 soup can milk
4 cups chopped cooked
   turkey

1 8-ounce package stuffing
   mix
1 cup cashews
1½ cups shredded medium
   Cheddar cheese

Sauté onion and celery in butter in skillet. Combine soup and milk in bowl; mix well. Add turkey and sautéed vegetables. Sprinkle ⅔ of the stuffing mix into buttered 9x13-inch baking pan. Layer turkey mixture, cashews, cheese and remaining stuffing mix in prepared dish. Bake at 300 degrees for 35 to 40 minutes or until bubbly and brown. Yield: 8 servings.

Approx Per Serving: Cal 605; T Fat 36 g; 54% Calories from Fat;
    Prot 36 g; Carbo 35 g; Fiber 2 g; Chol 117 mg; Sod 1243 mg.

Marian Downs, Hyrum, Utah

Faith is the best antidote for fear.

TURKEY ENCHILADAS

1½ pounds ground turkey
8 ounces turkey sausage
8 ounces lean ground beef
1 large onion, chopped
1 green bell pepper, chopped
9 mushrooms, sliced
½ bottle of Schilling's soup greens
2 large cloves of garlic, chopped

Salt and pepper to taste
¾ cup mild or hot salsa
1 8-ounce can tomato sauce
1 16-ounce can refried beans
12 large flour tortillas
2 cups each shredded Cheddar and Monterey Jack cheese
1 12-ounce jar salsa

Brown ground turkey, turkey sausage and ground beef with next 7 ingredients in skillet, stirring frequently; drain. Add ¾ cup salsa and tomato sauce. Simmer until liquid is reduced, stirring frequently. Spread refried beans down centers of tortillas. Layer with half the cheeses and turkey mixture. Roll tortillas to enclose filling; secure with wooden picks. Arrange in 9x13-inch baking pan sprayed with nonstick cooking spray. Top with half the remaining cheeses, 1 jar salsa and remaining cheeses. Bake, covered with heavy-duty foil, at 350 degrees for 30 minutes or until bubbly. Serve hot with shredded lettuce, sour cream and chopped tomatoes. Yield: 6 servings.

Approx Per Serving: Cal 1103; T Fat 56 g; 45% Calories from Fat; Prot 70 g; Carbo 87 g; Fiber 13 g; Chol 194 mg; Sod 1655 mg. Nutritional information does not include soup greens.

Joy Cummings, Sandy, Utah

HALIBUT AND SOUR CREAM BAKE

2 8-ounce halibut steaks, 1 inch thick
¼ cup sour cream
¼ cup mayonnaise
¼ cup sliced green onions

1 teaspoon lemon juice
¼ teaspoon salt
Red pepper to taste
¼ cup shredded Cheddar cheese

Cut halibut steaks into halves; arrange in 6x10-inch baking dish. Bake at 450 degrees for 12 to 15 minutes or until fish flakes easily. Combine next 6 ingredients in bowl; mix well. Spoon over fish; sprinkle with cheese. Bake at 450 degrees for 3 to 4 minutes longer or until sauce is heated through. Yield: 4 servings.

Approx Per Serving: Cal 260; T Fat 18 g; 64% Calories from Fat; Prot 21 g; Carbo 2 g; Fiber <1 g; Chol 51 mg; Sod 312 mg.

Georgene Baer, Providence, Utah

CRAB-STUFFED WHOLE SALMON

1 cup (or less) crab meat
1 cup shredded mozzarella
  cheese
2 tablespoons finely
  chopped celery
2 tablespoons finely
  chopped onion
1 cup sliced mushrooms

1 tablespoon soy sauce
1/2 cup melted butter
1 teaspoon seasoned salt
1 6 to 7-pound whole red or
  silver salmon
Lime juice to taste
Salt and pepper to taste

Combine crab meat, cheese, celery, onion, mushrooms, soy sauce, butter and seasoned salt in bowl; mix well. Butterfly and bone salmon. Drizzle with lime juice; sprinkle with salt and pepper. Spoon crab mixture into cavity of salmon. Wrap with foil; place in baking dish. Bake at 350 degrees for 1½ hours. May use 2 pieces salmon or imitation crab meat if preferred. Yield: 10 servings.

Approx Per Serving: Cal 491; T Fat 28 g; 53% Calories from Fat; Prot 56 g; Carbo 1 g; Fiber <1 g; Chol 187 mg; Sod 587 mg.

Merla Jorgensen, Pocatello, Idaho

CHINESE "CHICKEN"

1/4 cup chopped onion
2 cups chopped celery
1/4 cup chopped green bell
  pepper
1/4 cup margarine
1 6-ounce can chow mein
  noodles
2 9-ounce cans tuna

2 10-ounce cans cream of
  mushroom soup
1 4-ounce can mushrooms
1/4 cup chopped pimento
1/2 cup water
1/2 cup milk
8 ounces cashews

Sauté onion, celery and green pepper in margarine in skillet for 20 minutes. Reserve 1/2 cup noodles. Combine remaining noodles, tuna, soup, mushrooms, pimento, water, milk and cashews in bowl; mix well. Add sautéed vegetables; mix well. Spoon into 9x13-inch baking dish. Top with reserved noodles. Bake at 350 degrees for 20 to 25 minutes or until bubbly. May freeze dish without cashews, adding them at baking time. Yield: 12 servings.

Approx Per Serving: Cal 330; T Fat 20 g; 54% Calories from Fat; Prot 19 g; Carbo 20 g; Fiber 3 g; Chol 28 mg; Sod 786 mg.

Doris Wolfe, Boise, Idaho

SEAFOOD HOT DISH

1 7-ounce can albacore
   tuna, drained
2 7-ounce cans shrimp,
   drained
1 cup chopped celery
1 cup slivered almonds
1 cup mayonnaise-type salad
   dressing
3 cups cooked rice

1 10-ounce can cream of
   mushroom soup
1 soup can milk
1 4-ounce can mushrooms,
   drained
1 tablespoon lemon juice
1/2 small green bell pepper,
   chopped
1 cup crushed potato chips

Combine tuna, shrimp, celery, almonds, salad dressing, rice, soup, milk, mushrooms, lemon juice and green pepper in bowl; mix well. Spoon into 5x9-inch baking dish. Bake at 350 degrees for 45 minutes. Top with crushed potato chips. Bake for 15 minutes longer. Yield: 8 servings.

Approx Per Serving: Cal 492; T Fat 26 g; 47% Calories from Fat;
   Prot 27 g; Carbo 39 g; Fiber 3 g; Chol 113 mg; Sod 791 mg.

Carrol J. Walton, Salt Lake City, Utah

TUNA AND NOODLE CASSEROLE

3 ounces uncooked noodles
1 10-ounce can mushroom
   soup
1 6 1/2-ounce can tuna,
   drained
1 cup milk

1 2 1/2-ounce can mushrooms
1 cup shredded Cheddar
   cheese
1/2 cup sliced stuffed green
   olives
2 cups crushed potato chips

Cook noodles using package directions; drain. Combine soup, tuna and milk in saucepan. Bring to a boil. Add noodles, mushrooms, cheese and olives. Pour into buttered 1 1/2-quart casserole. Top with potato chips. Bake at 350 degrees for 30 minutes. Yield: 6 servings.

Approx Per Serving: Cal 374; T Fat 22 g; 53% Calories from Fat;
   Prot 19 g; Carbo 26 g; Fiber 2 g; Chol 31 mg; Sod 936 mg.

Dorothy Peterson, Logan, Utah

MINCED CLAM AND EGGPLANT CASSEROLE

1 large or 2 small eggplant,
unpeeled, chopped
Salt to taste
1 small onion, minced
3 tablespoons butter

2 7-ounce cans minced
clams
Pepper to taste
2 cups bread crumbs
1 tablespoon butter

Cook eggplant in boiling salted water in saucepan for 10 minutes; drain. Sauté onion in 3 tablespoons butter in skillet. Drain clams, reserving liquid. Add clams to onion. Alternate layers of eggplant and clam mixture in 1¾-quart baking dish until all ingredients are used, sprinkling layers lightly with salt and pepper. Top with bread crumbs. Pour reserved clam liquid over layers. Dot with 1 tablespoon butter. Bake at 350 degrees for 45 minutes. Yield: 6 servings.

Approx Per Serving: Cal 253; T Fat 14 g; 43% Calories from Fat;
Prot 11 g; Carbo 31 g; Fiber 4 g; Chol 64 mg; Sod 340 mg.

Florence L. Chamberlain, Caldwell, Idaho

HOT CRAB SOUFFLÉ

5 slices bread, cubed
½ cup mayonnaise
1 small onion, chopped
1 small green bell pepper,
chopped
1 cup chopped celery
1½ cups crab meat

5 slices bread
4 eggs
3 cups milk
1 10-ounce can cream of
mushroom soup
½ cup shredded Cheddar
cheese

Sprinkle cubed bread in 2-quart baking dish with 3-inch side. Combine mayonnaise, onion, green pepper and celery in bowl; mix well. Spread over cubed bread. Top with crab meat and bread slices. Beat eggs with milk in bowl. Pour over layers. Chill overnight. Spoon soup over top. Bake at 325 degrees for 1 hour. Top with cheese. Bake for 15 minutes longer. Yield: 8 servings.

Approx Per Serving: Cal 388; T Fat 24 g; 55% Calories from Fat;
Prot 17 g; Carbo 27 g; Fiber 1 g; Chol 160 mg; Sod 746 mg.

Alpha Burckardt, Boise, Idaho

LOBSTER NEWBURG

6 tablespoons butter
2 tablespoons flour
1½ cups light cream
3 egg yolks, beaten
1   5-ounce can lobster

3 tablespoons dry white wine
2 teaspoons lemon juice
¼ teaspoon salt
10 slices white bread, toasted

Melt butter in 12-inch skillet. Blend in flour. Add cream all at once. Cook until thickened, stirring constantly. Stir a small amount of hot mixture into egg yolks; stir egg yolks into hot mixture. Cook until thickened, stirring constantly. Add lobster, wine, lemon juice and salt. Cook until heated through. Cut toasted bread diagonally into quarters. Serve lobster on toast points. May substitute crab meat or shrimp for lobster or use a combination of seafood. Yield: 5 servings.

Approx Per Serving: Cal 449; T Fat 28 g; 57% Calories from Fat;
Prot 14 g; Carbo 34 g; Fiber 1 g; Chol 212 mg; Sod 653 mg.

Jan Lincoln, Helena, Montana

GARLIC-BROILED SHRIMP

½ cup melted unsalted butter
⅓ cup olive oil
1 tablespoon minced green
   onions
3 large cloves of garlic, minced
2 pounds large unpeeled
   shrimp, rinsed, deveined

1½ tablespoons fresh lemon
   juice
¼ cup minced parsley
¼ teaspoon salt
¼ teaspoon freshly ground
   pepper

Combine first 4 ingredients in shallow bowl; mix well. Add shrimp, coating well. Sprinkle with lemon juice, parsley, salt and pepper. Marinate for 30 minutes, turning frequently. Drain, reserving marinade. Arrange shrimp on rack in broiler pan. Broil 6 inches from heat source for 10 minutes, turning after 5 minutes. Bring reserved marinade to a boil in saucepan. Serve heated marinade with shrimp. Serve with rice, tossed salad, garlic bread and wine. Yield: 4 servings.

Approx Per Serving: Cal 547; T Fat 43 g; 71% Calories from Fat;
Prot 38 g; Carbo 2 g; Fiber <1 g; Chol 416 mg; Sod 545 mg.

Mary Lou Carlson, Helena, Montana

DOUBLE-BATCH SHRIMP FLORENTINE

4 10-ounce packages frozen
   chopped spinach, thawed,
   drained
3 pounds cooked shrimp
1/2 cup melted butter
1/2 cup flour
3 cups milk

1 cup dry white wine
1/2 cup chopped scallions
Salt, pepper and paprika to
   taste
2 cups shredded Cheddar
   cheese

Layer spinach and shrimp in two 9-inch pie plates lined with heavy-duty foil. Blend butter and flour in saucepan. Add milk, wine and scallions gradually. Cook over low heat until thickened, stirring constantly. Add seasonings. Pour over shrimp. Sprinkle with cheese. Bake at 350 degrees for 35 minutes. May bake 1 "batch" and freeze the other for future use. Bake frozen at 350 degrees for 1 hour or until bubbly. Yield: 8 servings.

Approx Per Serving: Cal 530; T Fat 26 g; 46% Calories from Fat;
   Prot 51 g; Carbo 19 g; Fiber 4 g; Chol 405 mg; Sod 815 mg.

Ruth Lovell, Caldwell, Idaho

TORTELINI WITH SHRIMP

1 8-ounce package spinach-
   cheese tortelini
1 8-ounce package cheese
   tortelini
1 small onion, sliced
1 clove of garlic, crushed
3/4 cup butter
1 pound shrimp, peeled,
   deveined

8 ounces plum tomatoes, cut
   into wedges
4 ounces boiled ham, cut
   into 1/4-inch strips
1 cup thawed frozen peas
1/2 cup grated Parmesan
   cheese
Freshly ground pepper to
   taste

Cook tortelini using package directions; keep warm. Sauté onion and garlic in butter in large skillet for 3 minutes. Add shrimp. Sauté for 3 minutes or until shrimp are pink. Add tomatoes, ham, peas and cheese. Cook for 1 minute. Toss with tortelini in serving bowl. Sprinkle with pepper. Garnish with additional cheese and fresh basil. Yield: 4 servings.

Approx Per Serving: Cal 955; T Fat 50 g; 48% Calories from Fat;
   Prot 50 g; Carbo 75 g; Fiber 7 g; Chol 320 mg; Sod 1511 mg.

June M. Fischer, Preston, Idaho

High Noon
Brunch Dishes

'89 H. CREEKMORE

EAGLE ROCK COUNCIL

Idaho Falls, Idaho

A simple homemade toy is helping children throughout southeastern Idaho cope in traumatic situations. For the past two years, the Telephone Pioneers have supplied hospitals, police and firemen with 12-inch Hug-A-Bears to be given to children in stressful circumstances. On occasion, custom bears have been made for special children. Seasonal bears are also made for Christmas and other holidays. Volunteers make about 100 bears a month. The bears cannot be purchased and only the Telephone Pioneers are authorized to create them. Their time is contributed, but the materials do cost money, and contributions of materials and money are welcomed.

In addition to the Hug-A-Bears, the Council has recently adopted a stretch of highway between Beach's Corner and Ucon and painted the picnic shelters at Tautphaus Park.

CHEESE CASSEROLE

2 4-ounce cans green
   chilies, drained, seeded
8 ounces Monterey Jack
   cheese, coarsely shredded
8 ounces Cheddar cheese,
   coarsely shredded

4 eggs, separated
3 tablespoons flour
1 cup milk
Salt and pepper to taste
2 tomatoes, sliced

Arrange chilies in casserole. Sprinkle cheeses on top. Beat egg whites until stiff peaks form. Combine egg yolks, flour, milk, salt and pepper in bowl; mix well. Fold gently into egg whites. Spoon over chilies; stir gently with fork. Bake at 350 degrees for 30 to 45 minutes or until set. Remove from oven. Arrange tomato slices on top. Yield: 8 servings.

Approx Per Serving: Cal 306; T Fat 22 g; 64% Calories from Fat; Prot 19 g; Carbo 9 g; Fiber 1 g; Chol 166 mg; Sod 379 mg.

Terri Rogers, Great Falls, Montana

CHEESE AND SAUSAGE CASSEROLE

2 pounds link sausage
8 slices bread, cubed
12 ounces sharp Cheddar
   cheese, shredded

4 eggs
2 1/2 cups milk
1 cup cream of mushroom
   soup

Cook sausage using package directions; drain. Layer bread cubes, sausage and cheese in greased 9x13-inch baking pan. Beat eggs with milk in bowl. Pour over layers. Chill, covered, in refrigerator, overnight. Spread soup over casserole. Bake at 325 degrees for 1 1/2 hours or until set. Yield: 8 servings.

Approx Per Serving: Cal 562; T Fat 40 g; 64% Calories from Fat; Prot 29 g; Carbo 21 g; Fiber 1 g; Chol 205 mg; Sod 1417 mg.

Donna Hager, Billings, Montana

*Any person who is always feeling sorry
for himself, should be.*

EGG AND SAUSAGE CASSEROLE

1 pound pork sausage
6 slices bread, cubed
8 ounces Cheddar cheese,
  shredded
6 eggs, beaten

1 cup milk
1 teaspoon dry mustard
1 teaspoon salt
12 ounces frozen hashed
  brown potatoes, thawed

Brown sausage in skillet, stirring until crumbly; drain. Place bread in 9x13-inch baking dish. Layer sausage and cheese on top. Combine eggs, milk and seasonings in bowl; mix well. Pour over cheese. Sprinkle potatoes over top. Chill, covered with foil, for 24 hours. Bake, covered, at 350 degrees for 35 minutes. Remove foil. Bake for 10 minutes longer. Yield: 12 servings.

Approx Per Serving: Cal 293; T Fat 19 g; 59% Calories from Fat;
  Prot 14 g; Carbo 17 g; Fiber 1 g; Chol 144 mg; Sod 649 mg.

Chuck Friederich, Eagle, Idaho

GRANDMA BONNIE'S ENCHILADAS

1 cup flour
2 cups yellow cornmeal
1 teaspoon salt
1 teaspoon baking powder
3 tablespoons shortening
2 1/2 cups water

12 ounces Cheddar cheese,
  shredded
1 cup chopped onion
1 6-ounce can enchilada
  sauce
7 to 14 eggs, fried to taste

Combine flour, cornmeal, salt and baking powder in bowl. Cut in shortening until crumbly. Add enough water to make fairly thin batter; mix well. Bake as for pancakes on preheated 400-degree griddle or electric skillet. Arrange in stacks of 3, spooning cheese, onion and enchilada sauce between layers. Top each stack with 1 or 2 fried eggs. Yield: 7 servings.

Approx Per Serving: Cal 626; T Fat 34 g; 49% Calories from Fat;
  Prot 30 g; Carbo 50 g; Fiber 4 g; Chol 477 mg; Sod 939 mg.

Sherlee A. Polglase, Great Falls, Montana

BREAKFAST PIZZA

1 pound sausage
1   8-count can crescent rolls
1 cup loose-pack hashed
   brown potatoes
1 cup shredded cheese
5 eggs

1/2 cup milk
1/2 teaspoon salt
1/8 teaspoon pepper
2 tablespoons Parmesan
   cheese

Cook sausage in skillet over medium heat until lightly browned, stirring until crumbly; drain. Separate rolls. Arrange in greased pizza pan, pressing to seal edges. Layer sausage, potatoes and shredded cheese over rolls. Combine eggs, milk and seasonings in bowl; mix well. Pour over layers. Sprinkle with Parmesan cheese. Bake at 375 degrees for 25 to 30 minutes or until set. Use 3 or 4 eggs for less full pan. Yield: 8 servings.

Approx Per Serving: Cal 359; T Fat 25 g; 63% Calories from Fat;
   Prot 15 g; Carbo 18 g; Fiber <1 g; Chol 171 mg; Sod 990 mg.

Dixie Dennis, Twin Falls, Idaho

CRUSTLESS QUICHE

2 cups chopped green onions
4 ounces fresh mushrooms,
   sliced
4 ounces cooked ham, cut
   into thin strips
3 tablespoons butter
2 1/2 cups whipping cream

6 eggs, beaten
1/2 teaspoon nutmeg
1/2 teaspoon salt
Pepper to taste
1 1/2 cups shredded Swiss
   cheese

Sauté green onions, mushrooms and ham in butter in skillet. Spoon into buttered 7x11-inch baking dish. Combine cream, eggs, seasonings and cheese in bowl; mix well. Pour over ham mixture. Bake at 375 degrees for 30 minutes or until set. Let stand for 10 minutes to cool slightly. Yield: 8 servings.

Approx Per Serving: Cal 467; T Fat 43 g; 82% Calories from Fat;
   Prot 16 g; Carbo 5 g; Fiber 1 g; Chol 301 mg; Sod 494 mg.

Bette Christensen, Logan, Utah

MEXICAN QUICHE

12 eggs, beaten
Salt and pepper to taste
1/2 teaspoon MSG
1 cup salsa
1/2 4-ounce can sliced olives
1 cup shredded mild cheese

1 cup shredded Monterey
  Jack cheese
1 large avocado, sliced
1 cup salsa
2 cups sour cream

Combine eggs, salt, pepper and MSG in bowl; beat well. Add 1 cup salsa and olives; mix well. Pour into greased 9x12-inch baking pan. Top with cheeses. Bake at 350 degrees for 30 minutes. Top with sliced avocado, remaining 1 cup salsa and sour cream. Yield: 10 servings.

Approx Per Serving: Cal 338; T Fat 29 g; 75% Calories from Fat;
    Prot 15 g; Carbo 7 g; Fiber 3 g; Chol 297 mg; Sod 634 mg.

Marilyn Wagner, Riverdale, Utah

ONION QUICHE

2 medium onions, grated
3 tablespoons butter
2 eggs, beaten
3/4 cup milk
1/2 teaspoon salt
1/8 teaspoon pepper

2 teaspoons flour
4 ounces Swiss cheese,
  shredded
2 ounces Parmesan cheese
1 unbaked 9-inch pie shell

Sauté onions in butter in skillet. Let stand until cool. Combine eggs, milk and seasonings in bowl; mix well. Sift flour into cooled onions. Add cheeses; mix well. Spoon into pie shell. Pour egg mixture over top. Bake at 350 degrees for 35 to 40 minutes or until set. Yield: 8 servings.

Approx Per Serving: Cal 281; T Fat 20 g; 63% Calories from Fat;
    Prot 11 g; Carbo 15 g; Fiber 1 g; Chol 86 mg; Sod 485 mg.

Sandy Kiser, Twin Falls, Idaho

SQUARE QUICHE

2 cups loose-pack hashed
   brown potatoes
2 cups mixed shredded
   Cheddar and Swiss cheese
6 eggs, beaten

¹/₄ cup chopped green bell
   pepper
¹/₄ cup chopped onion
¹/₄ cup chopped cooked ham
¹/₄ cup sliced mushrooms

Layer potatoes in greased 8-inch baking dish. Add half the mixed cheeses. Combine eggs, green pepper, onion, ham and mushrooms in bowl; mix well. Spoon over cheeses. Add remaining 1 cup cheese. Bake at 350 degrees for 40 minutes or until set. Yield: 6 servings.

Approx Per Serving: Cal 353; T Fat 23 g; 59% Calories from Fat;
   Prot 19 g; Carbo 17 g; Fiber 1 g; Chol 253 mg; Sod 331 mg.

Arloa Weiss, Billings, Montana

CHILI PEPPER CASSEROLE

2   4-ounce cans roasted
   peeled green chilies
2 cups chopped tomatoes
2 cups shredded Cheddar
   cheese

3 eggs, beaten
1 cup milk
¹/₂ cup biscuit mix
¹/₂ teaspoon salt

Remove stems and seeds from chilies. Rinse in cold water; drain. Arrange in greased 8x8-inch baking dish. Top with tomatoes and cheese. Combine eggs, milk, biscuit mix and salt in bowl; mix well. Pour over cheese. Bake at 350 degrees for 40 to 45 minutes or until golden brown. Yield: 6 servings.

Approx Per Serving: Cal 288; T Fat 18 g; 57% Calories from Fat;
   Prot 16 g; Carbo 16 g; Fiber 1 g; Chol 152 mg; Sod 603 mg.

Terri Rogers, Great Falls, Montana

CHILIES RELLENOS

1 28-ounce can whole green
  chilies
1 pound Monterey Jack
  cheese, cut into strips
4 ounces Cheddar cheese,
  shredded

Paprika to taste
5 eggs
1/4 cup flour
1 1/4 cups milk
1/2 teaspoon salt
Pepper to taste

Remove seeds from chilies; rinse and pat dry. Slip 1 strip Monterey Jack cheese into each pepper. Arrange half the chilies in greased 9x13-inch baking dish. Top with half the Cheddar cheese; sprinkle with paprika. Repeat layers. Beat eggs in bowl. Add flour gradually, beating until smooth. Add milk, salt and pepper; mix well. Pour over peppers. Bake at 350 degrees for 45 minutes or until set. Serve with nachos. Yield: 6 servings.

Approx Per Serving: Cal 527; T Fat 36 g; 60% Calories from Fat;
  Prot 33 g; Carbo 20 g; Fiber 2 g; Chol 273 mg; Sod 787 mg.

Betty L. Mann, Provo, Utah

CHILIES RELLENO SOUFFLÉ

6 egg yolks
1 cup evaporated milk
1 1/2 tablespoons flour
1/2 teaspoon salt
1/4 teaspoon pepper
1 28-ounce can green chilies

8 ounces Monterey Jack
  cheese, shredded
8 ounces sharp Cheddar
  cheese, shredded
6 egg whites, stiffly beaten
2 tomatoes, chopped, drained

Combine egg yolks, evaporated milk, flour, salt and pepper in bowl; mix well. Remove seeds from chilies; chop finely. Add with cheeses to egg yolk mixture. Fold in egg whites gently. Pour into buttered 9x13-inch baking dish. Bake at 325 degrees for 30 minutes. Add tomatoes. Bake for 20 to 30 minutes longer or until set. Yield: 8 servings.

Approx Per Serving: Cal 373; T Fat 25 g; 59% Calories from Fat;
  Prot 23 g; Carbo 16 g; Fiber 2 g; Chol 225 mg; Sod 547 mg.

Merla Jorgensen, Pocatello, Idaho

CHEESE-STUFFED PEPPERS

4 large green bell peppers
1 large tomato
2 teaspoons chopped fresh
　basil or 1/2 teaspoon dried
1/4 teaspoon salt

8 ounces sharp Cheddar
　cheese, cut into 1/4-inch
　cubes
8 ounces Swiss cheese, cut
　into 1/4-inch cubes

Cut green peppers into halves lengthwise; remove seeds. Place in colander. Steam for 6 to 8 minutes or until tender-crisp. Place in lightly greased baking dish. Scald tomato. Peel and chop. Combine tomato, basil, salt and cheeses in bowl; mix well. Fill green pepper shells completely with cheese mixture. Bake at 375 degrees for 20 minutes. May add chopped cooked chicken or turkey to cheese mixture. Yield: 8 servings.

Approx Per Serving: Cal 237; T Fat 18 g; 66% Calories from Fat;
　Prot 16 g; Carbo 5 g; Fiber 1 g; Chol 56 mg; Sod 320 mg.

Donna Hager, Billings, Montana

BUTTERMILK BISCUITS

2 cups flour
2 tablespoons baking powder
1/2 teaspoon salt
1 teaspoon shortening

1 cup plus 2 tablespoons
　buttermilk
1/8 teaspoon baking soda
1/2 cup oil

Sift flour, baking powder and salt together into bowl. Add shortening; mix well. Add mixture of buttermilk and baking soda. Mix for 30 strokes or until blended. Place dough on floured surface; sprinkle with flour. Pat to 1/2-inch thickness. Cut with round cutter. Dip each biscuit in oil; place on oiled baking sheet. Biscuits should touch. Bake in preheated 500-degree oven for 8 to 10 minutes or until browned. The less you handle the dough, the better the biscuit! Yield: 12 servings.

Approx Per Serving: Cal 171; T Fat 10 g; 52% Calories from Fat;
　Prot 3 g; Carbo 17 g; Fiber 1 g; Chol 1 mg; Sod 286 mg.

Terri Rogers, Great Falls, Montana

SOURDOUGH BISCUITS

These take a little practice before they melt in your mouth.

2 cups Sourdough Starter
1 teaspoon baking soda
1 teaspoon baking powder

⅓ cup sugar
½ teaspoon salt

Combine Sourdough Starter, baking soda, baking powder, sugar and salt in bowl; mix well. Knead on floured surface until smooth. Cut with biscuit cutter. Place in well greased 9x13-inch baking pan. Bake at 375 degrees for 20 minutes. Yield: 20 servings.

Approx Per Serving: Cal 407; T Fat 1 g; 2% Calories from Fat; Prot 11 g; Carbo 88 g; Fiber 3 g; Chol 0 mg; Sod 902 mg.

Sourdough Starter

2 cups unbleached flour
1 teaspoon salt
3 tablespoons sugar

1 envelope dry yeast
2 cups warm water

Combine dry ingredients in bowl. Add water gradually, stirring to mix well. Let stand, covered, in warm place for 3 to 5 days. After using 1 or 2 cups for recipe, add original ingredients and let stand for 10 to 12 hours. Use every 2 days or store in refrigerator for up to 2 weeks. Recipes made from refrigerated starter must stand at room temperature for 12 to 15 hours before baking to become active. Yield: 3 cups.

Irene Crane, Boise, Idaho

BUTTERMILK PANCAKES

1 cup flour
1 teaspoon baking soda
2 tablespoons sugar
¼ teaspoon salt

1 egg, beaten
¼ cup oil
1 cup buttermilk

Combine dry ingredients in bowl. Add mixture of egg, oil and buttermilk; mix well. Drop by spoonfuls onto hot greased griddle. Bake until brown on both sides. Yield: 6 servings.

Approx Per Serving: Cal 202; T Fat 11 g; 47% Calories from Fat; Prot 5 g; Carbo 22 g; Fiber 1 g; Chol 37 mg; Sod 281 mg.

Pat Hess, Providence, Utah

DUTCH BABY PANCAKES

⅓ cup butter
4 eggs

1 cup milk
1 cup flour

Melt butter in 9x13-inch baking pan in preheated 425-degree oven. Process eggs in blender container until blended. Add milk, processing constantly. Add flour. Process until smooth. Pour into hot prepared pan. Bake for 20 to 25 minutes or until golden brown. Serve immediately with fruit, syrup or confectioners' sugar. Yield: 6 servings.

Approx Per Serving: Cal 243; T Fat 15 g; 57% Calories from Fat; Prot 8 g; Carbo 18 g; Fiber 1 g; Chol 175 mg; Sod 149 mg.

Andree Maurice, Boise, Idaho

OLD-TIME PANCAKES

Serve with orange juice, Irish bacon and coffee.

1 cup unbleached flour,
** stirred with fork**
½ teaspoon baking powder
½ teaspoon baking soda
¼ teaspoon salt

1 tablespoon sugar
1 egg
1¼ cups buttermilk
2 tablespoons melted butter

Combine flour, baking powder, baking soda, salt and sugar in bowl. Beat egg in medium bowl until thick and lemon-colored. Add buttermilk and butter; beat until blended. Add flour mixture; stir just until moistened. Drop by ¼ cupfuls onto lightly greased 375-degree griddle. Bake until brown on both sides. Serve hot with butter and maple syrup. Yield: 13 servings.

Approx Per Serving: Cal 70; T Fat 3 g; 32% Calories from Fat; Prot 2 g; Carbo 9 g; Fiber <1 g; Chol 22 mg; Sod 130 mg.

Olga Fisher, Rupert, Idaho

Everyone's a manufacturer—some make good, others make trouble, still others make excuses.

CHERRY COFFEE CAKE

3 cups flour
1 teaspoon baking powder
1 teaspoon baking soda
1 cup sugar
1 teaspoon salt
1 cup margarine
2 eggs, beaten
1 cup sour cream
1 teaspoon vanilla extract

1 21-ounce can cherry pie
  filling
1/2 cup sugar
3 tablespoons melted
  margarine
1/2 cup flour
1/2 cup chopped pecans
1 teaspoon cinnamon

Sift 3 cups flour, baking powder, baking soda, 1 cup sugar and salt into bowl. Cut in margarine until crumbly. Mix eggs, sour cream and vanilla in bowl. Add to flour mixture; mix well. Spread half the batter in greased 9x13-inch baking pan. Spoon cherry pie filling over batter. Top with remaining batter. Combine 1/2 cup sugar, 3 tablespoons margarine, 1/2 cup flour, pecans and cinnamon in bowl; mix well. Sprinkle over top. Bake at 350 degrees for 35 minutes. Yield: 12 servings.

Approx Per Serving: Cal 526; T Fat 27 g; 45% Calories from Fat;
  Prot 6 g; Carbo 67 g; Fiber 2 g; Chol 44 mg; Sod 523 mg.

Colleen Rogan, Helena, Montana

QUICK COFFEE CAKE

1 2-layer package yellow
  cake mix
1 3-ounce package vanilla
  instant pudding mix
4 eggs
3/4 cup oil
3/4 cup water

1 teaspoon vanilla extract
1 teaspoon Molly McButter
  flavoring
1/4 cup sugar
1/4 cup chopped pecans
1 teaspoon cinnamon

Combine cake mix, pudding mix, eggs, oil, water and flavorings in mixer bowl. Beat at high speed for 8 minutes. Pour into greased and floured 9x13-inch baking pan. Sprinkle mixture of sugar, pecans and cinnamon on top. Bake at 350 degrees for 30 minutes or until coffee cake tests done. Yield: 12 servings.

Approx Per Serving: Cal 389; T Fat 21 g; 48% Calories from Fat;
  Prot 4 g; Carbo 47 g; Fiber <1 g; Chol 71 mg; Sod 332 mg.

Noreen Udall, Great Falls, Montana

MONKEY BREAD

½ cup chopped pecans
1   3-ounce package
  butterscotch pudding and
  pie filling mix

24 frozen dinner rolls
6 tablespoons margarine
½ cup packed brown sugar
¾ teaspoon cinnamon

Sprinkle pecans in greased bundt pan. Sprinkle pudding mix over pecans. Arrange dinner rolls in prepared pan. Combine margarine, brown sugar and cinnamon in saucepan; mix well. Heat until margarine melts. Pour over rolls. Let stand, covered, overnight. Bake at 350 degrees for 30 to 35 minutes or until golden brown. Yield: 24 servings.

Approx Per Serving: Cal 157; T Fat 7 g; 38% Calories from Fat;
  Prot 2 g; Carbo 22 g; Fiber 1 g; Chol <1 mg; Sod 214 mg.

Deloris Marking, Billings, Montana

APPLESAUCE MUFFINS

2 cups flour
1 tablespoon baking powder
½ teaspoon salt
¾ teaspoon cinnamon
⅔ cup sugar

1 egg, beaten
⅓ cup melted butter
¾ cup milk
½ cup applesauce

Sift first 5 ingredients together into bowl. Add egg, butter, milk and applesauce. Stir just until moistened. Fill paper-lined muffin cups ¾ full. Bake at 400 degrees for 20 minutes. Yield: 12 servings.

Approx Per Serving: Cal 185; T Fat 6 g; 30% Calories from Fat;
  Prot 3 g; Carbo 29 g; Fiber 1 g; Chol 34 mg; Sod 227 mg.

Barbara Hayes, Ogden, Utah

Give the birds crumbs; God gives you loaves.
English Proverb

FRUITY OAT BRAN MUFFINS

1/2 cup buttermilk
2 egg whites
11/2 tablespoons oil
1/3 cup honey
1/2 cup mashed banana
1/2 cup applesauce

21/4 cups oat bran
1 teaspoon cinnamon
1 teaspoon baking powder
1/2 teaspoon baking soda
1/4 teaspoon salt
1/2 cup raisins

Combine buttermilk, egg whites, oil and honey in bowl; mix well. Add banana and applesauce; mix well. Add oat bran, cinnamon, baking powder, baking soda and salt; mix well. Stir in raisins. Fill paper-lined muffin cups 1/2 full. Bake at 350 degrees for 25 minutes. Yield: 12 servings.

Approx Per Serving: Cal 124; T Fat 3 g; 15% Calories from Fat;
Prot 4 g; Carbo 29 g; Fiber 4 g; Chol <1 mg; Sod 131 mg.

Ilene Wilson, Logan, Utah

CINNAMON ROLLS

2 envelopes dry yeast
1/2 cup warm water
2 cups milk, scalded
1/2 cup shortening
4 cups flour
1 cup sugar
1 cup mashed potatoes
2 eggs, slightly beaten

2 teaspoons salt
1 cup flour
1 cup raisins
1/2 cup chopped pecans
2 cups flour
1/2 cup melted butter
1 tablespoon cinnamon
1/2 cup sugar

Dissolve yeast in warm water in bowl. Combine hot milk and shortening in bowl. Let stand until cool. Add 4 cups flour, 1 cup sugar, potatoes, eggs, salt and yeast; mix well. Stir in mixture of 1 cup flour, raisins and pecans. Add enough remaining 2 cups flour to make soft dough. Let rise until doubled in bulk. Divide into 2 portions. Roll each portion into rectangle. Brush with melted butter. Sprinkle with cinnamon and 1/2 cup sugar. Roll as for jelly roll; cut into 1-inch slices. Place on greased baking sheet. Let rise until doubled in bulk. Bake at 350 degrees for 20 minutes. Yield: 36 servings.

Approx Per Serving: Cal 211; T Fat 8 g; 32% Calories from Fat;
Prot 4 g; Carbo 33 g; Fiber 1 g; Chol 21 mg; Sod 169 mg.

Lucille Linford, Pocatello, Idaho

ORANGE BOWKNOTS

1 tablespoon yeast
1 tablespoon sugar
1/4 cup warm water
1 cup scalded milk, cooled
1/2 cup butter, softened
1/3 cup sugar
1 teaspoon salt
2 eggs

2 tablespoons grated orange
  rind
1/4 cup orange juice
5 to 6 cups flour
1 teaspoon grated orange rind
2 tablespoons orange juice
1 cup confectioners' sugar

Dissolve yeast and 1 tablespoon sugar in water in bowl. Add next 7 ingredients; mix well. Add enough flour to make soft dough. Let rise, covered, until doubled in bulk. Roll into two 10x18-inch rectangles. Cut into 3/4x10-inch strips. Tie each into knot, tucking ends under. Place on greased baking sheet. Bake at 350 degrees for 12 to 17 minutes or until golden brown. Glaze warm rolls with mixture of 1 teaspoon orange rind and remaining ingredients. Yield: 48 servings.

Approx Per Serving: Cal 98; T Fat 2 g; 23% Calories from Fat;
  Prot 2 g; Carbo 17 g; Fiber <1 g; Chol 15 mg; Sod 66 mg.

Evelyn Cameron, Blackfoot, Idaho

HIGHLAND OAT SCONES

1 1/2 cups flour
1/2 cup oat bran cereal
1/3 cup sugar
1 tablespoon baking powder
1/2 teaspoon salt
1/3 cup skim milk
1/3 cup melted margarine

1 egg
1/2 cup dark raisins
1 tablespoon melted
  margarine
1 tablespoon sugar
1/8 teaspoon cinnamon

Mix first 5 ingredients in bowl. Add milk, 1/3 cup margarine and egg; mix until moistened. Stir in raisins. Pat into 8-inch square on waxed paper. Cut into quarters. Cut each into 4 triangles. Brush with 1 tablespoon margarine. Sprinkle with mixture of 1 tablespoon sugar and cinnamon. Place on baking sheet. Bake at 375 degrees for 14 to 16 minutes or until golden brown. Yield: 16 servings.

Approx Per Serving: Cal 132; T Fat 5 g; 35% Calories from Fat;
  Prot 2 g; Carbo 20 g; Fiber 1 g; Chol 13 mg; Sod 201 mg.

Donna Hager, Billings, Montana

COUNTRY SCONES

1/2 cup dried currants
2 cups flour
3 tablespoons sugar
2 teaspoons baking powder
3/4 teaspoon salt
1/2 teaspoon baking soda

5 tablespoons butter
1 cup sour cream
1 egg, separated
1 teaspoon sugar
1/8 teaspoon cinnamon

Soak dried currants in hot water to cover in small bowl for 5 minutes. Drain well; set aside. Combine flour, 3 tablespoons sugar, baking powder, salt and baking soda in bowl. Cut in butter until crumbly. Add currants; mix well. Add mixture of sour cream and egg yolk; stir just until mixture clings together. Knead gently 10 or 12 times on lightly floured surface. Pat into 9-inch circle. Cut with 4-inch round cutter. Slice each circle into quarters; do not separate. Place on ungreased baking sheet. Brush with beaten egg white. Sprinkle with mixture of remaining 1 teaspoon sugar and cinnamon. Bake at 425 degrees for 15 to 18 minutes or until golden brown. Cool slightly on wire rack; break apart. Serve warm. Yield: 24 servings.

Approx Per Serving: Cal 99; T Fat 5 g; 43% Calories from Fat; Prot 2 g; Carbo 12 g; Fiber <1 g; Chol 20 mg; Sod 140 mg.

Donna Hager, Billings, Montana

BACON BREAD

This is great toasted!

4 cups flour
2/3 cup sugar
2 tablespoons baking powder
1 teaspoon baking soda
4 eggs
2 cups sour cream

2/3 cup milk
1 cup chopped pecans
1 pound bacon, crisp-fried,
  crumbled
1/4 cup melted butter

Sift dry ingredients into large bowl. Stir in mixture of eggs, sour cream and milk. Fold in pecans and bacon. Pour into 2 greased 5x9-inch loaf pans. Bake at 350 degrees for 50 to 55 minutes or until bread tests done. Brush with melted butter. Remove to wire rack to cool. Store in sealed plastic bags. Yield: 24 servings.

Approx Per Serving: Cal 315; T Fat 20 g; 57% Calories from Fat; Prot 10 g; Carbo 24 g; Fiber 1 g; Chol 66 mg; Sod 459 mg.

Joy Cummings, Sandy, Utah

Dough Punchers

Breads

'89 H. CREEKMORE

FRONTIER COUNCIL

Helena, Montana

Frontier Council held a "Hog Wild Fund Raiser Raffle" to raise funds for an educational center for the 4-H Community of Lewis and Clark County. The volunteer effort raised $2,500 for the "4-H Barn Raising." The funds will be used to help purchase a metal building that will be approximately 12,000 square feet in size. It will house a permanent livestock scale and space for a show/sale ring, indoor animal exhibits and storage for equipment.

When five U S West men from Helena and Butte took up arms and headed to Saudi, so did the Pioneers of the Frontier Council. An estimated 1,200 yellow ribbons were made and distributed by the Pioneers. T-shirts and sweat shirts were sold and pop cans collected and sold to raise funds for care packages sent by a Military Support Group from Helena. Sgt. Teddy, a camouflage Hug-A-Bear became the forerunner of 100 more bears sent to the children in Saudi by the Council. A video project carried messages from families and fellow employees to the men in Saudi.

CORN BREAD

1 cup flour
1/2 cup sugar
2 teaspoons baking powder
1/2 teaspoon baking soda
1 teaspoon salt

2 eggs, well beaten
1 1/2 cups buttermilk
3 tablespoons melted bacon
   drippings
1 1/2 cups cornmeal

Sift flour, sugar, baking powder, baking soda and salt together. Combine eggs, buttermilk and bacon drippings in bowl; mix well. Add cornmeal and sifted dry ingredients. Stir until just moistened. Pour into greased 9x9-inch baking pan. Bake at 400 degrees for 30 minutes or until golden brown. Yield: 9 servings.

Approx Per Serving: Cal 254; T Fat 7 g; 24% Calories from Fat;
   Prot 6 g; Carbo 42 g; Fiber 2 g; Chol 77 mg; Sod 461 mg.

Terri Rogers, Great Falls, Montana

MEXICAN CORN BREAD

1/2 cup flour
1 1/2 cups yellow cornmeal
1 tablespoon baking powder
1 teaspoon salt
1 cup milk
2 eggs, beaten

1   17-ounce can cream-style
   corn
1 cup shredded longhorn
   cheese
1/2 cup green chilies
1/4 cup corn oil

Mix flour, cornmeal, baking powder and salt in bowl. Add milk, eggs, corn, cheese, green chilies and oil; mix well. Pour into preheated greased shallow 9x13-inch baking pan. Bake at 350 degrees for 45 minutes or until golden brown. Cut into squares. Serve warm with Bert's Famous Award-Winning Chili (page 50) and tossed salad. Yield: 15 servings.

Approx Per Serving: Cal 175; T Fat 8 g; 39% Calories from Fat;
   Prot 5 g; Carbo 21 g; Fiber 2 g; Chol 39 mg; Sod 363 mg.

Mary Lou Carlson, Helena, Montana

*Whoever has a heart full of love always
has something to give.*

LINDA'S SWEET CORN BREAD

This is great served with clam chowder!

2 cups flour
1 cup cornmeal
1 tablespoon baking powder
1/2 teaspoon salt
5 egg yolks

1 1/4 cups evaporated milk
1 teaspoon vanilla extract
3/4 cup melted butter
1 1/2 cups sugar
5 egg whites

Mix flour, cornmeal, baking powder and salt together. Blend egg yolks, evaporated milk and vanilla in bowl; mix well. Combine butter and sugar in large bowl; mix well. Add dry ingredients and evaporated milk mixture alternately, beating well after each addition. Beat egg whites in mixer bowl until soft peaks form. Fold into batter. Spoon into greased 9x13-inch baking pan. Bake at 350 degrees for 30 to 35 minutes or until golden brown. Yield: 16 servings.

Approx Per Serving: Cal 290; T Fat 12 g; 38% Calories from Fat;
Prot 6 g; Carbo 40 g; Fiber 1 g; Chol 96 mg; Sod 241 mg.

Corinne G. Morrison, Leesburg, Florida

SPOON BREAD

1 cup butter, softened
1 cup sugar
4 eggs, beaten
1   17-ounce can cream-style
  corn
1 cup flour
1 cup cornmeal

4 teaspoons baking powder
1/4 teaspoon salt
1   4-ounce can chopped
  green chilies
1/2 cup shredded Tillamook
  cheese

Combine butter, sugar and eggs in bowl; mix well. Add corn; mix well. Add flour, cornmeal, baking powder and salt; mix well. Stir in green chilies and cheese. Spoon into 9x12-inch baking pan. Bake at 300 degrees for 1 hour or until golden brown. May substitute margarine for butter if desired. Yield: 15 servings.

Approx Per Serving: Cal 287; T Fat 15 g; 47% Calories from Fat;
Prot 5 g; Carbo 34 g; Fiber 2 g; Chol 94 mg; Sod 361 mg.

Martha Hamilton, Meridian, Idaho

SODA CRACKERS

1 cup butter
4 cups flour
1 tablespoon vinegar

3/4 cup milk
1/2 teaspoon baking soda
1/2 teaspoon salt

Cut butter into flour in bowl until crumbly. Blend vinegar and milk in small bowl. Stir in baking soda and salt. Add to flour mixture; mix well. Pat 1/5 inch thick on lightly floured surface. Cut into squares. Place on baking sheet. Bake at 375 degrees for 20 minutes or until golden. Yield: 24 servings.

Approx Per Serving: Cal 148; T Fat 8 g; 49% Calories from Fat; Prot 3 g; Carbo 16 g; Fiber 1 g; Chol 22 mg; Sod 130 mg.

Terri Rogers, Great Falls, Montana

FLOUR TORTILLAS

3 cups flour
Salt to taste

5 tablespoons shortening
1 cup warm water

Process flour, salt and shortening in food processor until crumbly. Add 1 cup warm water gradually, processing constantly until smooth. Shape into 12 balls; flatten into circles. Cook on medium-hot griddle until dry. Yield: 12 servings.

Approx Per Serving: Cal 161; T Fat 6 g; 32% Calories from Fat; Prot 3 g; Carbo 24 g; Fiber 1 g; Chol 0 mg; Sod 1 mg.

Terri Rogers, Great Falls, Montana

APPLESAUCE BREAD

2 cups flour
1 cup sugar
1 tablespoon cornstarch
2 teaspoons baking soda
1/4 teaspoon salt
1/2 teaspoon cinnamon

1/2 teaspoon cloves
3/4 teaspoon allspice
1/4 teaspoon nutmeg
1/2 cup oil
1 1/2 cups applesauce
1/2 cup each raisins and pecans

Combine all ingredients in bowl; mix well. Spoon into non-stick 5x9-inch loaf pan. Bake at 350 degrees for 1 hour or until loaf tests done. Cool on wire rack. Yield: 12 servings.

Approx Per Serving: Cal 237; T Fat 9 g; 35% Calories from Fat; Prot 2 g; Carbo 37 g; Fiber 1 g; Chol 0 mg; Sod 183 mg.

Marjorie Thomas, Boise, Idaho

BLUEBERRY-BANANA BREAD

*This bread is great for gift-giving, serving at parties
or just for a family treat.*

3/4 cup butter, softened
1 cup sugar
1 cup packed brown sugar
4 eggs
6 medium bananas, mashed
5 cups flour

1 tablespoon baking soda
1 teaspoon salt
1/2 cup buttermilk
1 cup chopped walnuts
2 cups blueberries
3 tablespoons brown sugar

Beat butter, sugar and 1 cup brown sugar in mixer bowl. Add eggs 1 at a time, beating well after each addition. Add mashed bananas; mix well. Stir in flour, baking soda and salt. Add buttermilk; mix well. Stir in walnuts and blueberries. Spoon into 3 greased 5x9-inch loaf pans. Sprinkle each loaf with 1 tablespoon brown sugar. Bake at 325 degrees for 1 hour and 10 minutes to 1 hour and 20 minutes or until loaves test done. Remove to wire rack to cool. Yield: 36 servings.

Approx Per Serving: Cal 199; T Fat 7 g; 30% Calories from Fat;
Prot 3 g; Carbo 32 g; Fiber 1 g; Chol 34 mg; Sod 176 mg.

Karren Fairbanks, Salt Lake City, Utah

CANNED BREAD

1 cup warm water
1 tablespoon dry yeast
2 tablespoons brown sugar
1/3 cup honey
1/3 cup oil

3 cups warm water
1 cup powdered milk
7 cups whole wheat flour
1 cup all-purpose flour
4 1/2 teaspoons salt

Mix 1 cup warm water, yeast and brown sugar in large bowl. Let stand for 5 minutes. Stir in honey. Add oil, 3 cups warm water, powdered milk, whole wheat flour, all-purpose flour and salt; mix well. Spoon into 3 greased 46-ounce juice cans. Place in preheated 300-degree oven. Turn off oven. Let stand in oven for 20 minutes. Increase oven temperature to 375 degrees. Bake for 50 to 60 minutes or until tops are brown. Cool in cans for 15 minutes. Remove to wire rack to cool completely. Yield: 36 servings.

Approx Per Serving: Cal 128; T Fat 3 g; 17% Calories from Fat;
Prot 4 g; Carbo 24 g; Fiber 3 g; Chol <1 mg; Sod 278 mg.

Rose Kriegen, Burley, Idaho

CHEESE BREAD

2 cups flour
1 tablespoon sugar
1 teaspoon baking powder
1/2 teaspoon salt
1/4 cup butter, softened

1 cup shredded Cheddar
  cheese
1 tablespoon grated onion
3/4 cup milk
1 egg, slightly beaten

Sift flour, sugar, baking powder and salt into bowl. Cut in butter 1/4 at a time until mixture resembles fine crumbs. Add cheese and onion; mix well. Stir in milk and egg until moistened. Spoon into greased 5x9-inch loaf pan. Bake at 350 degrees for 40 to 45 minutes or until loaf tests done. Cool on wire rack. Yield: 12 servings.

Approx Per Serving: Cal 168; T Fat 8 g; 44% Calories from Fat;
  Prot 6 g; Carbo 18 g; Fiber 1 g; Chol 40 mg; Sod 220 mg.

Georgia Beam, Billings, Montana

CRANBERRY BREAD

2 cups flour
1/2 teaspoon salt
1 1/2 teaspoons baking powder
1/2 teaspoon baking soda
1 cup sugar
1/4 cup melted margarine
1 tablespoon oil

1 egg, beaten
1/2 cup orange juice
1 tablespoon grated orange
  rind
1 1/2 cups chopped fresh
  cranberries
3/4 cup chopped pecans

Sift flour, salt, baking powder, baking soda and sugar together. Combine margarine, oil, egg, orange juice and orange rind in bowl; mix well. Stir in sifted dry ingredients until moistened. Stir in cranberries and pecans. Spoon into greased 4x8-inch loaf pan. Bake at 350 degrees for 1 hour or until loaf tests done. Cool on wire rack. Yield: 10 servings.

Approx Per Serving: Cal 302; T Fat 13 g; 37% Calories from Fat;
  Prot 4 g; Carbo 44 g; Fiber 2 g; Chol 21 mg; Sod 259 mg.

Barbara Hayes, Ogden, Utah

Only when you are silent can you learn something new.

DILLY BREAD

1 package dry yeast
1/4 cup warm water
1 cup creamed cottage cheese
2 tablespoons sugar
1 egg
1 tablespoon dried onion
  flakes
1 tablespoon butter

2 teaspoons dillseed
1 teaspoon salt
1/4 teaspoon baking soda
2 1/2 cups flour
2 tablespoons butter,
  softened
Salt to taste

Soften yeast in warm water in bowl. Heat cottage cheese in saucepan until lukewarm. Combine with yeast, sugar, egg, onion flakes, 1 tablespoon butter, dillseed, 1 teaspoon salt and baking soda in large mixer bowl; mix well. Add flour gradually, beating at low speed after each addition until stiff dough forms. Let rise covered in warm place for 50 to 60 minutes or until doubled in bulk. Stir dough down. Shape into well greased 8-inch round baking pan. Let rise in warm place for 30 to 40 minutes. Bake at 350 degrees for 40 to 50 minutes or until golden brown. Brush with 2 tablespoons butter; sprinkle with salt to taste. Yield: 8 servings.

Approx Per Serving: Cal 234; T Fat 7 g; 25% Calories from Fat;
    Prot 9 g; Carbo 34 g; Fiber 1 g; Chol 42 mg; Sod 445 mg.

Lucille Linford, Pocatello, Idaho

LEMON BREAD

1 2-layer package lemon
   cake mix
1 4-ounce package lemon
   instant pudding mix

4 eggs
1 cup water
1/2 cup oil
1/4 cup poppy seed

Combine cake mix, pudding mix, eggs, water, oil and poppy seed in mixer bowl; mix well. Pour into greased 9x11-inch baking pan. Bake at 350 degrees for 40 to 45 minutes or until bread tests done. Cool on wire rack. Yield: 10 servings.

Approx Per Serving: Cal 389; T Fat 17 g; 40% Calories from Fat;
    Prot 5 g; Carbo 54 g; Fiber <1 g; Chol 85 mg; Sod 418 mg.
    Nutritional information does not include poppy seed.

Boots McMillan, Helena, Montana

PUMPKIN BREAD

3¹/₃ cups flour
2 teaspoons baking soda
1 teaspoon salt
¹/₂ teaspoon baking powder
1 teaspoon cloves
1 teaspoon nutmeg
1 teaspoon cinnamon

3 cups sugar
4 eggs
2 cups canned pumpkin
1 cup oil
1¹/₂ cups raisins
1 cup chopped pecans

Sift flour, baking soda, salt, baking powder, cloves, nutmeg and cinnamon together. Beat sugar and eggs in mixer bowl. Add pumpkin and oil; mix well. Add dry ingredients gradually, beating well after each addition. Stir in raisins and pecans. Pour into 2 greased and floured 5x9-inch loaf pans. Bake at 325 degrees for 1 hour and 10 minutes or until loaves test done. Cool in pan. Yield: 24 servings.

Approx Per Serving: Cal 325; T Fat 14 g; 37% Calories from Fat;
    Prot 4 g; Carbo 49 g; Fiber 2 g; Chol 36 mg; Sod 179 mg.

Darlene Loveall, Sandy, Utah

STRAWBERRY BREAD

2 cups sugar
4 eggs, beaten
1¹/₄ cups oil
3 cups plus 2 tablespoons
    flour
¹/₂ teaspoon baking soda

1 teaspoon salt
1 tablespoon cinnamon
1¹/₄ cups chopped pecans
2 cups thawed frozen
    strawberries

Beat sugar, eggs and oil in mixer bowl. Add mixture of flour, baking soda, salt and cinnamon gradually, beating well after each addition. Stir in pecans and strawberries. Pour into 2 greased and floured 5x9-inch loaf pans. Bake at 375 degrees for 45 to 60 minutes or until loaves test done. Cool on wire rack. May bake in 5 miniature loaf pans. Yield: 24 servings.

Approx Per Serving: Cal 283; T Fat 17 g; 52% Calories from Fat;
    Prot 3 g; Carbo 31 g; Fiber 1 g; Chol 36 mg; Sod 118 mg.

Elaine Fielding, Orem, Utah

ZUCCHINI BREAD

2 cups raisins
3 cups flour
3 teaspoons cinnamon
1/4 teaspoon baking powder
2 teaspoons baking soda
1 teaspoon salt
Nutmeg to taste

1 cup sugar
1 cup packed brown sugar
1 cup vegetable oil
3 eggs
2 cups grated zucchini
3 teaspoons vanilla extract
1 cup chopped pecans

Plump raisins in hot water; drain. Mix next 6 ingredients together. Beat sugar, brown sugar, oil and eggs in mixer bowl. Add zucchini; mix well. Add dry ingredients gradually, mixing well after each addition. Stir in vanilla, raisins and pecans. Pour into 2 greased and floured 4x8-inch loaf pans. Bake at 350 degrees for 45 to 50 minutes or until loaves test done. Cool on wire rack. Yield: 20 servings.

Approx Per Serving: Cal 360; T Fat 16 g; 39% Calories from Fat;
Prot 4 g; Carbo 53 g; Fiber 2 g; Chol 32 mg; Sod 212 mg.

Ann Coulam, Salt Lake City, Utah

BEST ZUCCHINI BREAD

*This delicious old family recipe has an excellent texture
and is very moist.*

3 cups flour
1 teaspoon baking soda
1 teaspoon baking powder
1 teaspoon salt
3 teaspoons cinnamon
1/2 teaspoon nutmeg
3 cups sugar

3 eggs
1 cup vegetable oil
3 teaspoons vanilla extract
2 cups grated unpeeled
   zucchini
1 cup peeled grated apple
1 cup chopped pecans

Sift first 6 ingredients together. Beat sugar, eggs, oil and vanilla in large mixer bowl; mix well. Add sifted dry ingredients gradually, beating well after each addition. Stir in zucchini, apple and pecans. Pour into 2 greased and floured 5x9-inch loaf pans. Bake at 350 degrees for 45 to 60 minutes or until loaves test done. Remove from pans immediately. Cool on wire rack. Yield: 24 servings.

Approx Per Serving: Cal 284; T Fat 13 g; 42% Calories from Fat;
Prot 3 g; Carbo 39 g; Fiber 1 g; Chol 27 mg; Sod 147 mg.

Becky Powell, Salt Lake City, Utah

FRUITED MUFFINS

2 cups sifted flour
1/3 cup sugar
1 tablespoon baking powder
1 teaspoon salt
3/4 cup candied fruit mix
1 egg

1 cup milk
1/4 cup melted butter
1/4 cup candied fruit mix
1 tablespoon sugar
1 teaspoon grated lemon rind

Sift flour, 1/3 cup sugar, baking powder and salt in medium bowl. Stir in 3/4 cup fruit mix. Blend egg, milk and butter in small bowl. Add to dry ingredients. Stir gently just until liquid is absorbed; batter will be lumpy. Fill greased muffin cups 2/3 full. Sprinkle with remaining 1/4 cup fruit mix and mixture of 1 tablespoon sugar and lemon rind. Bake at 425 degrees for 20 minutes or until muffins test done. May substitute orange rind for lemon rind. Yield: 12 servings.

Approx Per Serving: Cal 210; T Fat 5 g; 22% Calories from Fat;
Prot 3 g; Carbo 38 g; Fiber 1 g; Chol 31 mg; Sod 307 mg.

Lucille Linford, Pocatello, Idaho

RASPBERRY MUFFINS

2 cups flour
1 tablespoon baking powder
1/2 teaspoon salt
2/3 cup sugar
1 egg, beaten

1/3 cup melted margarine
1/2 cup milk
1/2 cup sour cream
1 1/2 cups fresh raspberries

Sift flour, baking powder, salt and sugar in bowl. Stir in egg, margarine, milk and sour cream until moist. Fold in raspberries gently. Fill greased or paper-lined muffin cups full. Bake at 400 degrees for 20 minutes or until muffins test done. Yield: 12 servings.

Approx Per Serving: Cal 205; T Fat 8 g; 35% Calories from Fat;
Prot 4 g; Carbo 30 g; Fiber 2 g; Chol 23 mg; Sod 246 mg.

Barbara Hayes, Ogden, Utah

Happiness held is a seed. Happiness shared is the flower.

RHUBARB MUFFINS

2 cups flour
1/2 cup wheat germ
1 teaspoon baking soda
1 teaspoon baking powder
1/2 teaspoon salt
1 1/4 cups packed brown sugar
1/2 cup vegetable oil
1 egg

1 cup buttermilk
2 teaspoons vanilla extract
1 1/2 cups chopped rhubarb
1 1/2 cups chopped walnuts
1/3 cup sugar
1 teaspoon cinnamon
1 tablespoon melted butter

Mix flour, wheat germ, baking soda, baking powder and salt together. Beat brown sugar and oil in large bowl. Add egg, buttermilk and vanilla; mix well. Stir in rhubarb and walnuts. Beat in sifted dry ingredients just until blended. Fill paper-lined muffin cups 2/3 full. Top with mixture of sugar, cinnamon and melted butter. Bake at 350 degrees for 20 to 25 minutes or until muffins test done. Yield: 24 servings.

Approx Per Serving: Cal 209; T Fat 10 g; 43% Calories from Fat;
Prot 3 g; Carbo 27 g; Fiber 1 g; Chol 11 mg; Sod 117 mg.

Judy Frazer, Billings, Montana

ALL-BRAN ROLLS

1 cup All-Bran
1/2 cup margarine, softened
1 cup boiling water
2 tablespoons dry yeast
1/4 cup sugar

1 cup warm water
2 eggs, beaten
1 tablespoon sugar
1 teaspoon salt
5 cups flour

Combine All-Bran, margarine and boiling water in bowl; mix well. Let stand until cool. Dissolve yeast and 1/4 cup sugar in warm water in bowl. Combine eggs, 1 tablespoon sugar and salt in large bowl; mix well. Add cooled All-Bran mixture and yeast mixture; mix well. Stir in flour. Let rise, covered, in warm place until doubled in bulk. Shape into rolls. Place on greased baking sheet. Let rise, covered, until doubled in bulk. Bake at 400 degrees for 15 minutes or until golden brown.
Yield: 30 servings.

Approx Per Serving: Cal 125; T Fat 4 g; 26% Calories from Fat;
Prot 3 g; Carbo 20 g; Fiber 2 g; Chol 14 mg; Sod 144 mg.

Jean Ford, Smithfield, Utah

BEATEN BATTER ROLLS

3 packages dry yeast
1 teaspoon sugar
1/2 cup lukewarm water
1/2 cup margarine, softened
2 cups milk, scalded

3 eggs, beaten
1/4 cup sugar
6 cups flour
2 teaspoons salt

Dissolve yeast and 1 teaspoon sugar in water in bowl. Stir margarine into scalded milk. Combine with eggs and 1/4 cup sugar in bowl; mix well. Stir in mixture of flour and salt. Add yeast mixture; mix well. Let rise, covered, in warm place until doubled in bulk. Stir dough down. Let rise, covered, until doubled in bulk. Spoon into well-greased muffin cups. Let rise, covered, until doubled in bulk. Bake at 375 degrees for 12 to 15 minutes or until golden brown. May substitute shortening for margarine. Yield: 36 servings.

Approx Per Serving: Cal 121; T Fat 4 g; 28% Calories from Fat;
Prot 3 g; Carbo 18 g; Fiber 1 g; Chol 20 mg; Sod 160 mg.

Enid Larsen, Logan, Utah

NO-FAIL ROLLS

1/2 cup sugar
1/2 cup shortening
11/2 teaspoons salt
3 cups boiling water
2 yeast cakes

1 teaspoon sugar
1/4 cup warm water
2 eggs, beaten
8 cups flour

Combine 1/2 cup sugar, shortening and salt with 3 cups boiling water in large bowl. Let stand until lukewarm. Dissolve yeast cakes and 1 teaspoon sugar in 1/4 cup warm water in bowl. Add eggs to shortening mixture; mix well. Add 4 cups flour and yeast mixture; mix well. Stir in 3 cups flour; do not knead. Stir in remaining 1 cup flour gradually. Let rise, covered, in warm place until doubled in bulk. Spoon into greased muffin cups. Let rise, covered, until doubled in bulk. Bake at 350 degrees until golden brown. Yield: 48 servings.

Approx Per Serving: Cal 107; T Fat 3 g; 22% Calories from Fat;
Prot 3 g; Carbo 18 g; Fiber 1 g; Chol 9 mg; Sod 70 mg.

Lucille Linford, Pocatello, Idaho

CRESCENT ROLLS

1 cup milk, scalded
1 tablespoon dry yeast
1 tablespoon sugar
1/3 cup warm water
1/2 cup sugar

1/2 cup melted butter
3/4 teaspoon salt
3 eggs, beaten
31/4 to 4 cups flour

Let scalded milk stand until lukewarm. Combine yeast, 1 tablespoon sugar and 1/3 cup water in mixer bowl. Add milk, 1/2 cup sugar, butter, salt and eggs; mix well. Stir in enough flour to make soft dough. Let rise, covered, for 3 to 4 hours. Knead on lightly floured surface until smooth and elastic. Divide dough into 2 portions. Pat each portion into circle 1/4 inch thick on lightly floured surface. Cut into 16 wedges. Roll up from wide end. Shape into crescents on greased baking sheet. Let rise, lightly covered, for 4 to 6 hours. Bake at 375 degrees for 15 to 20 minutes or until golden brown. Yield: 32 servings.

Approx Per Serving: Cal 109; T Fat 4 g; 32% Calories from Fat; Prot 3 g; Carbo 16 g; Fiber <1 g; Chol 29 mg; Sod 84 mg.

Evelyn Cameron, Blackfoot, Idaho

GERMAN TWISTS

1 tablespoon dry yeast
1 cup sour cream, heated
1 cup shortening
31/2 cups flour

1 teaspoon salt
2 eggs, beaten
2 cups (about) sugar

Dissolve yeast in warm sour cream in bowl. Cut shortening into mixture of flour and salt in large bowl until crumbly. Add yeast mixture and eggs; mix well. Knead on lightly floured surface until smooth and elastic. Chill dough. Roll dough on lightly sugared surface. Sprinkle with sugar. Fold dough; roll again. Cut into 1x5-inch strips. Roll in sugar. Place on greased baking sheet. Let rise, covered, until doubled in bulk. Bake at 325 degrees for 10 to 15 minutes or until brown. Yield: 18 servings.

Approx Per Serving: Cal 312; T Fat 15 g; 43% Calories from Fat; Prot 4 g; Carbo 41 g; Fiber 1 g; Chol 29 mg; Sod 134 mg.

Boots McMillan, Helena, Montana

Cooking "Off the Range"

Microwave & Slow Cooker

'89 H. CREEKMORE

MAGIC VALLEY COUNCIL

Twin Falls, Idaho

Our club has been very actively involved in the Hug-A-Bear project. Every law enforcement agency from the State Police to the local City Police force now carries the Hug-A-Bears in their cars. Also the Same Day Operation Clinic has a number of the bears for each and every child who enters the facility. As the children come in for their operations they find their own special bear waiting for them on their bed and then they get to keep their new friend. We have done approximately 2,500 bears since the project began.

At Christmas every year we shop the local stores for toys and clothing items for local children. These gifts are wrapped and delivered to kids who would not receive any Christmas otherwise. We do Christmas food baskets for the needy and fill them with all sorts of items donated by our pioneers and purchase the rest with the money we have earned fund raising. And, Mental Health receives a ham dinner for all their people courtesy of the Magic Valley Club. Each year the number seems to grow since we started furnishing the dinner 10 years ago.

MINI TOSTADOS

1 cup refried beans
24 round tortilla chips
1/4 cup taco sauce

1/2 cup shredded Cheddar
  cheese
24 cherry tomato slices

Place 1 teaspoon beans on each tortilla chip. Top with 1/2 teaspoon taco sauce and 1/2 teaspoon cheese. Place 6 to 8 tostados at a time on paper towel-lined plate. Microwave on Medium for 1 to 3 minutes or until cheese melts, turning several times. Top each with tomato slice. Yield: 24 servings.

Approx Per Serving: Cal 52; T Fat 2 g; 38% Calories from Fat; Prot 2 g; Carbo 6 g; Fiber 2 g; Chol 2 mg; Sod 84 mg.

Angela Wagner, Riverdale, Utah

MICROWAVE LASAGNA

1 pound lean ground beef
3/4 cup tomato juice
3/4 cup tomato sauce
2 6-ounce cans tomato paste
1 onion, chopped
1 tablespoon oregano
2 teaspoons basil
1 teaspoon salt
1/2 teaspoon pepper
2 cloves of garlic, minced

2 teaspoons brown sugar
1 tablespoon Worcestershire
  sauce
8 ounces uncooked lasagna
  noodles
2 cups ricotta cheese
8 ounces mozzarella cheese,
  sliced
1 cup Parmesan cheese

Microwave ground beef in colander over glass casserole on High for 6 minutes; break into chunks. Combine with next 11 ingredients in bowl; mix well. Pour 1/3 cup sauce into 8x12-inch glass baking dish. Layer half the noodles, half the ricotta cheese and half the mozzarella cheese on top. Repeat layers with remaining noodles and ricotta cheese; top with remaining sauce. Sprinkle with Parmesan cheese. Microwave on Medium for 35 minutes. Place remaining mozzarella cheese on top. Microwave for 3 minutes. Let stand for 10 minutes. Yield: 6 servings.

Approx Per Serving: Cal 688; T Fat 35 g; 45% Calories from Fat; Prot 45 g; Carbo 51 g; Fiber 4 g; Chol 130 mg; Sod 1199 mg.

Thelma A. Newbry, Pocatello, Idaho

MEXICAN MANICOTTI

8 ounces ground beef
1 cup refried beans
1 teaspoon oregano
1/2 teaspoon cumin
8 uncooked manicotti shells
1 1/4 cups water

1 cup picante sauce
1 cup sour cream
1/4 cup chopped green onions
1/4 cup sliced olives
1/2 cup shredded Monterey
Jack cheese

Spoon mixture of ground beef, beans, oregano and cumin into manicotti shells. Arrange in 9x13-inch glass baking dish. Pour mixture of water and picante sauce over shells. Microwave on High for 10 minutes; turn shells over. Microwave on Medium for 17 to 19 minutes or until shells are tender. Top with mixture of sour cream, green onions and olives. Sprinkle with cheese. Microwave for several minutes or until cheese melts. Yield: 8 servings.

Approx Per Serving: Cal 310; T Fat 15 g; 42% Calories from Fat; Prot 14 g; Carbo 32 g; Fiber 5 g; Chol 38 mg; Sod 418 mg.

Linda P. Olsen, Logan, Utah

MMMMMMM GOOD CHICKEN AND RICE

1 cup rice, cooked
2 cups chopped cooked
  chicken
2 tablespoons chopped onion
1/4 cup toasted slivered
  almonds

1 10-ounce can cream of
  mushroom soup
1 tablespoon chicken
  bouillon
1/2 cup bread crumbs
1 tablespoon butter

Combine first 6 ingredients in bowl; mix well. Pour into 9-inch square glass casserole. Top with bread crumbs; dot with butter. Microwave on High for 15 minutes or until heated through. Yield: 4 servings.

Approx Per Serving: Cal 503; T Fat 19 g; 34% Calories from Fat; Prot 28 g; Carbo 54 g; Fiber 2 g; Chol 72 mg; Sod 1032 mg.

Leona E. Wolfe, Boise, Idaho

CHINESE CHICKEN

8 ounces chicken breast
  filets, cut into slivers
1 small onion, thinly sliced
1 teaspoon oil
3/4 cup chicken broth

1 cup frozen broccoli, baby
  carrots and water chestnuts
1 tablespoon soy sauce
3/4 cup uncooked minute rice

Combine chicken, onion and oil in 1½-quart glass baking dish. Microwave, covered, on High for 2 minutes. Add remaining ingredients. Microwave, covered, for 4 to 5 minutes longer. Let stand for 5 minutes. Fluff rice with fork. Yield: 4 servings.

Approx Per Serving: Cal 196; T Fat 2 g; 10% Calories from Fat;
  Prot 15 g; Carbo 30 g; Fiber 4 g; Chol 25 mg; Sod 456 mg.

Arloa Weiss, Billings, Montana

ITALIAN EGGPLANT BAKE

1/3 cup olive oil
1 large clove of garlic, minced
1/2 teaspoon basil
1/4 teaspoon oregano
8 1/2-inch thick peeled
  eggplant slices

1 15-ounce can tomato purée
1/4 teaspoon salt
1/4 teaspoon basil
1/4 teaspoon oregano
2 cups shredded mozzarella
  cheese

Combine first 4 ingredients in glass measuring cup. Microwave, covered with plastic wrap, on High for 45 seconds or until warm. Let stand for 5 minutes. Brush both sides of eggplant with oil mixture. Place on baking sheet. Drizzle with remaining oil mixture; toss to coat. Broil 4 inches from heat source for 4 to 6 minutes or until light brown; turn eggplant over. Broil for 4 to 6 minutes longer. Combine tomato purée, salt, 1/4 teaspoon basil and 1/4 teaspoon oregano in bowl; mix well. Spoon 1/4 cup sauce into 9-inch glass casserole. Arrange 4 eggplant slices on top. Sprinkle 1/4 cup cheese on each. Layer remaining eggplant and cheese on top. Spoon remaining sauce around eggplant. Microwave, covered with plastic wrap, on Medium-High for 7½ to 10 minutes or until bubbly, turning dish several times. Yield: 4 servings.

Approx Per Serving: Cal 373; T Fat 30 g; 70% Calories from Fat;
  Prot 13 g; Carbo 15 g; Fiber 4 g; Chol 44 mg; Sod 368 mg.

Marilyn Wagner, Riverdale, Utah

SUMMER VEGETABLE LASAGNA

3 tablespoons melted butter
1/4 cup flour
2 cups milk
1   4-ounce jar pimentos,
    drained, puréed
1   10-ounce package frozen
    chopped spinach, thawed,
    drained
2 large carrots, peeled,
    shredded

8 ounces ricotta cheese
1/2 cup grated Parmesan
    cheese
1 egg, slightly beaten
5 cooked lasagna noodles,
    cut into halves
8 ounces mozzarella cheese,
    shredded

Blend butter and flour in 4-cup glass bowl. Whisk in milk. Microwave on High for 5 to 7 minutes or until thickened, stirring twice. Stir in pimento purée. Combine spinach, carrots, ricotta cheese, Parmesan cheese and egg in bowl; mix well. Spoon 1/2 cup pimento sauce into 9-inch square glass baking dish. Layer noodles, cheese mixture, sauce and mozzarella cheese 1/3 at a time in prepared dish. Microwave, covered with waxed paper, on High for 10 to 13 minutes or until heated through and cheese melts. Garnish with parsley. Yield: 8 servings.

Approx Per Serving: Cal 322; T Fat 16 g; 44% Calories from Fat;
    Prot 19 g; Carbo 26 g; Fiber 2 g; Chol 75 mg; Sod 370 mg.

Erna Lou Sudbrock, Lewistown, Montana

SCAMPI

1/4 cup melted butter
3/4 cup olive oil
1/4 cup snipped fresh parsley
2 tablespoons lemon juice
2 cloves of garlic, minced

1/2 teaspoon salt
1/2 teaspoon pepper
11/2 pounds fresh medium
    shrimp, shelled

Combine first 7 ingredients in glass baking dish; mix well. Add shrimp; stir until coated. Microwave, covered, on Medium-High for 6 to 9 minutes or until shrimp turn pink, stirring twice. Let stand for 2 minutes. Serve over rice. Yield: 4 servings.

Approx Per Serving: Cal 600; T Fat 54 g; 80% Calories from Fat;
    Prot 29 g; Carbo 1 g; Fiber <1 g; Chol 296 mg; Sod 670 mg.

Merla Jorgensen, Pocatello, Idaho

QUICK "YUMMY" FUDGE

1 cup chocolate chips
1 14-ounce can sweetened
  condensed milk

Pinch of salt
1½ teaspoons vanilla extract
½ cup chopped pecans

Combine first 3 ingredients in 4-cup glass measuring cup. Microwave on Low for 5 minutes; mix well. Stir in vanilla and pecans. Pour into waxed paper-lined 8-inch square dish. Chill in refrigerator. Cut into squares. Yield: 16 servings.

Approx Per Serving: Cal 246; T Fat 18 g; 62% Calories from Fat;
  Prot 4 g; Carbo 22 g; Fiber 2 g; Chol 7 mg; Sod 31 mg.

Carla Wallace, Twin Falls, Idaho

MICROWAVE PEANUT BRITTLE

1 cup sugar
½ cup light corn syrup
1 cup salted peanuts

1 teaspoon butter
1 teaspoon vanilla extract
1 teaspoon baking soda

Combine sugar and corn syrup in 1½-quart glass casserole. Microwave on High for 4 minutes. Add peanuts. Microwave for 4 minutes. Add butter and vanilla. Microwave for 1 to 2 minutes longer. Stir in baking soda. Spread on buttered baking sheet. Let stand until cooled; break into pieces. Yield: 8 servings.

Approx Per Serving: Cal 265; T Fat 9 g; 30% Calories from Fat;
  Prot 5 g; Carbo 44 g; Fiber 2 g; Chol 1 mg; Sod 133 mg.

Arloa Weiss, Billings, Montana

CHEESE DIP

2 pounds Velveeta cheese,
  chopped
1 1-quart bottle of
  tomatoes, drained

½ 4-ounce can chopped
  jalapeño peppers

Combine all ingredients in large glass bowl. Microwave on High until cheese melts; mix well. Pour into slow cooker. Keep warm over low heat. Serve with nacho chips. Yield: 32 servings.

Approx Per Serving: Cal 112; T Fat 9 g; 71% Calories from Fat;
  Prot 7 g; Carbo 2 g; Fiber <1 g; Chol 27 mg; Sod 480 mg.

Marilyn Wagner, Riverdale, Utah

BARBECUED COCKTAIL MEATBALLS

2 pounds lean ground beef
1¼ cups finely chopped
   onion
½ teaspoon salt
¼ teaspoon pepper
1 teaspoon garlic salt
½ cup fine cracker crumbs

1 egg
¼ cup milk
2 tablespoons oil
1 18-ounce bottle of
   barbecue sauce
1 cup water

Combine first 8 ingredients in bowl; mix well. Shape by tablespoonfuls into meatballs. Brown in oil in skillet; drain. Place in slow cooker. Add mixture of barbecue sauce and water. Simmer on High for 1 to 2 hours. Serve warm. Yield: 75 servings.

Approx Per Serving: Cal 37; T Fat 2 g; 59% Calories from Fat;
   Prot 3 g; Carbo 1 g; Fiber <1 g; Chol 11 mg; Sod 99 mg.

Mary Lou Carlson, Helena, Montana

BARBECUED BEEF

1 4-pound rump roast
1 cup chopped onion
2 cups chili sauce
⅛ teaspoon onion salt
1½ cups catsup
2 cups water
2 tablespoons cornstarch

Dash of Worcestershire sauce
¼ cup white vinegar
Chili powder to taste
1 teaspoon paprika
½ teaspoon allspice
1 cup packed brown sugar

Place roast in roaster pan. Bake at 300 degrees for 2 hours; slice thin. Place in slow cooker. Add remaining ingredients. Cook on High for 2 to 3 hours or on Low for 5 to 6 hours. Serve on sandwich rolls or buns. Yield: 12 servings.

Approx Per Serving: Cal 361; T Fat 9 g; 22% Calories from Fat;
   Prot 30 g; Carbo 40 g; Fiber 1 g; Chol 85 mg; Sod 1022 mg.

Norma Harrison, St. George, Utah

He who hesitates gets leftovers.

SMOTHERED STEAK

1½ pounds round steak strips
⅓ cup flour
1 teaspoon salt
¼ teaspoon pepper
1 large onion, chopped

1 green bell pepper, sliced
1   16-ounce can tomatoes
1   4-ounce can mushrooms
2 tablespoons molasses
3 tablespoons soy sauce

Coat steak with flour, salt and pepper. Combine with remaining ingredients in slow cooker. Cook on High for 1 hour and on Low for 8 hours. Yield: 6 servings.

Approx Per Serving: Cal 225; T Fat 7 g; 28% Calories from Fat; Prot 24 g; Carbo 17 g; Fiber 2 g; Chol 64 mg; Sod 1115 mg.

Evelyn Cameron, Blackfoot, Idaho

CHILI

2 pounds ground beef,
  browned, drained
1 cup each chopped onions,
  celery and green bell pepper
4 cups tomatoes
2 tablespoons
  Worcestershire sauce

1 tablespoon chili powder
¼ cup packed brown sugar
1 tablespoon salt
2 tablespoons cumin
1 teaspoon mustard
1   28-ounce can chili beans
1   6-ounce can tomato sauce

Combine all ingredients in slow cooker. Cook on Low or High until heated through. Yield: 10 servings.

Approx Per Serving: Cal 313; T Fat 14 g; 39% Calories from Fat; Prot 23 g; Carbo 26 g; Fiber 8 g; Chol 59 mg; Sod 1279 mg.

Karen Gee, Ogden, Utah

CHICKEN ORIENTAL

1   5-pound chicken, cut up
½ cup soy sauce
¼ cup honey
1 clove of garlic, minced

¼ teaspoon ginger
½ teaspoon dry mustard
½ cup thinly sliced green
  onions

Combine all ingredients in slow cooker. Cook on Low for 6 hours or until tender. Yield: 8 servings.

Approx Per Serving: Cal 314; T Fat 11 g; 31% Calories from Fat; Prot 42 g; Carbo 11 g; Fiber <1 g; Chol 127 mg; Sod 1151 mg.

Evelyn Cameron, Blackfoot, Idaho

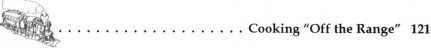

WORKING MOTHER'S DEEP-DISH CHICKEN PIE

1 chicken
2 bay leaves
1 medium onion, chopped
3 cups water
5 carrots, peeled, chopped
5 stalks celery, chopped

8 ounces fresh mushrooms
Salt and pepper to taste
1 cup cream
3 tablespoons flour
1 recipe pie pastry

Wash chicken. Place in slow cooker. Add bay leaves, onion and water. Cook on Low for 6 hours or until chicken is tender. Remove chicken. Let stand until cool. Bone and chop into bite-sized pieces. Pour pan juices into large saucepan. Remove bay leaves; skim surface. Add carrots and celery. Cook for 10 minutes. Add mushrooms, salt, pepper and cream. Add chicken. Stir in mixture of flour and a small amount of water. Cook until thickened, stirring constantly. Pour into deep-dish pie plate. Cover with pastry; seal edge. Bake at 400 degrees for 15 minutes or until crust is brown. May be frozen before baking.
Yield: 6 servings.

Approx Per Serving: Cal 566; T Fat 34 g; 53% Calories from Fat;
Prot 38 g; Carbo 28 g; Fiber 4 g; Chol 156 mg; Sod 347 mg.

Terri Rogers, Great Falls, Montana

CHICKEN RANCHERO

6 chicken breasts, skinned
Salt and pepper to taste
1 envelope enchilada sauce
  mix
1 6-ounce can tomato paste
1 tomato paste can water

2 cups shredded Monterey
  Jack cheese
4 cups cooked rice
1/2 cup chopped green onions
1 cup sour cream
1/2 cup chopped olives

Wash chicken. Sprinkle with salt and pepper. Place in slow cooker. Pour mixture of enchilada sauce mix, tomato paste and water over chicken. Cook on Low for 6 to 7 hours or until chicken is tender. Add cheese. Cook on High until cheese melts, stirring frequently. Serve on rice. Top with green onions, sour cream and olives. Yield: 4 servings.

Approx Per Serving: Cal 768; T Fat 37 g; 43% Calories from Fat;
Prot 45 g; Carbo 67 g; Fiber 5 g; Chol 132 mg; Sod 981 mg.

Darlene Loveall, Sandy, Utah

Bunkhouse Barbecues
Cooking Outdoors

'89 H. CREEKMORE

SNAKE RIVER COUNCIL

Pocatello, Idaho

One Council project this year enabled a resident of Pocatello to have new glasses. The lady had needed new glasses for about 10 years, but lived on a fixed income and could not afford the eye examination or the cost of the new glasses. The Council not only paid for the examination and the glasses but also committed to update the prescription when it was needed.

OUTDOOR COOKING

Cooking over a charcoal fire—on a grill or in a Dutch oven or skillet—is fun, easy, and adaptable to many recipes you normally bake, broil, or fry. Charcoal should be preheated for about 30 minutes for all types of cooking. The temperature may be gauged by how long you can hold your hand 4 inches above the coals: 2 seconds equals hot (400 degrees); 4 seconds equals medium (350 degrees); 5 seconds equals low (300 degrees). For **grilling**, use hot coals and greased grill rack. For added flavor, add mesquite, hickory or apple chips soaked in cold water to hot coals. **Pan frying** is done in a heavy skillet on rack over hot coals. Breads as well as meats may be prepared in this manner. For **Dutch oven cooking**, use enough coals to equal twice the diameter of the Dutch oven for medium heat or 3 times the diameter for high heat. Place half the coals underneath and half on the lid toward the edge. Cooking time will be about the same as for stove or oven. Several Dutch ovens may be stacked so that main dish, vegetable and desserts may be cooked at the same time.

DUTCH OVEN STEW

My father made this when he went on cattle drives.

2 pounds stew beef
8 medium potatoes, sliced
8 carrots, cut into chunks
2 bay leaves
1 envelope onion soup mix
1   10-ounce can cream of
    mushroom soup
1   10-ounce can cream of
    celery soup
1   8-ounce can tomato sauce

Layer beef and vegetables in Dutch oven. Place bay leaves on top. Pour mixture of soup mix, soups and tomato sauce on top. Cover with tight-fitting lid. Cover with coals. Bake until beef is tender. Discard bay leaves. May bake in oven at 325 degrees for 3 hours, 275 degrees for 6 hours or 250 degrees for 8 hours. Yield: 6 servings.

Approx Per Serving: Cal 630; T Fat 15 g; 21% Calories from Fat;
Prot 37 g; Carbo 88 g; Fiber 10 g; Chol 91 mg; Sod 1174 mg.

Rose Kriegen, Burley, Idaho

BARBECUED STEAK

8 8-ounce sirloin strip
 steaks
1 cup oil
2 cups red wine
1/2 4-ounce bottle of Heinz
 57 sauce
1/2 4-ounce bottle of A-1
 sauce
1 tablespoon Worcestershire
 sauce
1 teaspoon onion powder
1/2 teaspoon garlic powder
1 teaspoon salt
1/2 teaspoon whole ground
 pepper

Place steaks in shallow dish. Combine remaining ingredients in bowl; mix well. Pour over steaks. Marinate for 3 to 4 hours, turning steaks every hour. Grill over hot coals until done to taste, basting frequently with marinade. Yield: 8 servings.

Approx Per Serving: Cal 613; T Fat 40 g; 59% Calories from Fat;
 Prot 44 g; Carbo 7 g; Fiber <1 g; Chol 128 mg; Sod 358 mg.
 Nutritional information includes entire amount of marinade.

Eleanor Helderman, Boise, Idaho

HAMBURGERS ON THE GRILL

This also makes a great meat loaf!

2 pounds ground beef
1 egg, beaten
1/4 teaspoon oregano
1 teaspoon salt
1 teaspoon pepper
1/2 cup catsup
1 tablespoon Worcestershire
 sauce
1 cup shredded Cheddar
 cheese
1 cup chopped onion
8 hamburger buns

Combine ground beef, egg, seasonings, catsup, Worcestershire sauce, cheese and onion in bowl; mix well. Shape into patties. Grill over hot coals until done to taste. Serve on buns. Yield: 8 servings.

Approx Per Serving: Cal 452; T Fat 24 g; 48% Calories from Fat;
 Prot 30 g; Carbo 29 g; Fiber 2 g; Chol 116 mg; Sod 895 mg.

Judy Frazer, Billings, Montana

DAD'S BURGERS

3/4 cup boiling water
1/4 cup bulgur
1/3 cup whole natural
  almonds
1 pound lean ground beef
1/4 cup chopped green onions

1 teaspoon garlic salt
1 teaspoon basil
4 hamburger buns
4 lettuce leaves
1 tomato, sliced
1 red onion, sliced

Pour boiling water over bulgur in bowl. Let stand until cool. Place almonds in single layer on baking sheet. Bake at 350 degrees for 12 to 15 minutes or until lightly toasted, stirring occasionally. Let stand until cool. Chop coarsely. Drain bulgur well. Mix bulgur with almonds and next 4 ingredients in bowl. Shape into patties. Grill over hot coals until done to taste. Serve on buns with lettuce, tomato and onion. Yield: 4 servings.

Approx Per Serving: Cal 491; T Fat 25 g; 45% Calories from Fat;
  Prot 29 g; Carbo 38 g; Fiber 6 g; Chol 74 mg; Sod 856 mg.

Nancy Nielsen, Hyrum, Utah

CHICKEN TENDERS

1 pound chicken breast filets
1 onion, cut into quarters
1 green bell pepper, cut into
  squares
1 red bell pepper, cut into
  squares
8 ounces mushroom caps
1 clove of garlic, crushed
2 tablespoons lemon juice

1 teaspoon olive oil
1 small onion, chopped
1 tablespoon soy sauce
1/2 cup low-sodium soy sauce
1/2 teaspoon chili powder
1 teaspoon lemon juice
1/4 teaspoon crushed garlic
1/4 teaspoon finely chopped
  ginger

Cut chicken into 1-inch cubes. Thread onto skewers alternately with onion quarters, peppers and mushrooms. Place in shallow dish. Add mixture of next 5 ingredients. Marinate for 1 to 3 hours; drain. Mix 1/2 cup soy sauce and remaining ingredients in bowl. Grill chicken over hot coals until chicken is tender, basting frequently with sauce. Serve remaining sauce with chicken. Yield: 4 servings.

Approx Per Serving: Cal 174; T Fat 3 g; 14% Calories from Fat;
  Prot 26 g; Carbo 13 g; Fiber 3 g; Chol 49 mg; Sod 1859 mg.
  Nutritional information includes entire amount of marinade.

Debbie Dudgeon, Mesa, Arizona

GRILLED HALIBUT WITH TARTAR SAUCE

2 pounds halibut steaks
1/2 cup melted butter
2 teaspoons lemon juice
2 tablespoons minced fresh
  parsley
1 tablespoon minced fresh
  basil
1/2 cup mayonnaise
1/2 cup sour cream

1 tablespoon chopped green
  onions
1 tablespoon chopped parsley
2 tablespoons chopped sweet
  pickle
1/2 teaspoon dry mustard
1/2 teaspoon paprika
1/4 teaspoon salt
Pepper to taste

Grill halibut steaks over medium-hot coals for 6 minutes on each side or until fish flakes easily, brushing frequently with mixture of butter, lemon juice, 2 tablespoons parsley and basil. Combine mayonnaise and remaining ingredients in bowl; mix well. Serve with halibut. Yield: 8 servings.

Approx Per Serving: Cal 339; T Fat 28 g; 73% Calories from Fat;
  Prot 20 g; Carbo 3 g; Fiber <1 g; Chol 75 mg; Sod 326 mg.

Merla Jorgensen, Pocatello, Idaho

DUTCH OVEN POTATOES

6 large onions
7 pounds potatoes
Salt and pepper to taste
6 tablespoons oil

1 cup water
1 1/2 pounds Cheddar cheese,
  sliced

Slice onions and potatoes 1/8 inch thick. Cover bottom of Dutch oven with onions. Place 1-inch layer potatoes on top. Repeat layers until Dutch oven is filled, seasoning layers with salt and pepper to taste. Pour 1 1/2 tablespoons oil in each corner of Dutch oven. Add water; cover. Place on medium-hot coals. Cook for 45 minutes or until potatoes are tender. Top with cheese. Cook just until cheese melts. Yield: 20 servings.

Approx Per Serving: Cal 352; T Fat 15 g; 38% Calories from Fat;
  Prot 12 g; Carbo 44 g; Fiber 4 g; Chol 32 mg; Sod 500 mg.

E. Dale Henderson, Boise, Idaho

BUTTERMILK SCONES

2 cups buttermilk
2 cakes yeast
2 eggs, beaten
6 tablespoons oil
1 tablespoon baking powder

1 teaspoon salt
1/2 teaspoon baking soda
2 tablespoons sugar
5 cups flour
Oil for frying

Heat buttermilk in saucepan until warm. Add yeast. Let stand until dissolved. Add next 7 ingredients 1 at a time, mixing well after each addition. Dough will be soft. Let rise until doubled in bulk. Punch dough down. Store, covered, in refrigerator for up to 2 weeks. Pat out on floured surface to 3-inch thickness. Cut with knife. Fry in hot oil in skillet until browned on both sides. Yield: 36 servings.

Approx Per Serving: Cal 97; T Fat 3 g; 27% Calories from Fat;
Prot 3 g; Carbo 15 g; Fiber 1 g; Chol 12 mg; Sodium 117 mg.
Nutritional information does not include oil for frying.

Sarah H. Jensen, Richfield, Utah

INDIAN FRIED BREAD

3 tablespoons shortening
3 cups flour
1 teaspoon baking powder

1/2 teaspoon salt
3/4 cup (about) water
Oil for deep frying

Cut shortening into mixture of flour, baking powder and salt in bowl until crumbly. Add enough water to make soft dough; dough should not be sticky. Knead for 5 minutes. Let rest, covered with towel, for 3 minutes. Shape into 6 tennis ball-sized balls. Pat each into 8-inch circle. Fry in 1-inch hot oil in skillet until brown on both sides. Serve with beans, honey or cinnamon-sugar. Yield: 6 servings.

Approx Per Serving: Cal 285; T Fat 7 g; 23% Calories from Fat;
Prot 7 g; Carbo 48 g; Fiber 2 g; Chol 0 mg; Sod 234 mg.
Nutritional information does not include oil for deep frying.

Terri Rogers, Great Falls, Montana

SHEPHERD'S BREAD

1/2 cup sugar
1/2 cup shortening
3 cups very hot water
11/2 tablespoons yeast

2 cups flour
21/2 teaspoons salt
3 cups flour

Combine sugar, shortening and very hot water in bowl. Let stand until shortening melts. Add yeast. Let stand until dissolved. Add 2 cups flour and salt; mix well. Add enough remaining flour to make soft not sticky dough. Place in greased Dutch oven. Let rise to within 1/2 inch of top of pan; cover. Cook in hot coals for 40 to 45 minutes or until loaf tests done. May bake, covered, at 375 degrees for 12 minutes. Bake, uncovered, for 30 to 35 minutes longer. Yield: 12 servings.

Approx Per Serving: Cal 300; T Fat 9 g; 28% Calories from Fat;
   Prot 6 g; Carbo 48 g; Fiber 2 g; Chol 0 mg; Sod 446 mg.

Rose Kriegen, Burley, Idaho

HOT FUDGE CAKE

1/2 cup baking cocoa
1 cup packed brown sugar
2 cups warm water
1 16-ounce package
   miniature marshmallows

1 2-layer package devil's
   food cake mix
8 ounces whipped topping

Combine cocoa, brown sugar and water in 10- to 12-inch Dutch oven. Sprinkle marshmallows over cocoa mixture. Prepare cake mix using package directions. Pour over marshmallows, covering completely; cover. Place 5 to 7 hot coals on bottom and 14 to 16 coals on top of Dutch oven. Bake for 30 minutes or until cake tests done. Spoon into bowls. Top with whipped topping. May sprinkle chopped nuts or coconut over batter before cooking. May double recipe for 14-inch Dutch oven and 20 servings. May serve with ice cream. Yield: 15 servings.

Approx Per Serving: Cal 454; T Fat 13 g; 24% Calories from Fat;
   Prot 4 g; Carbo 86 g; Fiber 1 g; Chol 0 mg; Sod 205 mg.

Ric Anderson, Wellsville, Utah

Tumbleweeds and Sagebrush

Vegetables & Side Dishes

'89 H. Creekmore

TIMP COUNCIL

Provo, Utah

The Timp Council is involved in a yearly project with the Utah State Mental Hospital in Provo, Utah. Every October, in conjunction with the Hospitals' Haunted Castle, the Pioneers sell popcorn, candy, soda pop and hot drinks to the patrons waiting in line. The proceeds of the candy sale are then donated back to the State Mental Hospital in Provo, Utah in order to purchase additional equipment for the patients that the State budget does not allow for. In 1990 we raised over $1,200 that was used to purchase recreational equipment as well as books for the library.

In addition to the Halloween fund raiser the Pioneers along with the US West Foundation put on a very nice Christmas Dinner for the patients of the Hospital. The Foundation donates the money and the Pioneers provide the labor to serve dinner, provide Santa Claus and provide the entertainment for the evening. We also provide each patient with a bag of goodies at the conclusion. In 1991 the Pioneers and the Hospital are celebrating their Tenth Anniversary of this partnership.

BARBECUED BAKED BEANS

8 ounces bacon, chopped
1 large onion, chopped
1/2 green bell pepper, chopped
1   28-ounce can pork and
    beans

1/2 cup packed brown sugar
1/2   32-ounce bottle of catsup
1 tablespoon Worcestershire
    sauce

Cook bacon in skillet until brown; partially drain. Add onion and green pepper. Sauté until soft. Combine with remaining ingredients in ovenproof bean pot. Bake at 350 degrees for 3 hours. Yield: 6 servings.

Approx Per Serving: Cal 339; T Fat 8 g; 20% Calories from Fat;
    Prot 11 g; Carbo 60 g; Fiber 7 g; Chol 17 mg; Sod 1337 mg.

Doris Christensen, Salt Lake City, Utah

YE OL' BAKED BEANS

16 ounces ground beef
1 medium onion, chopped
8 ounces bacon, crisp-fried,
    crumbled
1   32-ounce can pork and
    beans
1   16-ounce can kidney
    beans, drained
1   15-ounce can lima beans,
    drained

1/3 cup packed brown sugar
1/3 cup sugar
1/4 cup barbecue sauce
1/4 cup catsup
2 tablespoons molasses
1 tablespoon prepared
    mustard
1/2 teaspoon chili powder

Brown ground beef with onion in skillet, stirring frequently; drain. Combine with bacon and beans in large bowl. Add mixture of brown sugar, sugar, barbecue sauce, catsup, molasses, mustard and chili powder; mix well. Spoon into large baking dish. Bake at 325 degrees for 1 to 2 hours. Yield: 8 servings.

Approx Per Serving: Cal 668; T Fat 27 g; 36% Calories from Fat;
    Prot 37 g; Carbo 72 g; Fiber 16 g; Chol 81 mg; Sod 1199 mg.

Linda Lay, Great Falls, Montana

BACON AND BEANS AND CARROTS

8 ounces bacon
2 pounds carrots
3 or 4 medium onions,
  chopped

4 16-ounce cans green beans
Salt and pepper to taste
3 or 4 8-ounce cans tomato
  sauce

Cut bacon into 1-inch pieces. Cut carrots into 2-inch sticks. Brown bacon well in large heavy saucepan; do not drain. Add onions. Cook until transparent. Add carrots, undrained green beans, salt and pepper; mix well. Top with tomato sauce. Simmer over low heat until of desired consistency. May substitute baby carrots for carrot sticks or fresh beans for canned beans. Yield: 12 servings.

Approx Per Serving: Cal 135; T Fat 3 g; 20% Calories from Fat;
  Prot 6 g; Carbo 24 g; Fiber 6 g; Chol 5 mg; Sod 954 mg.

Dorris Calton, Ogden, Utah

HARVEST CINNAMON BEANS

1/4 cup chopped onion
1/4 teaspoon cinnamon
1 tablespoon butter
1 1/2 pounds fresh green
  beans, cut into 1-inch
  pieces

1/2 cup chicken broth
1/8 teaspoon salt
Pepper to taste
2 tablespoons tomato paste

Sauté onion with cinnamon in butter in medium saucepan or 10-inch skillet until onion is tender but not brown. Add beans, chicken broth, salt and pepper. Bring to a boil; reduce heat. Cook, covered, for 20 minutes or until beans are tender. Stir in tomato paste gently. Serve at once. May substitute two 10-ounce packages thawed frozen cut green beans for fresh beans. Yield: 6 servings.

Approx Per Serving: Cal 58; T Fat 2 g; 30% Calories from Fat;
  Prot 3 g; Carbo 9 g; Fiber 3 g; Chol 5 mg; Sod 132 mg.

Ruth Lovell, Caldwell, Idaho

BROCCOLI CASSEROLE

1/2 cup cracker crumbs
1/4 cup sliced almonds
2 tablespoons melted butter
1/4 cup chopped onion
1/4 cup butter
2 tablespoons flour

1/2 cup water
1   8-ounce jar cheese spread
2   10-ounce packages frozen
    chopped broccoli, thawed
3 eggs, beaten

Combine cracker crumbs, almonds and 2 tablespoons melted butter in bowl; mix well. Sauté onion in 1/4 cup butter in saucepan. Stir in flour. Add water, mixing well. Cook until thickened, stirring constantly. Stir in cheese spread. Combine with broccoli in bowl. Add eggs; mix gently. Spoon into greased 1 1/2-quart baking dish. Sprinkle with cracker crumb mixture. Bake at 350 degrees for 1 hour. Yield: 6 servings.

Approx Per Serving: Cal 355; T Fat 26 g; 65% Calories from Fat;
    Prot 15 g; Carbo 17 g; Fiber 4 g; Chol 164 mg; Sod 693 mg.

Arloa Weiss, Billings, Montana

CHEESY BROCCOLI SOUP

1 or 2 bunches fresh broccoli,
    chopped
1/2 cup melted butter
1/2 cup flour

4 or 5 cups milk
1 cup Cheez Whiz
Salt and pepper to taste

Cook broccoli in a small amount of water until tender; drain. Blend butter and flour in saucepan. Cook for several minutes. Stir in milk. Cook until thickened, stirring constantly. Stir in Cheez Whiz. Add broccoli, salt and pepper. Simmer until heated through. Serve hot. Yield: 6 servings.

Approx Per Serving: Cal 454; T Fat 32 g; 61% Calories from Fat;
    Prot 19 g; Carbo 26 g; Fiber 4 g; Chol 93 mg; Sod 695 mg.

Marilyn Olsen, Logan, Utah

MARINATED CARROTS

2 pounds carrots, sliced
1 10-ounce can tomato soup
1 cup sugar
3/4 cup vinegar
1 teaspoon Worcestershire
  sauce

1/3 cup oil
1 green bell pepper, chopped
1 onion, chopped
1 teaspoon dry mustard
1 teaspoon pepper

Cook carrots in water in saucepan until tender; drain. Combine soup, sugar, vinegar, Worcestershire sauce, oil, green pepper, onion, dry mustard and pepper in bowl; mix well. Add carrots. Marinate in refrigerator overnight. May substitute 5 cans sliced carrots for fresh carrots. Yield: 12 servings.

Approx Per Serving: Cal 176; T Fat 7 g; 32% Calories from Fat;
  Prot 1 g; Carbo 30 g; Fiber 3 g; Chol 0 mg; Sod 196 mg.

Marie Clark, Nampa, Idaho

SCALLOPED CORN

1/4 cup chopped onion
1/4 cup chopped green bell
  pepper
2 tablespoons butter
2 tablespoons flour
1/2 teaspoon paprika
1/4 teaspoon dry mustard

1 teaspoon salt
Pepper to taste
1/4 cup milk
2 cups fresh or frozen corn
1 egg, beaten
1/3 cup cracker crumbs
1 tablespoon melted butter

Sauté onion and green pepper in 2 tablespoons butter in saucepan; remove from heat. Stir in flour, paprika, dry mustard, salt and pepper. Cook over low heat until thickened, stirring constantly; remove from heat. Stir in milk gradually. Bring to a boil, stirring constantly. Stir in corn and egg. Spoon into 1-quart baking dish. Top with mixture of cracker crumbs and 1 tablespoon melted butter. Bake at 350 degrees for 30 to 35 minutes or until brown. Yield: 4 servings.

Approx Per Serving: Cal 220; T Fat 12 g; 48% Calories from Fat;
  Prot 5 g; Carbo 25 g; Fiber 4 g; Chol 81 mg; Sod 732 mg.

Irene Stewart Kemph, Miles City, Montana

CORN AND VEGETABLE CASSEROLE

1 17-ounce can cream-style
  corn
1/2 cup finely grated carrots
1 tablespoon grated green
  bell pepper
1/2 cup chopped celery
1 tablespoon chopped onion
2 eggs, beaten

1/2 cup cracker crumbs
1/4 cup melted butter
1/4 cup evaporated milk
6 drops of Tabasco sauce
1 tablespoon sugar
1/2 teaspoon salt
1/2 cup shredded Cheddar
  cheese

Combine corn, carrots, green pepper, celery, onion, eggs, cracker crumbs, butter, evaporated milk, Tabasco sauce, sugar and salt in bowl; mix well. Spoon into 3x8x8-inch baking dish. Top with cheese. Bake at 350 degrees for 30 minutes. Yield: 8 servings.

Approx Per Serving: Cal 186; T Fat 11 g; 51% Calories from Fat;
    Prot 5 g; Carbo 19 g; Fiber 2 g; Chol 80 mg; Sod 500 mg.

Irene Crane, Boise, Idaho

SWEET ONION CASSEROLE

4 cups chopped Walla Walla
  onions
2 tablespoons butter
1 10-ounce can cream of
  chicken soup
1 soup can milk
3/4 cup shredded Swiss
  cheese

1 teaspoon Worcestershire
  sauce
1 teaspoon paprika
6 1/2-inch slices French
  bread
2 tablespoons butter,
  softened

Sauté onions in 2 tablespoons butter in skillet. Spread in shallow baking dish. Combine soup, milk, cheese, Worcestershire sauce and paprika in bowl; mix well. Spoon over onions. Spread bread with softened butter. Arrange on top of casserole. Bake at 350 degrees for 25 minutes. Yield: 8 servings.

Approx Per Serving: Cal 248; T Fat 13 g; 48% Calories from Fat;
    Prot 9 g; Carbo 24 g; Fiber 2 g; Chol 33 mg; Sod 529 mg.

Donna Hager, Billings, Montana

ONION PIE

4 medium onions, thinly
  sliced into rings
2 tablespoons butter
1 unbaked 9-inch pie shell
1 cup shredded Swiss cheese

2 eggs, beaten
1 cup half and half
3/4 teaspoon salt
Pepper to taste
Paprika to taste

Sauté onions in butter in skillet. Spread in pie shell. Sprinkle with cheese. Combine eggs, half and half, salt and pepper in mixer bowl. Beat until smooth. Pour over onions and cheese. Sprinkle with paprika. Bake at 425 degrees for 15 minutes; reduce temperature to 350 degrees. Bake for 30 minutes longer. Let stand for 15 minutes before serving. Yield: 6 servings.

Approx Per Serving: Cal 370; T Fat 26 g; 62% Calories from Fat;
  Prot 12 g; Carbo 24 g; Fiber 2 g; Chol 113 mg; Sod 573 mg.

Jan Keif, St. George, Utah

FRENCH PEAS

4 slices bacon, chopped
1 tablespoon chopped onion
1 tablespoon flour
1 cup light cream
1 cup chopped mushrooms

2 tablespoons butter
2 cups frozen peas
1/2 teaspoon salt
Pepper to taste

Fry bacon partially in saucepan. Add onion. Sauté until tender. Stir in flour. Add cream. Cook until thickened, stirring constantly. Sauté mushrooms in butter in skillet for 5 minutes; drain on paper towel. Add mushrooms and peas to cream sauce. Season with salt and pepper. Cook until heated through. Yield: 4 servings.

Approx Per Serving: Cal 332; T Fat 28 g; 74% Calories from Fat;
  Prot 8 g; Carbo 14 g; Fiber 4 g; Chol 88 mg; Sod 526 mg.

Marie Clark, Nampa, Idaho

AU GRATIN POTATOES

8 potatoes, cooked, peeled
1/2 cup melted butter
1 10-ounce can cream of
celery soup
1 10-ounce can cream of
chicken soup

2 cups sour cream
1 onion, chopped
2 cups shredded Cheddar
cheese
Salt and pepper to taste
1 cup crushed cornflakes

Grate potatoes into 9x13-inch baking dish sprayed with non-stick cooking spray. Drizzle with butter. Combine soups, sour cream, onion, cheese, salt and pepper in bowl; mix well. Pour over potatoes. Top with crushed cornflakes. Bake at 350 degrees for 45 minutes. Yield: 10 servings.

Approx Per Serving: Cal 464; T Fat 29 g; 56% Calories from Fat; Prot 12 g; Carbo 40 g; Fiber 2 g; Chol 74 mg; Sod 770 mg.

Leona P. Geary, Logan, Utah

CHEESE POTATOES

5 medium potatoes
2 tablespoons butter
1/2 cup shredded American
cheese

1/4 cup milk
1 teaspoon salt
1/2 teaspoon pepper

Bake potatoes at 400 degrees for 1 hour. Cool enough to handle easily. Cut thin lengthwise slice from each potato; press ends toward center gently. Remove potato pulp, reserving 4 shells. Combine pulp with butter, cheese, milk, salt and pepper in mixer bowl; beat until smooth. Spoon into reserved shells; place on baking sheet. Bake for 15 minutes longer. May garnish with additional cheese or substitute Cheddar cheese for American cheese. Yield: 4 servings.

Approx Per Serving: Cal 388; T Fat 11 g; 25% Calories from Fat; Prot 10 g; Carbo 65 g; Fiber 6 g; Chol 31 mg; Sod 810 mg.

Michelle Groothof, Boise, Idaho

GOLDEN PARMESAN POTATOES

1/4 cup sifted flour
1/4 cup grated Parmesan
  cheese
2 tablespoons chopped parsley

3/4 teaspoon salt
1/8 teaspoon pepper
6 large potatoes, peeled
1/3 cup melted butter

Combine first 5 ingredients in bag. Slice each potato into 4 wedges. Moisten and place in flour mixture in bag; shake to coat well. Arrange in melted butter in 9x13-inch baking dish. Bake at 375 degrees for 1 hour, turning to brown evenly. Yield: 8 servings.

Approx Per Serving: Cal 257; T Fat 9 g; 29% Calories from Fat; Prot 5 g; Carbo 41 g; Fiber 4 g; Chol 23 mg; Sod 323 mg.

Evelyn R. Damschen, Anaconda, Montana

BAKED POTATO SPEARS

1 cup mayonnaise-type salad
  dressing
1/4 cup grated Parmesan cheese
1/4 cup milk
1 tablespoon chopped chives

3 large potatoes
1/4 cup mayonnaise-type
  salad dressing
1/4 teaspoon onion salt
1/4 teaspoon pepper

Combine 1 cup salad dressing, cheese, milk and chives in bowl; mix well. Chill for several hours. Slice potatoes into wedges. Brush with 1/4 cup salad dressing; sprinkle with seasonings. Place on greased 10x15-inch baking sheet. Bake in preheated 375-degree oven for 50 minutes. Serve with cheese dip. Yield: 4 servings.

Approx Per Serving: Cal 484; T Fat 27 g; 49% Calories from Fat; Prot 7 g; Carbo 57 g; Fiber 4 g; Chol 25 mg; Sod 768 mg.

Hazel M. Johnson, Murray, Utah

SAUERKRAUT

6 cups (about) coarsely
  chopped cabbage

1 teaspoon sugar
1 teaspoon salt

Pack cabbage tightly into 1-quart wide-mouth jar. Add sugar and salt. Fill sterilized jar with boiling water; seal. Let stand for 3 weeks. Yield: 6 servings.

Approx Per Serving: Cal 19; T Fat <1 g; 5% Calories from Fat; Prot 1 g; Carbo 4 g; Fiber 2 g; Chol 0 mg; Sod 367 mg.

Arloa Weiss, Billings, Montana

SUMMER SQUASH CASSEROLE

6 cups chopped yellow
  squash
1/4 cup chopped onion
Salt to taste
1 10-ounce can cream of
  chicken soup

1 cup sour cream
1 cup shredded carrots
1 8-ounce package herb-
  seasoned stuffing mix
1/2 cup melted butter

Cook squash with onion in salted water in saucepan for 5 minutes; drain. Combine soup and sour cream in bowl; mix well. Stir in carrots. Fold in squash mixture. Combine stuffing mix and butter in bowl. Layer half the stuffing mixture, all the squash mixture and remaining stuffing mixture in 9x13-inch baking dish. Bake at 350 degrees for 25 to 30 minutes or until bubbly. Yield: 8 servings.

Approx Per Serving: Cal 329; T Fat 21 g; 56% Calories from Fat;
  Prot 7 g; Carbo 30 g; Fiber 2 g; Chol 47 mg; Sod 775 mg.

Karren Fairbanks, Salt Lake City, Utah

SWEET POTATO PIE

3 cups mashed cooked sweet
  potatoes
2 eggs, slightly beaten
1/3 stick margarine, melted
1/2 teaspoon salt

3/4 cup milk
1 cup packed brown sugar
1/3 cup milk
1/3 cup margarine, softened
1 cup chopped pecans

Combine sweet potatoes, eggs, melted margarine, salt and milk in casserole; mix well. Top with mixture of brown sugar, milk, 1/3 cup softened margarine and pecans. Bake at 350 degrees for 30 minutes. Yield: 8 servings.

Approx Per Serving: Cal 465; T Fat 24 g; 45% Calories from Fat;
  Prot 6 g; Carbo 60 g; Fiber 3 g; Chol 58 mg; Sod 383 mg.

Ruth Davis, Filer, Idaho

No kindness is ever wasted.

NANCY'S SWEET POTATO CASSEROLE

3 cups mashed cooked sweet
  potatoes
3/4 cup sugar
2 eggs
1/2 cup milk
1/4 cup melted margarine

1 teaspoon vanilla extract
1/2 teaspoon salt
1/4 cup melted margarine
1 cup packed brown sugar
1/2 cup self-rising flour
1 cup chopped pecans

Combine sweet potatoes, sugar, eggs, milk, 1/4 cup margarine, vanilla and salt in bowl; mix well. Spoon into buttered 9x9-inch baking dish. Combine 1/4 cup margarine, brown sugar, flour and pecans in bowl; mix well. Sprinkle over casserole. Bake at 350 degrees for 30 minutes. Yield: 8 servings.

Approx Per Serving: Cal 531; T Fat 24 g; 39% Calories from Fat;
  Prot 6 g; Carbo 77 g; Fiber 3 g; Chol 55 mg; Sod 459 mg.

Corinne G. Morrison, Leesburg, Florida

ZUCCHINI CASSEROLE

6 cups chopped zucchini
1 small onion, chopped
1 cup grated carrots
1 10-ounce can cream of
  chicken soup

1 cup sour cream
1 6-ounce package stove-
  top stuffing mix
1 pound ground beef

Combine zucchini, onion and carrots with water to cover in saucepan. Cook for 15 minutes or until tender; drain. Stir in soup and sour cream. Prepare stuffing mix using package directions. Brown ground beef in skillet, stirring until crumbly; drain. Add to stuffing mix. Spoon half the stuffing mixture into 9x13-inch baking dish sprayed with nonstick cooking spray. Top with zucchini mixture and remaining stuffing. Bake at 350 degrees for 30 minutes. Yield: 8 servings.

Approx Per Serving: Cal 310; T Fat 21 g; 60% Calories from Fat;
  Prot 15 g; Carbo 17 g; Fiber 2 g; Chol 52 mg; Sod 524 mg.

Scott Hess, Providence, Utah

ZUCCHINI IN DILL CREAM SAUCE

2¼ pounds unpeeled
zucchini, cut into strips
¼ cup finely chopped onion
½ cup water
1 teaspoon instant chicken
bouillon
½ teaspoon dillweed

1 teaspoon salt
2 tablespoons melted butter
2 teaspoons sugar
1 teaspoon lemon juice
2 tablespoons flour
½ cup sour cream

Combine zucchini, onion, water, bouillon, dillweed and salt in saucepan. Bring to a boil; reduce heat. Simmer, covered, for 5 minutes or until tender-crisp; do not drain. Add butter, sugar and lemon juice; remove from heat. Blend flour and sour cream in bowl. Stir half the hot liquid from zucchini into sour cream mixture; stir sour cream mixture into saucepan. Cook until thickened, stirring constantly. Yield: 6 servings.

Approx Per Serving: Cal 119; T Fat 8 g; 59% Calories from Fat;
   Prot 3 g; Carbo 10 g; Fiber 2 g; Chol 19 mg; Sod 594 mg.

Ruth Lovell, Caldwell, Idaho

CREAM OF ZUCCHINI SOUP

8 ounces onions, chopped
2 tablespoons butter
1½ pounds zucchini, sliced
3 cups chicken broth
½ cup half and half
⅛ teaspoon nutmeg

Cayenne pepper to taste
⅛ teaspoon salt
⅛ teaspoon pepper
1 cup shredded Cheddar
cheese

Sauté onions in butter in 3-quart saucepan. Add zucchini, chicken broth, half and half, nutmeg, cayenne pepper, salt and pepper; mix well. Bring to a boil; reduce heat. Simmer until zucchini is tender. Process in blender until smooth. Return to saucepan. Add cheese. Heat just until cheese melts; do not boil. Yield: 6 servings.

Approx Per Serving: Cal 185; T Fat 13 g; 64% Calories from Fat;
   Prot 10 g; Carbo 8 g; Fiber 2 g; Chol 38 mg; Sod 593 mg.

Florence L. Chamberlain, Caldwell, Idaho

MEATLESS CASSEROLE

1 cup chopped celery
1 cup grated carrots
1/4 cup chopped onion
1/2 cup chopped green bell
 pepper
1/2 cup mayonnaise
1/2 cup slivered almonds
2 cups cooked rice

2 tablespoons soy sauce
1 4-ounce can mushrooms,
 drained
1/2 cup crushed wheat crackers
2 tablespoons butter
1/2 cup crushed wheat crackers
1/2 cup slivered almonds

Combine celery, carrots, onion, green pepper, mayonnaise, 1/2 cup almonds, rice, soy sauce, mushrooms and 1/2 cup cracker crumbs in bowl; mix well. Spoon into 2-quart casserole. Top with mixture of butter, remaining 1/2 cup cracker crumbs and 1/2 cup almonds. Bake at 350 degrees for 30 minutes. Yield: 8 servings.

Approx Per Serving: Cal 405; T Fat 26 g; 57% Calories from Fat;
 Prot 8 g; Carbo 37 g; Fiber 5 g; Chol 16 mg; Sod 684 mg.

Betty L. Mann, Provo, Utah

SQUASH AND APPLE CASSEROLE

1 medium butternut or acorn
 squash
3 cups sliced apples
Brown sugar substitute to
 equal 1/2 cup packed
 brown sugar

1/4 cup melted margarine
1 tablespoon flour
1/2 teaspoon nutmeg
1/2 teaspoon salt
1/4 cup chopped walnuts

Cut squash into halves lengthwise, discarding seeds. Cut into small pieces. Layer squash and apples in baking dish. Combine brown sugar substitute, margarine, flour, nutmeg and salt in bowl; mix well. Sprinkle brown sugar mixture and walnuts over layers. Bake, covered with foil, at 350 degrees for 50 minutes or until squash is tender. May bake squash halves at 350 degrees for 35 minutes, fill centers with apples, sprinkle with brown sugar mixture and walnuts and bake until squash is tender. Yield: 8 servings.

Approx Per Serving: Cal 150; T Fat 8 g; 48% Calories from Fat;
 Prot 2 g; Carbo 19 g; Fiber 4 g; Chol 0 mg; Sod 250 mg.

Donna Hager, Billings, Montana

DRESSING CASSEROLE

1 24-ounce loaf day-old
bread
8 ounces pork sausage
1 large onion, chopped
2 stalks celery, chopped
2 eggs, beaten
2 tablespoons (heaping)
grated Parmesan cheese

2 tablespoons chopped
parsley
1 teaspoon sage
1 teaspoon poultry seasoning
1 teaspoon salt
2/3 cup chicken bouillon
1/2 cup melted butter

Cube bread into bowl. Brown sausage in skillet, stirring until crumbly. Remove sausage with slotted spoon, adding to bread in bowl. Drain skillet, reserving 1 tablespoon drippings. Sauté onion and celery in reserved drippings in skillet for 10 minutes. Add to bread mixture with eggs, cheese, parsley, sage, poultry seasoning and salt; mix well. Stir in bouillon and butter. Spoon into oiled 9x13-inch baking dish. Bake at 350 degrees for 30 minutes. Yield: 8 servings.

Approx Per Serving: Cal 413; T Fat 21 g; 46% Calories from Fat;
Prot 13 g; Carbo 43 g; Fiber 2 g; Chol 96 mg; Sod 1081 mg.

June M. Fischer, Preston, Idaho

DRESSING FOR HAM

1/2 cup butter, softened
1 cup sugar
4 eggs

1 cup drained crushed
pineapple
5 slices bread, cubed

Cream butter and sugar in mixer bowl until light. Beat in eggs. Add pineapple; mix well. Fold in bread cubes. Spoon into 1 1/2-quart baking dish. Bake at 350 degrees for 45 minutes. Yield: 6 servings.

Approx Per Serving: Cal 401; T Fat 20 g; 44% Calories from Fat;
Prot 6 g; Carbo 51 g; Fiber 1 g; Chol 183 mg; Sod 296 mg.

Mardi Millons, Helena, Montana

FETTUCINI À LA PIMENTO

1 16-ounce package fettucini
6 to 8 quarts boiling water
1 tablespoon salt
1/2 cup butter, softened
1/2 cup whipping cream
1/2 cup grated Parmesan
   cheese

1 clove of garlic, finely
   chopped
2 tablespoons finely
   chopped parsley
1 tablespoon chopped
   pimento
Salt and pepper to taste

Combine pasta with 6 to 8 quarts boiling water and 1 table-spoon salt in saucepan. Cook until tender. Cream butter in mixer bowl until light. Beat in cream. Add cheese, garlic, parsley and pimento; mix well. Drain pasta. Add to pimento mixture with salt and pepper to taste; toss to coat well. Yield: 6 servings.

Approx Per Serving: Cal 515; T Fat 26 g; 45% Calories from Fat;
   Prot 13 g; Carbo 58 g; Fiber 3 g; Chol 74 mg; Sod 1330 mg.

Merla Jorgensen, Pocatello, Idaho

FETTUCINI PRIMAVERA

1 12-ounce package fettucini
1 pound asparagus, cut into
   1-inch pieces
2 red bell peppers, cut into
   strips
2 carrots, sliced
1 cup frozen peas

1 cup whipping cream
1 cup grated Parmesan cheese
2 tablespoons butter
1 egg, beaten
1/4 teaspoon salt
1/4 teaspoon cracked pepper

Cook pasta until nearly tender using package directions. Add asparagus, bell peppers, carrots and peas. Cook for 3 minutes longer; drain. Combine cream, cheese, butter, egg, salt and pepper in small saucepan. Cook over low heat for 5 minutes or until slightly thickened, stirring constantly. Pour over pasta, tossing to coat well. Spoon into serving bowl. Yield: 6 servings.

Approx Per Serving: Cal 508; T Fat 25 g; 43% Calories from Fat;
   Prot 19 g; Carbo 55 g; Fiber 6 g; Chol 111 mg; Sod 438 mg.

Annette Rich, Salt Lake City, Utah

RICE CASSEROLE

1/2 green bell pepper, chopped
1 small onion, chopped
1 tablespoon butter
2 4-ounce cans mushrooms, drained
2 10-ounce cans beef consommé
1 cup uncooked long grain rice

Sauté green pepper and onion in butter in large skillet. Add mushrooms; mix well. Add consommé; mix well. Place rice in buttered 2- or 3-quart baking dish. Pour consommé mixture over rice. Bake, covered with foil, at 140 degrees for 40 minutes. Turn back 1 corner of foil. Bake for 20 minutes longer. Yield: 8 servings.

Approx Per Serving: Cal 61; T Fat 2 g; 26% Calories from Fat;
Prot 2 g; Carbo 9 g; Fiber 1 g; Chol 4 mg; Sod 497 mg.

Dorothy Ewer, Logan, Utah

GOURMET RICE

1 cup instant rice
2 cups water
3 chicken bouillon cubes
1 teaspoon salt
1/2 cup chopped green bell pepper
1/2 cup chopped green onions
1/4 cup butter
1/2 cup sliced black olives
3 tablespoons chopped pimento

Combine rice, water, bouillon cubes and salt in 2-quart saucepan. Cook for 25 minutes or until water is absorbed. Sauté green pepper and green onions in butter in skillet until tender. Add to rice. Add olives and pimento; mix well. Heat to serving temperature. May add 1/4 cup chopped celery or use red or yellow bell peppers if preferred. Yield: 4 servings.

Approx Per Serving: Cal 253; T Fat 18 g; 61% Calories from Fat;
Prot 3 g; Carbo 23 g; Fiber 3 g; Chol 31 mg; Sod 1709 mg.

Robert L. Stommel, Idaho Falls, Idaho

SPANISH RICE

8 ounces extra-lean ground
 beef
1 medium onion, chopped
1 medium green bell pepper,
 chopped
1 cup uncooked rice
2 tablespoons
 Worcestershire sauce

1/2 cup tomato sauce
1 1/2 cups water
1 teaspoon chili powder
Tabasco sauce to taste
Garlic powder, thyme, salt
 and pepper to taste

Brown ground beef with onion and green pepper in large skillet, stirring frequently; drain. Add rice, Worcestershire sauce, tomato sauce, water, chili powder, Tabasco sauce, garlic powder, thyme, salt and pepper; mix well. Bring to a boil; reduce heat. Simmer for 20 minutes. May increase amount of ground beef for a 1-dish meal. Yield: 6 servings.

Approx Per Serving: Cal 212; T Fat 6 g; 24% Calories from Fat;
 Prot 10 g; Carbo 30 g; Fiber 1 g; Chol 25 mg; Sod 197 mg.

Imogene Sweeney, Boise, Idaho

QUICK SPANISH RICE

8 ounces ground beef
1 medium onion, sliced
1/2 cup chopped green bell
 pepper
1 cup uncooked instant rice
2 8-ounce cans tomato sauce

1 3/4 cups hot water
1 tablespoon prepared
 mustard
1 teaspoon salt
Pepper to taste

Brown ground beef in skillet, stirring until crumbly; drain. Add onion, green pepper and rice. Cook until brown, stirring constantly. Add tomato sauce, water, mustard, salt and pepper; mix well. Bring to a boil; reduce heat. Simmer, covered, for 25 minutes. Yield: 4 servings.

Approx Per Serving: Cal 258; T Fat 9 g; 29% Calories from Fat;
 Prot 15 g; Carbo 32 g; Fiber 3 g; Chol 37 mg; Sod 1301 mg.

Wyn K. Doney, Preston, Idaho

HALF-SUGAR PEAR JAM

4 pounds ripe Bartlett pears   **2 cups sugar**
¼ cup lemon juice

Peel pears. Cut pears into quarters, removing cores. Cut crosswise into thin slices. Toss with lemon juice in bowl. Layer pears and sugar ½ at a time in heavy 4-quart saucepan. Let stand for 3 hours. Stir to mix. Bring to a boil; reduce heat. Simmer for 10 minutes. Remove pears to bowl with slotted spoon. Cook syrup for 20 to 30 minutes or to 230 degrees on candy thermometer, spun-thread stage, stirring occasionally. Stir in pears. Cook for 1 minute longer. Ladle into 2 hot sterilized 1-pint jars, leaving ¼-inch headspace; seal with 2-piece lids. Process in hot water bath for 15 minutes. May store in refrigerator for up to 3 weeks or freeze for up to 1 year if preferred. Yield: 64 servings.

Approx Per Serving: Cal 41; T Fat <1 g; 2% Calories from Fat;
   Prot <1 g; Carbo 11 g; Fiber 1 g; Chol 0 mg; Sod <1 mg.

Marna C. Buffo, Provo, Utah

BREAD AND BUTTER PICKLES

12 medium cucumbers, sliced   **½ teaspoon mustard seed**
½ cup salt   **¼ teaspoon celery seed**
1½ cups vinegar   **½ teaspoon turmeric**
2 cups sugar   **6 small onions, sliced**
1 teaspoon dry mustard

Sprinkle cucumbers with salt in bowl; weight with plate. Let stand for 1 hour. Rinse and drain. Combine vinegar, sugar, dry mustard, mustard seed, celery seed and turmeric in saucepan. Bring to a boil. Add cucumbers and onions. Bring to a boil. Cook for 5 minutes. Ladle into 5 hot sterilized 1-pint jars, leaving ¼-inch headspace; seal with 2-piece lids. Yield: 80 servings.

Approx Per Serving: Cal 29; T Fat <1 g; 3% Calories from Fat;
   Prot <1 g; Carbo 7 g; Fiber 1 g; Chol 0 mg; Sod 641 mg.

Judy Frazer, Billings, Montana

HOMEMADE EGG NOODLES

3 eggs
2 cups flour

1 teaspoon baking powder
1/2 teaspoon salt

Beat eggs in bowl. Add flour, baking powder and salt; mix well to form dough. Roll on lightly floured surface. Cut as desired. Cook in water or soup base for 15 minutes or until tender. Yield: 8 servings.

Approx Per Serving: Cal 144; T Fat 2 g; 15% Calories from Fat; Prot 6 g; Carbo 24 g; Fiber 1 g; Chol 80 mg; Sod 201 mg.

Donna Farnes, Boise, Idaho

BARBECUE SAUCE

1/4 cup catsup
2 to 3 tablespoons brown
  sugar

1 tablespoon Worcestershire
  sauce
3 dashes of liquid smoke

Combine catsup, brown sugar, Worcestershire sauce and liquid smoke in saucepan; mix well. Simmer for several minutes or until heated through. Yield: 8 servings.

Approx Per Serving: Cal 30; T Fat <1 g; 1% Calories from Fat; Prot <1 g; Carbo 7 g; Fiber <1 g; Chol 0 mg; Sod 110 mg. Nutritional information does not include liquid smoke.

Wyn K. Doney, Preston, Idaho

TARTAR SAUCE

4 teaspoons lemon juice
1 tablespoon minced onion
3/4 cup mayonnaise
1/4 cup sour cream

1 teaspoon sugar
1/4 teaspoon dillweed
1/2 teaspoon seasoned salt

Combine lemon juice, onion, mayonnaise, sour cream, sugar, dillweed and seasoned salt in bowl; mix well. Let stand for 30 minutes. Serve with fish. Yield: 16 servings.

Approx Per Serving: Cal 83; T Fat 9 g; 95% Calories from Fat; Prot <1 g; Carbo 1 g; Fiber <1 g; Chol 8 mg; Sod 127 mg.

Martha Hamilton, Meridian, Idaho

The Chuck Wagon

Cooking for a Crowd

'89' H. CREEKMORE

TREASURE VALLEY COUNCIL

Boise, Idaho

A recent Council project was the conversion of a surplus concrete waste-treatment tank to a counseling and youth outreach center for the Ada County Sheriff's Department. Marietta Wroten, a newly-retired U S West employee, served as chairperson for the Pioneer portion of the work. Pioneer volunteers helped to complete and paint the interior walls and wood trim and to paint the outside. The result is a first-class facility, which was dedicated at an Open House in January of 1991.

HOT HATS

4 ounces dry yeast
22 cups warm water
6 ounces sugar
4 ounces nonfat dry milk
4 ounces baking powder
16 ounces baker's margarine
25 pounds flour

Salt to taste
40 cups chopped cooked ham
40 cups shredded Swiss
  cheese
6 eggs, beaten
2¹/₂ cups sesame seed

Dissolve yeast in warm water in large mixer bowl. Let stand for 5 minutes. Beat at low speed for 1 minute. Add sugar, milk powder, baking powder and margarine. Beat at low speed for 1 minute. Add flour and salt. Beat for 6 minutes. Chill in refrigerator for 12 hours. Roll dough ¹/₄ inch thick on floured surface. Cut into ovals 5 inches in diameter. Place ¹/₂ cup mixed ham and cheese on 1 end of each oval. Brush edge with egg. Fold dough over to enclose filling; roll up edge to seal. Brush with egg; sprinkle with sesame seed. Place on baking sheet. Bake at 555 degrees for 10 minutes or until golden brown. (For 10 sandwiches, use 1¹/₂ teaspoons yeast, 1³/₈ cups water, 2¹/₄ teaspoons sugar, 1¹/₂ teaspoons nonfat dry milk, 1¹/₂ teaspoons baking powder, 1 tablespoon baker's margarine, 3 cups flour, 2¹/₂ cups each ham and cheese, 1 tablespoon egg and 2¹/₂ table-spoons sesame seed.) Yield: 160 servings.

Approx Per Serving: Cal 466; T Fat 14 g; 28% Calories from Fat;
    Prot 26 g; Carbo 57 g; Fiber 2 g; Chol 53 mg; Sod 652 mg.

Terri Rogers, Great Falls, Montana

SHRIMP SOUP

2 quarts tomato juice
2 12-ounce bottles of
  cocktail sauce
1 7-ounce bottle of catsup
1 bunch celery, chopped

2 tablespoons prepared
  horseradish
1¹/₂ pounds cooked fresh
  shrimp

Combine all ingredients in 1-gallon jar. Chill for several hours. Yield: 16 servings.

Approx Per Serving: Cal 126; T Fat 1 g; 4% Calories from Fat;
    Prot 11 g; Carbo 19 g; Fiber 1 g; Chol 83 mg; Sod 961 mg.

Merla Jorgensen, Pocatello, Idaho

ALBONDIGAS SOUP

This Spanish meatball soup freezes well and makes a real meal with bread.

2 pounds lean ground veal
1 cup bread crumbs
2 eggs, beaten
2 (or more) onions, chopped
4 cloves of garlic, minced
2 tablespoons oil
8 carrots, sliced
8 stalks celery, sliced

2 green bell peppers,
　chopped
1　28-ounce can tomatoes,
　chopped
1 cup salsa (or to taste)
8 cups beef broth
1¹/₂ teaspoons cumin
Salt and pepper to taste

Combine ground veal, bread crumbs and eggs in bowl; mix well. Shape into small meatballs. Place on rack in 12x15-inch baking pan. Bake at 350 degrees for 40 minutes. Sauté onions and garlic in oil in large stockpot for 5 minutes. Add carrots, celery and green peppers. Cook for 15 minutes. Add tomatoes, salsa, broth and seasonings. Simmer for 20 minutes. Add meatballs. Simmer for 20 minutes longer. May substitute lean ground beef for ground veal. Yield: 15 servings.

Approx Per Serving: Cal 192; T Fat 6 g; 28% Calories from Fat;
　Prot 20 g; Carbo 15 g; Fiber 3 g; Chol 91 mg; Sod 648 mg.

Evelyn R. Damschen, Anaconda, Montana

CREAMY AMBROSIA

1　10-ounce jar maraschino
　cherries
1　20-ounce can pineapple
　chunks
2 bananas, sliced
1 cup seedless green grape
　halves

1　11-ounce can mandarin
　oranges
1　16-ounce can sliced peaches
1 cup shredded coconut
1　4-ounce package lemon
　instant pudding mix
8 ounces whipped topping

Drain cherries. Do not drain remaining fruit. Combine fruit and coconut in large bowl. Sprinkle pudding mix over fruit; stir gently. Let stand for 5 minutes. Fold in whipped topping. Spoon into serving bowl. Chill, covered, for 4 hours or until completely chilled. Yield: 20 servings.

Approx Per Serving: Cal 155; T Fat 4 g; 24% Calories from Fat;
　Prot 1 g; Carbo 31 g; Fiber 2 g; Chol 0 mg; Sod 45 mg.

Sherlee A. Polglase, Great Falls, Montana

MACARONI SALAD

*Mom liked to serve this sweet salad in the hot summer months
with cold cuts or barbecue.*

2 pounds macaroni shells
12 green onions, chopped
2 medium tomatoes, chopped
1 green bell pepper, chopped
4 slices cheese, chopped
4 eggs, chopped
1/2 cup thinly sliced celery
1/2 cup grated carrot
1/2 cup grated cabbage

1 cup sandwich spread
1 cup reduced-calorie
 mayonnaise-type salad
 dressing
1/4 cup sweet pickle juice
4 packages artificial
 sweetener
2 hard-boiled eggs, sliced

Cook macaroni using package directions; drain. Spray with
cold water; drain. Combine with green onions, tomatoes, green
pepper, cheese, chopped eggs, celery, carrot and cabbage in dish-
pan; mix well. Combine sandwich spread, salad dressing, pickle
juice and sweetener in small bowl; mix well. Add enough to
macaroni mixture to coat generously; mix well. Arrange sliced
eggs on top. Yield: 16 servings.

Approx Per Serving: Cal 370; T Fat 14 g; 33% Calories from Fat;
 Prot 12 g; Carbo 50 g; Fiber 3 g; Chol 94 mg; Sod 319 mg.

Mary Maureen Ozburn, Twin Falls, Idaho

WONDERFUL SALAD DRESSING

1 cup sugar
1 cup vinegar
1 cup oil
1 cup catsup
1 teaspoon salt

1 teaspoon pepper
1 teaspoon garlic salt
2 teaspoons dried onion
 flakes
1/8 teaspoon MSG

Combine all ingredients in 1-quart jar; cover. Shake until
well mixed. Chill for 24 hours. Shake before serving.
Yield: 64 servings.

Approx Per Serving: Cal 47; T Fat 3 g; 63% Calories from Fat;
 Prot <1 g; Carbo 4 g; Fiber <1 g; Chol 0 mg; Sod 118 mg.

Dorris Calton, Ogden, Utah

TACO SALAD FOR-A-CROWD

1 pound lean ground beef
1 16-ounce can refried
  beans with sausage
1 envelope taco seasoning mix
6 green onions, chopped
1 6-ounce can sliced black
  olives
1 head lettuce, shredded
1 tomato, chopped
8 ounces Cheddar cheese,
  shredded
8 ounces mozzarella cheese,
  shredded
1 15-ounce package nacho
  cheese-flavored tortilla
  chips, crushed
1 cup sour cream
1 cup salsa
1 cup mayonnaise-type salad
  dressing

Brown ground beef in skillet, stirring until crumbly; drain. Add refried beans and taco seasoning mix; mix well. Cook until heated through. Let stand until slightly cool. Combine green onions, olives, lettuce and tomato in large bowl. Add cheeses, crushed chips and ground beef mixture; toss to mix well. Pour mixture of sour cream, salsa and salad dressing over salad; toss to mix well. Garnish with whole tortilla chips and black olives around edge. Yield: 30 servings.

Approx Per Serving: Cal 242; T Fat 16 g; 60% Calories from Fat;
   Prot 9 g; Carbo 16 g; Fiber 2 g; Chol 31 mg; Sod 470 mg.

Sherlee A. Polglase, Great Falls, Montana

BARBECUE FOR ONE HUNDRED

15 pounds ground beef
3 large onions, chopped
1/2 cup lemon juice
4 cups catsup
2 28-ounce cans tomato
  sauce
1 cup packed brown sugar
1/4 cup prepared mustard
1 8-ounce bottle of
  barbecue sauce
3 tablespoons salt
1/2 cup vinegar
1 large green bell pepper,
  chopped
1 8-ounce package celery
  hearts, chopped

Brown ground beef with onions in large stockpot, stirring until ground beef is crumbly; drain. Add remaining ingredients; mix well. Simmer for 2 hours. Yield: 100 servings.

Approx Per Serving: Cal 169; T Fat 10 g; 52% Calories from Fat;
   Prot 13 g; Carbo 7 g; Fiber 1 g; Chol 44 mg; Sod 470 mg.

Lucille Linford, Pocatello, Idaho

CALICO BEANS

8 ounces bacon, crisp-fried, crumbled
1 pound ground chuck
1 cup chopped onion
1/2 cup catsup
3/4 cup packed brown sugar
2 teaspoons prepared mustard
4 teaspoons white vinegar
Several drops of Tabasco sauce
1/2 teaspoon salt
1 tablespoon horseradish
1   30-ounce can pork and beans, drained
1   15-ounce can kidney beans, drained
2   15-ounce cans lima beans, drained
1   15-ounce can garbanzo beans, drained

Combine all ingredients in large baking pan; mix well. Bake at 350 degrees for 1 hour. Serve hot. Yield: 30 servings.

Approx Per Serving: Cal 202; T Fat 7 g; 30% Calories from Fat; Prot 11 g; Carbo 25 g; Fiber 6 g; Chol 18 mg; Sod 383 mg.

Sherlee A. Polglase, Great Falls, Montana

CHUCK WAGON BEANS

This recipe is an annual favorite in our hunting camp.

1 pound bacon, chopped
2 pounds ground beef
2 large onions, chopped
2   28-ounce cans pork and beans
2   14-ounce cans stewed tomatoes
1 cup packed brown sugar
1/2 cup catsup
2 stalks celery, chopped
2 large bay leaves
Salt and pepper to taste
Garlic powder to taste
Soy sauce to taste

Brown bacon in large stockpot. Add ground beef and onions. Cook until ground beef is brown, stirring frequently; drain. Add remaining ingredients; mix well. Simmer for 1 1/2 to 2 hours. Yield: 20 servings.

Approx Per Serving: Cal 296; T Fat 11 g; 34% Calories from Fat; Prot 16 g; Carbo 35 g; Fiber 5 g; Chol 41 mg; Sod 557 mg.

Chuck Friederich, Eagle, Idaho

HAM AND POTATOES AU GRATIN

3¼ pounds potatoes, sliced
    ¼ inch thick
½ cup chopped onion
½ cup chopped green bell
    pepper
½ cup shortening
1½ cups flour
13 cups milk, scalded

8 ounces sharp Cheddar
    cheese, shredded
½ ounce Worcestershire
    sauce
2½ pounds cooked ham,
    cubed
6 cups bread crumbs
½ cup melted butter

Cook potatoes in a small amount of water in large saucepan until almost tender; drain and set aside. Sauté onion and green pepper in shortening in stockpot. Stir in flour. Stir in hot milk gradually. Cook for 15 minutes or until thickened, stirring constantly. Add potatoes, cheese, Worcestershire sauce and ham; mix well. Pour into deep 12x15-inch baking pan. Sprinkle with mixture of bread crumbs and butter. Bake at 375 degrees for 30 to 45 minutes or until golden brown. Yield: 25 servings.

Approx Per Serving: Cal 420; T Fat 19 g; 40% Calories from Fat;
    Prot 23 g; Carbo 40 g; Fiber 2 g; Chol 63 mg; Sod 929 mg.

Nancy Nielsen, Hyrum, Utah

SWEET AND SOUR PORK

15 pounds lean pork
    shoulder
1¼ cups oil
10   20-ounce cans pineapple
    chunks

3⅓ cups vinegar
2½ cups packed brown sugar
1¼ cups cornstarch
5 teaspoons salt
10 tablespoons soy sauce

Cut pork into ½x2-inch strips. Brown oil in stockpot; drain. Drain pineapple, reserving juice. Add enough water to juice to measure 15 cups. Combine juice, vinegar, brown sugar, cornstarch, salt and soy sauce in large saucepan. Cook until thickened, stirring constantly. Add to pork. Simmer, covered, for 1 hour or until pork is tender. Add pineapple and serve. (To serve 4, use 1½ pounds pork, 2 tablespoons oil, 1 can pineapple, ⅓ cup vinegar, ¼ cup packed brown sugar, 2 tablespoons cornstarch, ½ teaspoon salt and 1 tablespoon soy sauce.) Yield: 40 servings.

Approx Per Serving: Cal 490; T Fat 18 g; 33% Calories from Fat;
    Prot 34 g; Carbo 48 g; Fiber 1 g; Chol 104 mg; Sod 614 mg.

Lucille Linford, Pocatello, Idaho

CHICKEN BREAST SUPREME

25 pounds 4-ounce chicken
  breast filets
1½ cups melted margarine
4 cups chopped mushrooms
½ cup melted margarine
1 gallon milk

¼ cup chicken base
½ teaspoon white pepper
1½ cups margarine, softened
2 cups flour
3 cups sour cream

Place chicken breasts on baking sheet sprayed with nonstick cooking spray. Drizzle with 1½ cups melted margarine. Bake at 350 degrees for 20 minutes. Place in 3 large 2-inch deep baking pans. Sauté mushrooms in remaining ½ cup melted margarine in skillet. Spoon over chicken. Scald milk in large double boiler. Add chicken base and white pepper. Add mixture of softened margarine and flour gradually, whisking constantly. Simmer for 5 minutes. Whisk in sour cream. Pour over chicken; cover with foil. Bake at 325 degrees for 1 hour. Yield: 100 servings.

Approx Per Serving: Cal 186; T Fat 10 g; 47% Calories from Fat;
  Prot 21 g; Carbo 3 g; Fiber <1 g; Chol 55 mg; Sod 143 mg.

Hazel M. Johnson, Murray, Utah

HAWAIIAN DISH FOR-A-PARTY

8 chickens
20 cups cooked rice
8 cups chicken gravy
12 medium onions, chopped
16 cups chopped celery
16 green bell peppers,
  chopped
25 medium tomatoes,
  chopped

8 cups shredded coconut
9 cups crushed pineapple
4 4-ounce packages slivered
  almonds
6 8-ounce cans Chinese
  noodles
8 cups shredded Cheddar
  cheese

Cook chickens in a small amount of water in large stockpot. Remove skin and bones; chop into bite-sized pieces. Arrange over rice on serving platter. Arrange remaining ingredients in individual serving dishes around chicken. Guests should layer ingredients on plate as desired. Yield: 33 servings.

Approx Per Serving: Cal 1083; T Fat 49 g; 40% Calories from Fat;
  Prot 70 g; Carbo 95 g; Fiber 11 g; Chol 182 mg; Sod 1125 mg.

Lucille Linford, Pocatello, Idaho

LEMON-BAKED CHICKEN

25 pounds 4-ounce chicken
  breast filets
9 cups sliced celery
4 cups chopped onions
6 lemons, thinly sliced
1 cup chopped parsley
1/2 cup cooking sherry

1/4 cup whole sweet basil
2 tablespoons garlic powder
2 tablespoons seasoned salt
1 tablespoon white pepper
1/4 cup chicken base
12 cups boiling water

Place chicken breasts in 5 deep 12x15-inch baking pans. Top with celery and onions. Arrange lemon slices in attractive pattern over chicken. Sprinkle parsley, sherry and mixture of seasonings over chicken. Dissolve chicken base in boiling water. Ladle over chicken; cover with foil. Bake at 350 degrees for 1 1/2 hours. Yield: 100 servings.

Approx Per Serving: Cal 101; T Fat 1 g; 10% Calories from Fat;
  Prot 20 g; Carbo 2 g; Fiber <1 g; Chol 49 mg; Sod 195 mg.

Hazel M. Johnson, Murray, Utah

NINE-LAYER CHICKEN CASSEROLE

6 slices white bread, trimmed
4 cups chopped cooked
  chicken
8 ounces mushrooms, sliced
2 tablespoons margarine
1   8-ounce can water
  chestnuts, drained, chopped
1/2 cup mayonnaise
6 ounces Monterey Jack
  cheese, thinly sliced

4 ounces American cheese,
  sliced
3 eggs, beaten
1 1/2 cups milk
1   10-ounce can cream of
  mushroom soup
1   10-ounce can cream of
  chicken soup
1/4 cup melted margarine
2/3 cup dried bread crumbs

Layer bread and chicken in buttered 9x13-inch baking pan. Sauté mushrooms in 2 tablespoons margarine in skillet. Spoon over chicken. Spoon mixture of water chestnuts and mayonnaise over mushrooms. Top with cheese slices. Pour mixture of eggs, milk and soups over layers. Chill for 3 to 24 hours. Bake at 325 degrees for 1 1/4 hours. Sprinkle with mixture of melted margarine and crumbs. Bake for 15 minutes longer. Yield: 12 servings.

Approx Per Serving: Cal 451; T Fat 30 g; 60% Calories from Fat;
  Prot 25 g; Carbo 20 g; Fiber 1 g; Chol 129 mg; Sod 892 mg.

Louise Petersen, Glendive, Montana

BOB'S AWARD-WINNING TURKEY MEAT LOAF

2½ pounds lean ground
  turkey
8 ounces lean ground beef
2 envelopes
  onion-mushroom soup mix
2 cups crushed herb-
  seasoned stuffing mix
2 eggs, beaten

1 cup water
¼ cup catsup
2 tablespoons steak sauce
2 tablespoons
  Worcestershire sauce
1 10-ounce can cream of
  mushroom soup

Combine ground turkey, ground beef, soup mix, stuffing mix, eggs, water, catsup, steak and Worcestershire sauces in large bowl; mix well. Pack into 3-quart casserole. Pour mushroom soup over top. Bake, covered, at 350 degrees for 1 hour. Bake, uncovered, for 30 minutes longer or until cooked through. Yield: 12 servings.

Approx Per Serving: Cal 304; T Fat 16 g; 47% Calories from Fat; Prot 25 g; Carbo 15 g; Fiber <1 g; Chol 108 mg; Sod 725 mg.

Bob Millons, Helena, Montana

TRIPLE BEAN CASSEROLE

This is delicious hot or cold.

1 16-ounce can lima beans,
  drained
1 31-ounce can pork and
  beans in sauce
1 15-ounce can red kidney
  beans, drained
1 large onion, chopped

1 7½-ounce can tomatoes,
  chopped
¼ cup packed brown sugar
1 tablespoon Worcestershire
  sauce
½ teaspoon dry mustard
½ cup bacon bits

Combine all ingredients in 2-quart casserole; mix well. Bake, covered, at 375 degrees for 40 minutes. Bake, uncovered, for 25 to 30 minutes longer or until of desired consistency. Yield: 20 servings.

Approx Per Serving: Cal 124; T Fat 2 g; 11% Calories from Fat; Prot 6 g; Carbo 23 g; Fiber 7 g; Chol 3 mg; Sod 294 mg.

Barbara Hamilton, Boise, Idaho

SOUR CREAM POTATO CASSEROLE

1 2-pound package frozen
   southern-style potatoes
1/2 cup melted butter
2 10-ounce cans cream of
   chicken soup
2 cups sour cream

1/2 teaspoon salt
1 onion, chopped
2 cups grated Cheddar cheese
2 cups crushed cornflakes
1/4 cup melted butter

Spread potatoes in 8x12-inch baking pan. Combine 1/2 cup melted butter, soup, sour cream, salt and onion in bowl; mix well. Pour over potatoes. Sprinkle with cheese. Top with mixture of cornflake crumbs and 1/4 cup melted butter. Bake at 350 degrees for 40 minutes. Yield: 12 servings.

Approx Per Serving: Cal 506; T Fat 39 g; 67% Calories from Fat;
    Prot 10 g; Carbo 33 g; Fiber 1 g; Chol 72 mg; Sod 867 mg.

Ione Raymond, Logan, Utah

TEXAS POTATOES

1 2-pound package frozen
   hashed brown potatoes
1 medium onion, chopped
1 cup shredded Cheddar
   cheese
1/2 cup butter

2 10-ounce cans cream of
   chicken soup
4 cups sour cream
3 cups cornflake crumbs
1/4 cup melted butter

Combine potatoes, onion and cheese in large bowl; mix well. Heat 1/2 cup butter and soup in saucepan until butter melts; remove from heat. Stir in sour cream. Pour over potato mixture; stir gently. Spoon into 9x13-inch baking dish. Top with mixture of cornflake crumbs and remaining 1/4 cup melted butter. Bake at 350 degrees for 45 minutes. Serve hot. Yield: 15 servings.

Approx Per Serving: Cal 466; T Fat 34 g; 64% Calories from Fat;
    Prot 8 g; Carbo 35 g; Fiber 2 g; Chol 63 mg; Sod 643 mg.

Betty Raye Partridge, West Jordan, Utah

VEGETABLE CASSEROLE

6 cups frozen or blanched
fresh mixed carrots,
broccoli and cauliflower
2 cups mushroom soup

1   16-ounce jar process
cheese spread
1   6-ounce can French-fried
onion rings

Layer vegetables in 9x13-inch baking pan. Heat soup and cheese spread in saucepan until cheese spread melts, stirring occasionally. Pour over vegetables. Bake at 370 degrees for 30 minutes. Sprinkle onion rings over top. Bake for 10 minutes longer. Yield: 12 servings.

Approx Per Serving: Cal 236; T Fat 15 g; 57% Calories from Fat;
Prot 11 g; Carbo 16 g; Fiber 3 g; Chol 30 mg; Sod 838 mg.

Arloa Weiss, Billings, Montana

PILAF

This is an excellent side dish with ham, turkey, chicken or beef.

1   8-ounce can mushroom
pieces
1 large onion, chopped
1 teaspoon oregano

1 cup margarine
2 cups uncooked brown rice
3   10-ounce cans consommé

Drain mushrooms, reserving liquid. Add enough water to reserved liquid to measure 2 cups. Sauté mushrooms and onion with oregano in margarine in 4-quart saucepan. Add rice, 2 cups liquid and consommé. Simmer for 20 minutes. Pour into large casserole. Bake, covered, at 350 degrees for 40 minutes or until rice is tender. Yield: 15 servings.

Approx Per Serving: Cal 214; T Fat 13 g; 54% Calories from Fat;
Prot 4 g; Carbo 21 g; Fiber 1 g; Chol <1 mg; Sod 390 mg.

Ellenor Berntson, Salt Lake City, Utah

Life is what happens when you're making other plans.

DILL PICKLES

7 quarts cucumbers
14 sprigs of dill
4 cloves of garlic
12 cups water

4½ cups vinegar
1 cup canning salt
½ teaspoon alum

Wash cucumbers; rub off spines. Place 1 sprig of dill and ¼ clove of garlic in 14 sterilized 1-pint jars. Pack cucumbers into jars. Combine water, vinegar, salt and alum in large saucepan. Bring to a boil. Cook for 5 minutes. Pour over cucumbers; seal with 2-piece lids. Process in hot water bath for 10 minutes. Yield: 140 servings.

Approx Per Serving: Cal 2; T Fat <1 g; 2% Calories from Fat; Prot <1 g; Carbo 1 g; Fiber <1 g; Chol 0 mg; Sod 731 mg.

Merla Jorgensen, Pocatello, Idaho

REFRIGERATOR PICKLES

1 gallon large cucumbers
3 large onions
4 cups sugar
4 cups vinegar

½ cup pickling salt
1⅓ teaspoons turmeric
1½ teaspoons celery seed
1½ teaspoons mustard seed

Slice cucumbers and onions. Pack into 8 sterilized 1-pint jars. Combine sugar, vinegar, salt, turmeric, celery seed and mustard seed in saucepan. Bring to a boil. Let stand until cool. Pour over cucumbers; seal. Let stand in refrigerator for 2 weeks. Store in refrigerator. Yield: 80 servings.

Approx Per Serving g: Cal 48; T Fat <1 g; 1% Calories from Fat; Prot <1 g; Carbo 12 g; Fiber 1 g; Chol 0 mg; Sod 641 mg.

Bernice Farner, Meridian, Idaho

*Many can rise to the occasion, but few
know when to sit down.*

SALSA

4 quarts tomatoes, peeled, chopped
1 cup chopped green bell pepper
2 cups chopped onions
5 jalapeño peppers, seeded, finely chopped

3/4 cup sugar
3 tablespoons salt
2 1/4 teaspoons paprika
2 tablespoons garlic powder
2 tablespoons seasoned salt
1/4 cup lemon juice

Combine vegetables, sugar, seasonings and lemon juice in large saucepan. Cook over low heat until thickened, stirring occasionally. Pour into 8 hot sterilized jars leaving 1/2-inch headspace; seal with 2-piece lids. Process in boiling water bath for 10 minutes. Yield: 64 servings.

Approx Per Serving: Cal 22; T Fat <1 g; 5% Calories from Fat; Prot 1 g; Carbo 5 g; Fiber 1 g; Chol 0 mg; Sod 504 mg.

Sarah H. Jensen, Richfield, Utah

ZUCCHINI MARMALADE

This tastes similar to orange marmalade.

5 pounds zucchini, peeled, seeded
2 whole oranges, seeded
1/2 cup maraschino cherries with juice

5 pounds sugar
1 20-ounce can juice-pack crushed pineapple
Juice of 2 lemons

Grind zucchini, whole oranges and cherries. Combine with sugar, pineapple and lemon juice in large heavy baking pan (such as Dutch oven); mix well. Bake at 350 degrees for 4 hours. Pour into 6 hot sterilized 1/2-pint jars; seal. May be cooked on top of the stove until thickened, stirring frequently. Yield: 200 servings.

Approx Per Serving: Cal 48; T Fat <1 g; 0% Calories from Fat; Prot <1 g; Carbo 12 g; Fiber <1 g; Chol 0 mg; Sod 1 mg.

Luella Merriman, Great Falls, Montana

BRAN MUFFINS

1 cup boiling water
1 cup bran flakes
2 cups All-Bran
1/2 cup shortening
1 cup packed brown sugar
1/2 cup sugar
2 eggs

2 cups buttermilk
2 1/2 cups flour
2 1/2 teaspoons baking soda
1 teaspoon baking powder
1/2 teaspoon salt
1 teaspoon vanilla extract

Pour boiling water over cereal in bowl. Let stand until softened. Cream shortening, brown sugar and sugar in mixer bowl for 2 minutes. Add eggs. Beat for 30 seconds. Add buttermilk. Stir for 1 minute. Sift flour, baking soda, baking powder and salt together. Add to creamed mixture gradually, mixing well after each addition. Stir for 1 minute. Add vanilla and cereal mixture; mix well. Store in tightly covered container in refrigerator for up to 6 weeks. Fill greased muffin cups 3/4 full. Bake at 400 degrees for 20 minutes. May add dates, raisins or nuts to batter if desired. Yield: 72 servings.

Approx Per Serving: Cal 58; T Fat 2 g; 25% Calories from Fat;
   Prot 1 g; Carbo 10 g; Fiber 1 g; Chol 6 mg; Sod 90 mg.

Selma Simper, Blackfoot, Idaho

WESTERN ZUCCHINI BREAD

3 eggs, beaten
1 cup oil
2 cups grated zucchini,
   drained
1 teaspoon vanilla extract
3 cups sugar
3 1/2 cups flour

1 teaspoon salt
1 teaspoon baking soda
1 teaspoon baking powder
1/2 cup chopped walnuts
2 teaspoons cinnamon
1 teaspoon nutmeg

Combine eggs, oil, zucchini and vanilla in bowl; mix well. Combine sugar, flour, salt, baking soda, baking powder, walnuts and spices in bowl. Add to zucchini mixture; mix well. Pour into 3 greased and floured 5x9-inch loaf pans. Bake at 350 degrees for 1 hour. May add chocolate chips to batter. Yield: 36 servings.

Approx Per Serving: Cal 181; T Fat 8 g; 38% Calories from Fat;
   Prot 2 g; Carbo 27 g; Fiber 1 g; Chol 18 mg; Sod 98 mg.

Marna C. Buffo, Provo, Utah

· · · · · · · · · · · · · · · · · · · ·

CARAMEL CORN

Do not eat more than 5 pounds at a time!

2¹/₂ cups packed brown sugar
1 cup light corn syrup
¹/₂ cup margarine

1   14-ounce can sweetened
    condensed milk
8 quarts popped popcorn

Combine brown sugar, corn syrup and margarine in large saucepan. Cook to 234 to 240 degrees on candy thermometer, soft-ball stage. Remove from heat; stir in condensed milk. Pour over popped popcorn; mix lightly until evenly coated. Spread on waxed paper-lined surface to cool. Break into pieces. Yield: 32 servings.

Approx Per Serving: Cal 188; T Fat 4 g; 20% Calories from Fat;
    Prot 2 g; Carbo 37 g; Fiber 1 g; Chol 4 mg; Sod 62 mg.

Gary L. Ferrin, Idaho Falls, Idaho

CARAMELS

1 cup packed brown sugar
¹/₂ cup butter
1   14-ounce can sweetened
    condensed milk

1 cup sugar
1 cup light corn syrup

Combine all ingredients in large saucepan. Cook over medium heat to 245 degrees on candy thermometer, hard-ball stage, stirring constantly. Pour into buttered 9x13-inch dish. Let stand until firm. Cut into squares. Wrap in waxed paper. Yield: 80 servings.

Approx Per Serving: Cal 57; T Fat 2 g; 24% Calories from Fat;
    Prot <1 g; Carbo 11 g; Fiber 0 g; Chol 5 mg; Sod 19 mg.

Nancy Snow, Ogden, Utah

*The world stands aside to let anyone pass who
knows where he's going.*

CEREAL TREAT

4 cups Cherrios
4 cups Kix
4 cups Special-K
4 cups Rice Chex
2 cups sugar

1 cup butter
3/4 cup light corn syrup
1/8 teaspoon salt
1 cup cream
1 teaspoon vanilla extract

Combine cereals in large container. Combine sugar, butter, corn syrup and salt in large saucepan. Bring to a boil. Cook, covered, for 1 minute to dissolve sugar. Add cream. Cook to 234 to 240 degrees on candy thermometer, soft-ball stage. Add vanilla. Pour over cereal; mix until cereal is coated. Spread on waxed paper-lined surface to cool. Break into pieces. Yield: 32 servings.

Approx Per Serving: Cal 189; T Fat 9 g; 41% Calories from Fat;
Prot 2 g; Carbo 27 g; Fiber 1 g; Chol 26 mg; Sod 173 mg.

Wyn K. Doney, Preston, Idaho

BEST BROWNIES

2 cups sugar
2 cups flour
5 tablespoons baking cocoa
1/2 teaspoon salt
1 cup shortening
4 eggs, beaten
1/2 cup milk

1 cup chopped pecans
1 cup sugar
1/2 cup cream
1 cup chocolate chips
1 cup miniature
   marshmallows

Combine 2 cups sugar, flour, cocoa and salt in bowl. Cream shortening, eggs and milk in bowl until blended. Add sugar mixture; mix just until blended. Stir in pecans. Spread in 12x15-inch baking pan. Bake at 350 degrees for 30 minutes or until brownies test done. Bring 1 cup sugar and cream to a boil in saucepan. Cook for 1 minute. Add chocolate chips and marshmallows. Stir until smooth. Spread frosting immediately over warm brownies. Cut into squares. Yield: 180 servings.

Approx Per Serving: Cal 43; T Fat 2 g; 48% Calories from Fat;
Prot <1 g; Carbo 5 g; Fiber <1 g; Chol 6 mg; Sod 9 mg.

Evelyn R. Damschen, Anaconda, Montana

CHOCOLATE CHIP COOKIES

2 cups butter, softened
2 cups sugar
2 cups packed brown sugar
2 teaspoons vanilla extract
7 cups flour
1 teaspoon salt
2 teaspoons baking powder
2 teaspoons baking soda
4 cups chocolate chips
1   8-ounce chocolate bar, grated
2 cups chopped pecans

Cream butter, sugars and vanilla in mixer bowl until light and fluffy. Combine flour, salt, baking powder and baking soda. Add to creamed mixture; mix well. Add chocolate chips, grated chocolate and pecans; mix well. Shape into golf ball-sized balls. Place on greased cookie sheet. Bake at 375 degrees for 10 to 12 minutes or until brown. Yield: 112 servings.

Approx Per Serving: Cal 145; T Fat 8 g; 45% Calories from Fat;
    Prot 1 g; Carbo 19 g; Fiber 1 g; Chol 9 mg; Sod 72 mg.

Nancy Nielsen, Hyrum, Utah

MONSTER COOKIES

12 eggs, beaten
4 cups sugar
2   1-pound packages brown sugar
1 tablespoon vanilla extract
1 tablespoon light corn syrup
2 cups margarine, softened
3 pounds peanut butter
8 teaspoons baking soda
18 cups quick-cooking oats
1 pound chocolate chips
1 pound "M & M's" Chocolate Candies

Combine eggs, sugars, vanilla and corn syrup in large bowl; mix well. Add margarine and peanut butter; mix well. Stir in mixture of baking soda and oats. Add chocolate chips and candies. Drop by spoonfuls onto greased cookie sheets; flatten. Bake at 350 degrees for 15 minutes. Let stand on cookie sheet for several minutes. Remove to wire rack to cool. Yield: 80 servings.

Approx Per Serving: Cal 362; T Fat 19 g; 46% Calories from Fat;
    Prot 9 g; Carbo 43 g; Fiber 3 g; Chol 32 mg; Sod 222 mg.

Arloa Weiss, Billings, Montana

NUTMEG COOKIES

2/3 cup butter, softened
2 cups sugar
1 egg
1 cup sour cream
1 teaspoon baking soda
1 teaspoon salt

1 1/2 teaspoons nutmeg
5 1/2 cups flour
1 cup sugar
2 tablespoons flour
1 cup water
2 cups chopped raisins

Cream butter and sugar in mixer bowl until light and fluffy. Add egg. Beat until smooth. Add sour cream; mix well. Add mixture of baking soda, salt, nutmeg and flour; mix well. Roll on floured surface. Cut half the cookies with doughnut cutter. Remove center of cutter. Cut remaining cookies. Place solid cookies on greased baking sheet. Combine 1 cup sugar, 2 tablespoons flour, water and raisins in saucepan. Cook until thickened and moisture evaporates. Let stand until cool. Place 1 teaspoon filling on each cookie. Top with remaining cookies; seal edges with fork. Bake at 350 degrees for 15 minutes. Remove to wire rack to cool. Yield: 75 servings.

Approx Per Serving: Cal 100; T Fat 2 g; 22% Calories from Fat;
Prot 1 g; Carbo 19 g; Fiber 1 g; Chol 9 mg; Sod 56 mg.

Hazel M. Johnson, Murray, Utah

SPRITZ COOKIES

2 cups butter, softened
1 1/2 cups sugar
4 egg yolks

1/2 teaspoon almond extract
5 cups flour

Cream butter until light. Add sugar gradually, beating until fluffy. Add egg yolks; mix well. Stir in flavoring. Add flour gradually, mixing well after each addition. Chill for 20 to 30 minutes if dough is sticky. Press through cookie press 1 inch apart on cold ungreased cookie sheets. Bake at 425 degrees for 8 minutes or until light brown. Remove to wire rack to cool. Store in airtight container. May decorate with sugar sprinkles before baking. Yield: 96 servings.

Approx Per Serving: Cal 72; T Fat 4 g; 51% Calories from Fat;
Prot 1 g; Carbo 8 g; Fiber <1 g; Chol 19 mg; Sod 33 mg.

Gina Stinchfield, Helena, Montana

SOUR CREAM COOKIES

1 1-pound package light
  brown sugar
1¹/2 cups margarine
4 eggs
2 cups sour cream
6 cups flour
1 teaspoon salt
1 teaspoon (heaping) baking
  soda
1 teaspoon (heaping) baking
  powder
2 teaspoons vanilla extract
2 cups chocolate chips
1 8-ounce package
  shredded coconut
1 cup chopped pecans
1 cup sugar
1 teaspoon cinnamon

Cream brown sugar and margarine in mixer bowl until light
and fluffy. Add eggs; mix well. Add sour cream; mix well. Add
mixture of flour, salt, baking soda and baking powder gradually,
mixing well after each addition. Blend in vanilla. Fold in chocolate
chips, coconut and pecans. Shape by teaspoonfuls into balls. Coat
with mixture of 1 cup sugar and cinnamon. Place on greased
cookie sheet. Bake at 375 degrees for 10 to 12 minutes.
Yield: 120 servings.

Approx Per Serving: Cal 105; T Fat 6 g; 47% Calories from Fat;
  Prot 1 g; Carbo 13 g; Fiber 1 g; Chol 9 mg; Sod 66 mg.

Shirley Allen, Boise, Idaho

SUGAR COOKIES

2²/3 cups shortening
3 cups sugar
1 tablespoon plus 1 teaspoon
  vanilla extract
4 eggs
¹/4 cup milk
8 cups flour
2 tablespoons baking powder
1 teaspoon salt

Cream shortening and sugar in mixer bowl until light and
fluffy. Add vanilla; mix well. Beat in eggs 1 at a time. Add
milk; mix until blended. Add mixture of flour, baking powder
and salt gradually, beating well after each addition. Shape into
balls. Place on greased cookie sheet. Flatten slightly with bottom
of glass coated with sugar. Bake at 375 degrees for 8 to 12 minutes
or until light brown. Do not overbake. These cookies should
be thick and soft. Yield: 96 servings.

Approx Per Serving: Cal 117; T Fat 6 g; 46% Calories from Fat;
  Prot 1 g; Carbo 14 g; Fiber <1 g; Chol 9 mg; Sod 46 mg.

Karren Fairbanks, Salt Lake City, Utah

APRICOT SYRUP

4 cups apricot purée	3 tablespoons lemon juice
1 cup water	4 cups sugar

Combine apricot purée, water and lemon juice in large saucepan. Stir until sugar dissolves. Bring to a boil over medium-high heat. Cook for 5 minutes; remove from heat. Skim foam. Pour into 4 hot sterilized 1-pint jars, leaving 1/2-inch headspace; seal with 2-piece lids. Serve on waffles, pancakes or ice cream. Yield: 64 servings.

Approx Per Serving: Cal 56; T Fat <1 g; 0% Calories from Fat; Prot <1 g; Carbo 14 g; Fiber <1 g; Chol 0 mg; Sod 1 mg.

Marna C. Buffo, Provo, Utah

HOME-CANNED PIE FILLING PIES

4 cups sugar	3 quarts sliced peeled apples
1 cup cornstarch	2 quarts apricots, pitted
1 tablespoon cinnamon	18 tablespoons lemon gelatin
1 teaspoon nutmeg	9 unbaked pie shells
1 teaspoon salt	4 1/2 cups sugar
10 cups water	4 1/2 cups flour
3 tablespoons lemon juice	2 1/4 cups butter
2 quarts fresh cherries, pitted	4 1/2 teaspoons cinnamon
2 quarts sliced peeled peaches	2 1/4 teaspoons ginger

Combine 4 cups sugar, cornstarch, 1 tablespoon cinnamon, nutmeg, salt and water in saucepan. Cook until thickened and clear, stirring constantly. Stir in lemon juice. Fill 9 hot sterilized 1-quart jars 1/3 full with sauce. Place cherries in 2 jars, peaches in 2 jars, apples in 3 jars and apricots in 2 jars; push fruit down with wooden spoon until jar is full to neck. Seal with 2-piece lids. Process in boiling water bath for 20 minutes. Sprinkle 2 tablespoons dry gelatin in each pie shell. Add 1 quart pie filling to each prepared pie shell. Top each with mixture of 1/2 cup sugar, 1/2 cup flour, 1/4 cup butter, 1/2 teaspoon cinnamon and 1/4 teaspoon ginger. Cover edges with foil. Bake at 375 degrees for 30 minutes; remove foil. Bake for 30 minutes longer. Filling also makes good 2-crust pies or cobblers. Yield: 54 servings.

Approx Per Serving: Cal 444; T Fat 18 g; 36% Calories from Fat; Prot 4 g; Carbo 69 g; Fiber 2 g; Chol 21 mg; Sod 304 mg.

Karren Fairbanks, Salt Lake City, Utah

. . . .

The Last Chance

Desserts

'89 H. Creekmore

WASATCH COUNCIL

Ogden, Utah

Every year at Easter, the Future and Regular Pioneers have an Easter Egg Hunt at the Utah School for the Blind in Ogden with "beeper eggs." The children trade the eggs for a small basket with candy and other goodies.

At Halloween and Christmas, Council volunteers give parties for the children at the Canyon View School for the Handicapped. For the Halloween party, they go in costume and pass out bags of treats. At Christmas, Santa Claus takes small gifts and candy.

ALOTOBOUREKO

3 cups sugar
3 cups water
Juice of 1/4 lemon
3/4 cup dry Cream of Wheat
  cereal
2 tablespoons flour

Salt to taste
2 cups sugar
4 cups milk
5 eggs, well beaten
3/4 cup butter, melted
1 pound phyllo dough

Combine 3 cups sugar, water and lemon juice in saucepan. Bring to a boil, stirring until sugar dissolves. Boil for 12 to 15 minutes. Let stand until completely cooled. Mix cereal and flour in saucepan. Add salt and sugar to taste. Stir in milk. Cook cereal using package directions. Stir a small amount of hot cereal into eggs; stir eggs into hot cereal. Butter bottom of 9x13-inch baking pan. Layer 6 sheets of phyllo in pan, brushing each sheet with butter. Add cereal mixture. Add 8 sheets of phyllo, brushing each sheet with butter. Pour remaining butter over top. Bake at 325 degrees for 1 hour. Drizzle sugar syrup over hot dessert, starting at corners and allowing syrup to be absorbed. Do not use all the syrup if dessert does not absorb it. Yield: 24 servings.

Approx Per Serving: Cal 315; T Fat 8 g; 23% Calories from Fat;
  Prot 5 g; Carbo 54 g; Fiber 1 g; Chol 65 mg; Sod 148 mg.

Georgia Beam, Billings, Montana

APPLE CRUMBLE

3 or 4 apples, peeled, sliced
1/2 cup packed brown sugar

6 tablespoons butter
1/3 cup cracker crumbs

Place apples in buttered baking dish. Combine brown sugar, butter and crumbs in small bowl; mix until crumbly. Sprinkle over apples. Bake at 400 degrees for 20 to 30 minutes or until apples are tender and top is golden brown. Serve with ice cream or whipped cream. Yield: 6 servings.

Approx Per Serving: Cal 237; T Fat 12 g; 45% Calories from Fat;
  Prot <1 g; Carbo 34 g; Fiber 2 g; Chol 33 mg; Sod 165 mg.

Phyllis Lee, Great Falls, Montana

APPLE SQUARES

3 eggs
1³/₄ cups sugar
2 cups sifted flour
1 teaspoon cinnamon
1 teaspoon baking powder
¹/₂ teaspoon salt
1 cup oil
1 teaspoon vanilla extract

2 cups thinly sliced apples
³/₄ cup chopped walnuts
2¹/₂ cups confectioners' sugar
¹/₃ cup sour cream
¹/₄ cup butter, softened
³/₄ teaspoon vanilla extract
¹/₈ teaspoon salt

Beat eggs with sugar in mixer bowl until fluffy. Sift in flour, cinnamon, baking powder and ¹/₂ teaspoon salt; mix well. Add oil and 1 teaspoon vanilla. Fold in apples and walnuts. Pour into greased and floured 9x13-inch baking pan. Bake at 350 degrees for 45 to 50 minutes or until golden brown. Let stand until cool. Combine confectioners' sugar, sour cream, butter, ³/₄ teaspoon vanilla and ¹/₈ teaspoon salt in mixer bowl; beat until smooth and creamy. Spread over top. Cut into squares. Yield: 18 servings.

Approx Per Serving: Cal 378; T Fat 20 g; 46% Calories from Fat;
    Prot 3 g; Carbo 49 g; Fiber 1 g; Chol 44 mg; Sod 129 mg.

Karren Fairbanks, Salt Lake City, Utah

BOB'S AWARD-WINNING CHEESECAKE

1³/₄ cups graham cracker
    crumbs
¹/₄ cup chopped walnuts
¹/₂ teaspoon cinnamon
¹/₂ cup melted butter
3 eggs
1 cup sugar

16 ounces cream cheese,
    softened
¹/₄ teaspoon salt
2 teaspoons vanilla extract
¹/₄ teaspoon almond extract
1¹/₂ cups sour cream

Combine crumbs, walnuts, cinnamon and butter in bowl; mix well. Press over bottom of 10-inch springform pan. Beat eggs in mixer bowl. Add sugar, cream cheese, salt and flavorings; beat until smooth. Blend in sour cream. Pour into prepared pan. Bake at 375 degrees for 35 minutes. Cool. Chill in pan. Place on serving plate; remove side of pan. Add favorite topping such as strawberries or blueberries. Yield: 16 servings.

Approx Per Serving: Cal 329; T Fat 24 g; 64% Calories from Fat;
    Prot 5 g; Carbo 25 g; Fiber <1 g; Chol 96 mg; Sod 271 mg.

Bob Millons, Helena, Montana

LEMONY CHEESECAKE

1½ cups graham cracker crumbs
½ teaspoon cinnamon
3 tablespoons sugar
¼ cup unsalted butter
24 ounces cream cheese
1¼ cups sugar

6 egg yolks
2 cups sour cream
⅓ cup flour
2 teaspoons vanilla extract
Grated rind of 1 lemon
Juice of ½ lemon
6 egg whites, stiffly beaten

Press 12-inch square foil around side of 9-inch springform pan. Combine crumbs, cinnamon, 3 tablespoons sugar and melted butter in bowl; mix well. Press ¾ cup mixture over bottom and side of pan. Chill in refrigerator. Beat softened cream cheese in mixer bowl at low speed. Add 1¼ cups sugar gradually, beating until light and fluffy. Beat in egg yolks 1 at a time. Add next 5 ingredients; beat until smooth. Fold in egg whites gently. Pour into prepared pan. Bake at 350 degrees for 1¼ hours or until golden. Turn off oven. Let stand in oven for 1 hour. Cool on wire rack. Sprinkle remaining crumb mixture over top. Chill overnight. Place on serving plate; remove side of pan. Garnish with sprinkle of confectioners' sugar. Yield: 12 servings.

Approx Per Serving: Cal 525; T Fat 36 g; 61% Calories from Fat; Prot 10 g; Carbo 42 g; Fiber <1 g; Chol 196 mg; Sod 311 mg.

Bobbi Rintala, Salem, Oregon

PINEAPPLE CHEESECAKE

1½ tablespoons unflavored gelatin
1 cup diet lemon-lime soda
4 slices juice-pack pineapple
¼ cup pineapple juice

1 teaspoon vanilla extract
1 teaspoon lemon juice
Artificial sweetener to equal ⅓ cup sugar
1⅓ cups ricotta cheese

Soften gelatin in ¼ cup cold soda in blender container. Heat remaining soda in saucepan; pour into blender. Process until gelatin dissolves. Add remaining ingredients; process until smooth and creamy. Pour into pie plate. Chill until firm. May substitute cream soda for lemon-lime soda and add ½ teaspoon coconut extract. Yield: 8 servings.

Approx Per Serving: Cal 109; T Fat 5 g; 46% Calories from Fat; Prot 7 g; Carbo 7 g; Fiber 1 g; Chol 21 mg; Sod 40 mg.

Patty E. Henderson, Boise, Idaho

CHOCOLATE-CHERRY ICE CREAM

1 cup slivered almonds
2 cups sugar
1 cup baking cocoa
6 egg yolks, beaten
6 cups cream

1 teaspoon almond extract
1/2 teaspoon vanilla extract
1 cup drained chopped
  maraschino cherries

Spread almonds in shallow baking pan. Toast at 350 degrees for 8 to 10 minutes or until golden brown, stirring occasionally. Let stand until cool. Chop coarsely and set aside. Mix sugar and cocoa in large saucepan. Add egg yolks and 2 cups cream; mix well. Cook over medium heat until very hot, stirring constantly; do not boil. Cool to room temperature. Stir in remaining 4 cups cream and flavorings. Chill for 6 hours or longer. Pour into 5-quart ice cream freezer. Freeze using manufacturer's instructions. Fold in cherries and almonds. Repack freezer cylinder in ice and salt. Let stand for several hours. Yield: 15 servings.

Approx Per Serving: Cal 542; T Fat 43 g; 69% Calories from Fat;
    Prot 6 g; Carbo 38 g; Fiber 3 g; Chol 216 mg; Sod 42 mg.

Nancy Nielsen, Hyrum, Utah

CHOCOLATE ICEBOX DESSERT

1 cup flour
1/4 cup packed brown sugar
1/2 cup melted butter
1/2 cup finely chopped pecans
8 ounces cream cheese,
  softened
1 cup confectioners' sugar

8 ounces whipped topping
2 4-ounce packages
  chocolate instant pudding
  mix
4 cups milk
8 ounces whipped topping
1/2 cup chopped pecans

Combine flour, brown sugar, butter and 1/2 cup pecans in bowl; mix well. Pat over bottom of 9x13-inch baking dish. Bake at 350 degrees for 15 minutes or until light brown. Let stand until cool. Combine cream cheese, confectioners' sugar and 8 ounces whipped topping in mixer bowl; beat until fluffy. Spread over cooled baked layer. Chill in refrigerator. Prepare pudding mix with milk using package directions. Spoon over cream cheese layer. Chill until set. Spread remaining whipped topping over top. Sprinkle with 1/2 cup pecans. Yield: 15 servings.

Approx Per Serving: Cal 427; T Fat 27 g; 55% Calories from Fat;
    Prot 5 g; Carbo 44 g; Fiber 1 g; Chol 42 mg; Sod 234 mg.

Mehl Ree Strate, Orem, Utah

RICH PUDDING DESSERT

1 cup flour
1/2 cup chopped pecans
1/2 cup butter, softened
8 ounces cream cheese,
  softened
1 cup confectioners' sugar
1 6-ounce package vanilla
  instant pudding mix

1 6-ounce package
  chocolate instant pudding
  mix
4 cups milk
3 cups whipped cream
1 4-ounce milk chocolate
  candy bar, grated

Combine flour, pecans and butter in bowl; mix well. Press over bottom of 9x13-inch baking dish. Bake at 350 degrees for 15 minutes. Let stand until cool. Beat cream cheese and confectioners' sugar in mixer bowl until smooth. Spread over cooled crust. Combine pudding mixes and milk in bowl; prepare using package directions. Fold in 1½ cups whipped cream. Pour over cream cheese layer. Top with remaining 1½ cups whipped cream; sprinkle candy over top. Chill until serving time. Yield: 15 servings.

Approx Per Serving: Cal 439; T Fat 28 g; 55% Calories from Fat;
  Prot 6 g; Carbo 45 g; Fiber 1 g; Chol 76 mg; Sod 291 mg.

LuDean Pehrson, Logan, Utah

HOT FUDGE SAUCE

1/4 cup baking cocoa
1/4 cup flour
2 cups sugar
1 12-ounce can evaporated
  milk

2 tablespoons butter
1 teaspoon vanilla extract

Combine cocoa, flour and sugar in saucepan. Stir in evaporated milk. Add butter. Bring to a boil, stirring constantly. Cook over low heat for 3 to 5 minutes; remove from heat. Stir in vanilla. Yield: 30 servings.

Approx Per Serving: Cal 80; T Fat 2 g; 20% Calories from Fat;
  Prot 1 g; Carbo 16 g; Fiber <1 g; Chol 5 mg; Sod 19 mg.

Darla Wheeler, Brigham City, Utah

CHOCOLATE TEMPTATION

1 cup flour
1/2 cup butter, softened
1/2 cup packed brown sugar
1 cup chopped pecans
8 ounces cream cheese, softened
1 cup confectioners' sugar
12 ounces whipped topping

1   4-ounce package butter brickle instant pudding mix
1   4-ounce package chocolate instant pudding mix
2 cups milk
1   1½-ounce toffee candy bar, crushed

Combine flour, butter, brown sugar and pecans in bowl; mix well. Press over bottom of 9x13-inch baking dish. Bake at 350 degrees for 20 minutes. Let stand until cool. Beat cream cheese with confectioners' sugar in mixer bowl until smooth. Blend in 1 cup whipped topping. Spread over cooled crust. Combine pudding mixes and milk in bowl; prepare using package directions. Spread over cream cheese layer. Top with remaining whipped topping. Sprinkle with candy. Chill until serving time. Yield: 12 servings.

Approx Per Serving: Cal 520; T Fat 32 g; 54% Calories from Fat;
   Prot 5 g; Carbo 56 g; Fiber 1 g; Chol 47 mg; Sod 285 mg.

Ethel R. Grigg, Kuna, Idaho

MINIATURE CREAM PUFFS

1 cup water
1/2 cup butter

1 cup flour
4 eggs

Bring water and butter to a full rolling boil in saucepan. Add flour. Cook over low heat for 1 minute, stirring vigorously until mixture forms ball; remove from heat. Add eggs. Beat until smooth and glossy. Drop by slightly rounded teaspoonfuls onto ungreased baking sheet. Bake at 400 degrees for 25 minutes or until puffed, golden brown and dry. Remove to wire rack. Let stand away from drafts until cooled. Cut tops from puffs; scoop out soft dough. Fill with favorite fillings. Yield: 24 servings.

Approx Per Serving: Cal 66; T Fat 5 g; 66% Calories from Fat;
   Prot 2 g; Carbo 4 g; Fiber <1 g; Chol 46 mg; Sod 44 mg.

Arloa Weiss, Billings, Montana

SHERBET ICE CREAM

1 cup chopped maraschino
  cherries
Juice of 3 lemons
1 8-ounce can crushed
  pineapple

1 12-ounce can evaporated
  milk
1 1/2 cups sugar
6 cups milk

Combine cherries, lemon juice, pineapple, evaporated milk and sugar in large bowl; mix well. Stir in milk. Pour into ice cream freezer container. Freeze using manufacturer's instructions. Tastes best when freshly made. Yield: 15 servings.

Approx Per Serving: Cal 199; T Fat 5 g; 22% Calories from Fat;
  Prot 5 g; Carbo 35 g; Fiber <1 g; Chol 20 mg; Sod 66 mg.

Nancy Snow, Ogden, Utah

PINK LEMONADE DESSERT

55 Ritz crackers, crushed
1/2 cup confectioners' sugar
1/2 cup melted butter
2 cups whipping cream,
  whipped
1 14-ounce can sweetened
  condensed milk

1 6-ounce can frozen pink
  lemonade concentrate,
  thawed
1/2 cup crushed pecans

Combine cracker crumbs, confectioners' sugar and butter in bowl; mix well. Press 3/4 of the mixture over bottom of 9x13-inch baking dish. Blend whipped cream, condensed milk and lemonade concentrate in bowl. Pour over crumb layer. Sprinkle remaining crumb mixture and pecans over top. Chill for 6 hours before serving. Yield: 20 servings.

Approx Per Serving: Cal 275; T Fat 20 g; 62% Calories from Fat;
  Prot 3 g; Carbo 25 g; Fiber <1 g; Chol 52 mg; Sod 156 mg.

Sarah H. Jensen, Richfield, Utah

*There is no machine that can take the place
of a good neighbor.*

MANDARIN ORANGE GELATIN DESSERT

2 3-ounce packages orange
   gelatin
2 cups boiling water
1 12-ounce can frozen
   orange juice concentrate
1 8-ounce can crushed
   pineapple, drained
1 6-ounce can mandarin
   oranges, drained

1 4-ounce package lemon
   instant pudding mix
2 cups milk
1 cup whipping cream,
   whipped
1/2 cup shredded Cheddar
   cheese

Dissolve gelatin in boiling water in bowl. Add orange juice concentrate; stir until melted. Add drained fruit. Pour into 9x13-inch dish. Chill until set. Prepare pudding mix with milk using package directions. Fold in whipped cream. Spread over congealed gelatin layer. Top with cheese. Chill for several hours to overnight. Yield: 20 servings.

Approx Per Serving: Cal 158; T Fat 6 g; 34% Calories from Fat;
   Prot 3 g; Carbo 24 g; Fiber <1 g; Chol 23 mg; Sod 98 mg.

Ruth Davis, Filer, Idaho

PUMPKIN DESSERT

6 eggs
1 28-ounce can pumpkin
1 1/2 cups sugar
1/2 cup packed brown sugar
1 teaspoon salt
1 teaspoon ginger

1/2 teaspoon cloves
2 cups evaporated milk
1 2-layer package yellow
   cake mix
1/2 cup margarine, softened

Beat eggs in large bowl. Add pumpkin, sugar, brown sugar, salt, ginger, cloves and evaporated milk; mix well. Pour into 9x13-inch baking dish. Combine cake mix and margarine in bowl; mix until crumbly. Sprinkle over pumpkin mixture. Bake at 350 degrees for 45 minutes. Yield: 20 servings.

Approx Per Serving: Cal 300; T Fat 10 g; 31% Calories from Fat;
   Prot 5 g; Carbo 48 g; Fiber 1 g; Chol 71 mg; Sod 369 mg.

Terri Rogers, Great Falls, Montana

SOPAPILLAS

2 cups flour
1 cup baking mix
1 teaspoon salt

1 teaspoon baking powder
1 cup (about) warm water
Oil for deep frying

Combine flour, baking mix, salt and baking powder in bowl; mix well. Add enough warm water to make medium dough, kneading by hand in bowl. Divide into meatball-sized portions. Roll each into medium thick 4- to 5-inch diameter circle. Deep-fry in hot oil until puffed and golden brown; drain on paper towels. Serve with butter and honey, jelly or confectioners' sugar. Yield: 15 servings.

Approx Per Serving: Cal 97; T Fat 1 g; 13% Calories from Fat;
    Prot 2 g; Carbo 18 g; Fiber <1 g; Chol 0 mg; Sod 270 mg.
    Nutritional information does not include oil for deep frying.

Georgia Beam, Billings, Montana

SUMMER FROZEN DELIGHT

1 16-ounce can sliced
    peaches
1 15-ounce can apricots
1 10-ounce package frozen
    strawberries, thawed

2 medium bananas, sliced
1 cup pineapple juice
1 6-ounce can frozen orange
    juice concentrate, thawed
1/4 cup lemon juice

Combine undrained peaches, apricots and strawberries in large bowl. Add bananas, pineapple juice, orange juice concentrate and lemon juice; mix well. Ladle into 5 1/2-ounce paper cups; cover tightly with foil and place on tray. Freeze until firm. Peel paper cup from frozen treat as you eat. Home canned peaches and apricots are best. Yield: 12 servings.

Approx Per Serving: Cal 119; T Fat <1 g; 2% Calories from Fat;
    Prot 1 g; Carbo 31 g; Fiber 2 g; Chol 0 mg; Sod 5 mg.

Bertha Bateman, Logan, Utah

*How silent the woods would be if only
the best birds sang.*

ENGLISH TRIFFLES

1 6-ounce package
   strawberry-banana gelatin
1 6-ounce package lemon-
   lime gelatin

4 bananas, sliced
12 (about) Twinkies, sliced
   lengthwise

Prepare gelatins individually using package directions. Chill until partially set. Pour lemon-lime gelatin into 4-quart parfait bowl. Layer bananas, Twinkies and strawberry-banana gelatin on top. Chill for 3 to 4 hours or until set. Garnish each serving with whipped topping and fresh fruit in season. Yield: 12 servings.

Approx Per Serving: Cal 283; T Fat 4 g; 13% Calories from Fat;
   Prot 4 g; Carbo 59 g; Fiber 1 g; Chol 0 mg; Sod 279 mg.

Shirley Winn, Richmond, Utah

COCONUT IMPOSSIBLE PIE

4 eggs
1 cup sugar
1/2 cup flour
2 cups milk

2 teaspoons vanilla extract
2 teaspoons butter
1 cup coconut

Combine all ingredients in blender container. Process until well mixed. Pour into buttered 9-inch pie plate. Bake at 400 degrees for 30 minutes or until set. Yield: 6 servings.

Approx Per Serving: Cal 363; T Fat 13 g; 33% Calories from Fat;
   Prot 8 g; Carbo 53 g; Fiber 2 g; Chol 156 mg; Sod 132 mg.

Sherry Mosher, Ogden, Utah

HOT FUDGE PIE

2 eggs
4 teaspoons baking cocoa
1 cup sugar
1/2 cup melted margarine

1 teaspoon vanilla extract
1/2 cup flour
1/4 cup boiling water

Beat eggs in bowl. Add remaining ingredients; mix well. Pour into buttered 9-inch round baking pan. Bake at 325 degrees for 30 minutes. Serve with ice cream or whipped cream. Yield: 6 servings.

Approx Per Serving: Cal 334; T Fat 17 g; 46% Calories from Fat;
   Prot 3 g; Carbo 42 g; Fiber 1 g; Chol 71 mg; Sod 203 mg.

Linda P. Olsen, Logan, Utah

. . . .

ANGEL PIE

4 egg whites
1/4 teaspoon cream of tartar
1 cup sugar
4 egg yolks

1/2 cup sugar
1 tablespoon lemon juice
Grated rind of 1 lemon
1 cup whipping cream

Beat egg whites in mixer bowl until glossy. Add cream of tartar and 1 cup sugar gradually, beating until stiff peaks form. Spread over bottom and side of buttered pie plate. Bake at 300 degrees for 1 1/2 hours. Let stand until completely cooled. Beat egg yolks in double boiler. Add 1/2 cup sugar, lemon juice and rind; mix well. Cook until thickened, stirring constantly. Cool completely. Whip whipping cream in bowl. Fold in cooked mixture. Spoon into meringue crust. Chill for 24 hours or longer. Yield: 8 servings.

Approx Per Serving: Cal 287; T Fat 14 g; 42% Calories from Fat; Prot 4 g; Carbo 39 g; Fiber <1 g; Chol 147 mg; Sod 41 mg.

Vi Thomson, Missoula, Montana

APPLE PIE

4 1/2 cups sliced peeled tart
  apples
1/4 cup (or more) water
3/4 cup sugar
1 1/2 tablespoons flour

1 teaspoon cinnamon
1 recipe 2-crust pie pastry
2 tablespoons butter
Several drops of lemon juice
1 tablespoon milk

Simmer apples in water in saucepan until apples wilt. Mix sugar, flour and cinnamon in small bowl. Sprinkle half the mixture over pastry-lined pie plate. Lift apple slices from cooking liquid with slotted spoon; place in pie plate. Add 1/4 cup cooking liquid. Sprinkle with remaining sugar mixture. Dot with butter; sprinkle with lemon juice. Top with remaining pastry, sealing edge and cutting vents. Brush with milk and sprinkle with additional sugar. Bake at 425 degrees for 30 to 40 minutes or until golden brown. Yield: 6 servings.

Approx Per Serving: Cal 520; T Fat 22 g; 38% Calories from Fat; Prot 4 g; Carbo 62 g; Fiber 3 g; Chol 10 mg; Sod 401 mg.

Nancy Nielsen, Hyrum, Utah

SOUR CREAM LEMON PIE

1 4-ounce package lemon
   pudding and pie filling mix
3/4 cup sugar
3 cups water
3 egg yolks, beaten

8 ounces cream cheese
1 cup sour cream
1 baked 9-inch deep-dish pie
   shell
8 ounces whipped topping

Combine pie filling, sugar, water and egg yolks in double boiler. Cook until thickened, stirring constantly; turn off heat. Add cream cheese; beat until smooth. Stir in sour cream. Pour into pie shell. Let stand until cool. Spread whipped topping over top. Chill for 2 hours or longer. Yield: 6 servings.

Approx Per Serving: Cal 690; T Fat 44 g; 56% Calories from Fat;
   Prot 8 g; Carbo 69 g; Fiber 1 g; Chol 165 mg; Sod 472 mg.

Eleanor Helderman, Boise, Idaho

MACADAMIA NUT CREAM PIE

1/2 cup sugar
1/4 cup cornstarch
1/8 teaspoon salt
2 cups milk
3 egg yolks
1 tablespoon butter
1/2 cup whipping cream
2 tablespoons coffee liqueur

1/2 cup coarsely chopped
   macadamia nuts
1 baked 9-inch pie shell
1/2 cup whipping cream
1 tablespoon superfine sugar
1 tablespoon coffee liqueur
1/4 cup macadamia nuts

Combine 1/2 cup sugar, cornstarch and salt in 2-quart saucepan; mix well. Stir in milk gradually. Add egg yolks; mix well. Cook over medium-low heat for 10 minutes or until thickened to consistency of mayonnaise, stirring constantly; remove from heat. Stir in butter until melted. Pour into bowl. Cover surface with plastic wrap. Chill in refrigerator. Whip 1/2 cup whipping cream and 2 tablespoons liqueur in mixer bowl until soft peaks form. Fold into cooked mixture. Fold in chopped macadamia nuts. Pour into pie shell. Chill in refrigerator. Whip 1/2 cup whipping cream, superfine sugar and 1 tablespoon coffee liqueur in mixer bowl until soft peaks form. Spread over pie. Garnish with thinly sliced macadamia nuts in center and whole macadamia nuts around edge. Chill until set. Yield: 8 servings.

Approx Per Serving: Cal 467; T Fat 33 g; 64% Calories from Fat;
   Prot 6 g; Carbo 36 g; Fiber 1 g; Chol 133 mg; Sod 224 mg.

Shirley Allen, Boise, Idaho

MARGARITA PIE

1¼ cups finely crushed
  pretzels
1 tablespoon sugar
½ cup melted butter
6 cups vanilla ice cream,
  softened

6 tablespoons frozen limeade
  concentrate, thawed
3 tablespoons Tequila
1 tablespoon Triple Sec
1½ teaspoons grated lime
  rind

Combine pretzels, sugar and butter in bowl; mix well. Press over bottom and side of 9-inch pie plate. Freeze for 1 hour. Combine ice cream, limeade concentrate, Tequila, Triple Sec and lime rind in bowl; blend well. Spoon into frozen shell. Freeze for several hours to overnight. Let stand at room temperature for 15 to 20 minutes. Cut into wedges. Garnish with twisted lime slices. Yield: 6 servings.

Approx Per Serving: Cal 475; T Fat 30 g; 56% Calories from Fat; Prot 5 g; Carbo 47 g; Fiber <1 g; Chol 100 mg; Sod 322 mg.

Nancy Nielsen, Hyrum, Utah

MARSHMALLOW CREAM PEACH PIE

1½ cups graham cracker
  crumbs
⅓ cup confectioners' sugar
½ cup melted butter
18 large marshmallows

¼ cup milk
1 cup whipping cream,
  whipped
3 cups chopped peeled
  peaches

Combine crumbs, confectioners' sugar and butter in bowl; mix well. Press over bottom and side of pie plate. Chill until firm. Combine marshmallows and milk in saucepan. Cook over low heat until marshmallows melt, stirring constantly. Let stand until cool and thickened. Beat until smooth. Fold into whipped cream gently. Fold in peaches gently. Spoon into prepared pie shell. Chill for several hours or until firm. Yield: 6 servings.

Approx Per Serving: Cal 520; T Fat 30 g; 50% Calories from Fat; Prot 5 g; Carbo 63 g; Fiber 2 g; Chol 56 mg; Sod 356 mg.

Boots McMillan, Helena, Montana

RHUBARB ORANGE CREAM PIE

1 recipe 1-crust pie pastry
3 egg whites
1/4 cup sugar
3 egg yolks, beaten
1/4 cup butter, softened
3 tablespoons frozen orange
  juice concentrate, thawed

1 cup sugar
1/4 cup flour
1/4 teaspoon salt
2 1/2 cups 1/2-inch rhubarb
  pieces
1/3 cup chopped pecans

Line 9-inch pie plate with high fluted rim with pastry. Beat egg whites in mixer bowl until stiff peaks form. Add 1/4 cup sugar gradually, beating constantly until very stiff. Beat egg yolks with butter and orange juice concentrate in bowl. Add 1 cup sugar, flour and salt; mix well. Stir in rhubarb. Fold gently into stiffly beaten egg whites. Pour into pastry-lined pie plate. Sprinkle with pecans. Place on bottom rack of 375-degree oven. Bake for 15 minutes. Reduce temperature to 325 degrees. Bake for 45 to 50 minutes longer or until set and golden brown. Yield: 6 servings.

Approx Per Serving: Cal 505; T Fat 25 g; 44% Calories from Fat;
  Prot 7 g; Carbo 66 g; Fiber 3 g; Chol 127 mg; Sod 375 mg.

Irene Crane, Boise, Idaho

STRAWBERRY MERINGUE PIE

3 egg whites
1/2 teaspoon baking powder
1 cup sugar
10 soda crackers, finely
  crushed

1/2 cup chopped pecans
4 cups sliced strawberries
1/2 cup whipping cream,
  whipped
Sugar to taste

Beat egg whites with baking powder in mixer bowl until soft peaks form. Add 1 cup sugar gradually, beating until stiff peaks form. Fold in cracker crumbs and pecans gently. Spread in buttered 9-inch pie plate. Bake at 300 degrees for 30 minutes. Cool completely. Meringue crust will puff up while baking to fill pie plate but sink slightly while cooling to allow room for berries. Spoon strawberries into center. Sweeten whipped cream as desired. Spread whipped cream over berries, covering to edge of meringue crust. Chill for several hours to overnight. Yield: 6 servings.

Approx Per Serving: Cal 322; T Fat 15 g; 40% Calories from Fat;
  Prot 4 g; Carbo 47 g; Fiber 3 g; Chol 29 mg; Sod 127 mg.

Marilyn R. Privrasky, Salt Lake City, Utah

Grubstakes

Cakes

'89 H. CREEKMORE

WESTERN MONTANA COUNCIL

Missoula, Montana

Council member Bill Morrelles has been repairing radios for the Western Montana Radio Reading Service, a nonprofit radio service serving the blind and print-impaired. The special radios are on loan to subscribers at no charge.

For the second year, Council members have assisted to plant and care for flowers at the Missoula Community Medical and Rehabilitation Centers. In addition, council members pay "dues" of $1.00 each month to the Christmas Stocking Club in order to purchase stockings and "stuffers" for the residents of the Flor Haven Personal Care Home in Missoula.

GOLDEN ANGEL CAKE

4 egg yolks
1 tablespoon cold water
1¹/₂ cups sugar
1 teaspoon vanilla extract
¹/₂ cup boiling water

1¹/₂ cups flour, sifted
¹/₂ teaspoon salt
4 egg whites
¹/₂ teaspoon cream of tartar

Beat egg yolks with cold water in large bowl. Add sugar. Beat until smooth. Add vanilla, boiling water, flour and salt; mix well. Combine egg whites and cream of tartar in mixer bowl. Beat until stiff peaks form. Fold into flour mixture. Spoon into ungreased angel food cake pan. Cut through batter 1 inch from center of pan with knife. Bake at 350 degrees for 1 hour. Cool in pan for 10 minutes. Invert on funnel to cool completely. Loosen cake from side of pan. Invert onto serving plate. Yield: 16 servings.

Approx Per Serving: Cal 132; T Fat 2 g; 10% Calories from Fat;
Prot 3 g; Carbo 27 g; Fiber <1 g; Chol 53 mg; Sod 82 mg.

Joyce Harmon, Brigham City, Utah

APPLE CAKE PUDDING

2 cups flour
1 teaspoon salt
2 teaspoons baking soda
2 teaspoons cinnamon
2 teaspoons nutmeg
2 cups sugar
2 eggs, beaten
1 cup oil

6 large apples, grated
1 cup chopped walnuts
1 cup packed brown sugar
1 cup sugar
¹/₂ cup margarine
1 cup evaporated milk
1 tablespoon vanilla extract

Sift flour, salt, baking soda, cinnamon and nutmeg together. Cream 2 cups sugar, eggs and oil in mixer bowl until light and fluffy. Stir in flour mixture. Add apples and walnuts; mix well. Spoon into greased and floured 9x13-inch cake pan. Bake at 350 degrees for 40 minutes. Combine brown sugar, remaining 1 cup sugar, margarine, evaporated milk and vanilla in saucepan. Cook over medium heat until sugar is dissolved, stirring frequently; do not boil. Pour over warm or cold cake. May top with whipped cream or ice cream. Yield: 20 servings.

Approx Per Serving: Cal 439; T Fat 21 g; 42% Calories from Fat;
Prot 4 g; Carbo 62 g; Fiber 2 g; Chol 25 mg; Sod 270 mg.

Sarah H. Jensen, Richfield, Utah

SLICED RAW APPLE CAKE

4 cups thinly sliced apples
1 cup chopped dates
2 cups sugar
1 cup oil
1 teaspoon vanilla extract
3 cups flour

1/2 teaspoon each nutmeg,
cinnamon and salt
2 teaspoons baking soda
2 tablespoons confectioners'
sugar

Mix apples, dates and sugar in bowl. Let stand for 1 hour. Stir in oil and vanilla. Sift next 5 ingredients together. Stir into apple mixture. Spoon into greased and floured bundt pan. Bake at 350 degrees for 1¼ hours. Cool in pan for 10 minutes. Invert onto wire rack. Sprinkle with confectioners' sugar. Yield: 16 servings.

Approx Per Serving: Cal 349; T Fat 14 g; 35% Calories from Fat; Prot 3 g; Carbo 55 g; Fiber 2 g; Chol 0 mg; Sod 171 mg.

Marna C. Buffo, Provo, Utah

BANANA NUT CAKE

3 cups sifted flour
1 tablespoon baking powder
3/4 cup margarine, softened
1½ cups sugar
1 cup mashed bananas
2 teaspoons vanilla extract
1/2 cup chopped walnuts
3 eggs, separated
1½ cups milk

1 teaspoon baking soda
2 teaspoons vinegar
1   4-ounce package vanilla
pudding and pie filling mix
1/2 cup milk
6 to 7 tablespoons shortening
6 tablespoons butter,
softened
2 cups confectioners' sugar

Sift flour and baking powder together 3 times. Combine margarine, sugar, bananas, 1 teaspoon vanilla and walnuts in mixer bowl. Beat until fluffy. Add egg yolks, beating until light. Stir in flour mixture and mixture of 1½ cups milk, baking soda and vinegar. Fold in stiffly beaten egg whites. Spoon into 2 greased and floured 9-inch cake pans. Bake at 375 degrees for 30 minutes. Cool in pans for 10 minutes. Invert onto wire rack. Combine pudding mix and 1/2 cup milk in saucepan. Cook over medium heat until thickened, stirring constantly. Let stand to cool. Add remaining ingredients. Beat until smooth. Frost cooled cake. Yield: 12 servings.

Approx Per Serving: Cal 629; T Fat 31 g; 43% Calories from Fat; Prot 7 g; Carbo 84 g; Fiber 2 g; Chol 74 mg; Sod 430 mg.

Anna Godfrey, Smithfield, Utah

BASIC CAKE

1 cup packed brown sugar
1¾ cups plus 2 tablespoons
  flour
½ teaspoon salt
1 teaspoon baking soda
2 teaspoons cinnamon
½ teaspoon cloves
⅛ teaspoon mace

⅛ teaspoon ginger
⅛ teaspoon allspice
2 eggs
1 cup oil
1 teaspoon maple extract
1 cup chopped pecans
1¼ cups applesauce

Sift first 9 ingredients together into bowl. Stir in eggs, oil and flavoring. Add pecans and applesauce; mix well. Spoon into 2 greased and floured 9-inch cake pans. Bake at 350 degrees for 30 minutes. Cool in pans for 10 minutes. Remove to wire racks to cool completely. May substitute white sugar for brown sugar; may substitute pumpkin for applesauce. May also substitute baby prunes or apricots, mashed bananas or mincemeat for applesauce, omitting mace, ginger and allspice. Yield: 12 servings.

Approx Per Serving: Cal 409; T Fat 26 g; 56% Calories from Fat;
  Prot 4 g; Carbo 42 g; Fiber 2 g; Chol 36 mg; Sod 180 mg.

Lucille Linford, Pocatello, Idaho

CARROT SPICE CAKE

1½ cups grated carrots
1½ cups sugar
1½ cups water
1 cup raisins
¼ cup margarine
1 teaspoon cinnamon
1 teaspoon cloves

1 teaspoon nutmeg
2 cups flour, sifted
2 teaspoons baking soda
¼ teaspoon salt
½ cup chopped walnuts
  (optional)

Combine carrots, sugar, water, raisins, margarine, cinnamon, cloves and nutmeg in saucepan; mix well. Boil for 5 minutes, stirring frequently. Cool to room temperature. Add flour, baking soda, salt and walnuts; mix well. Spoon into greased and floured 9-inch tube pan. Bake at 375 degrees for 50 minutes. Cool in pan for 10 minutes. Invert onto serving plate. May spread with favorite frosting. Yield: 10 servings.

Approx Per Serving: Cal 335; T Fat 9 g; 22% Calories from Fat;
  Prot 4 g; Carbo 63 g; Fiber 2 g; Chol 0 mg; Sod 280 mg.

Rita Winterberger, Huson, Montana

CREAM CHEESE-FROSTED CARROT CAKES

2 cups sugar
1¼ cups oil
4 eggs
2¼ cups flour
2 teaspoons baking soda
2 teaspoons cinnamon
1 teaspoon salt
3 cups grated carrots
1 cup chopped pecans

1 1-pound package
   confectioners' sugar
8 ounces cream cheese,
   softened
½ cup butter, softened
2 teaspoons vanilla extract
½ cup chopped pecans
¼ cup evaporated milk

Cream sugar and oil in mixer bowl until light and fluffy. Beat in eggs. Add flour, baking soda, cinnamon and salt; mix well. Stir in carrots and 1 cup pecans. Spoon into 3 greased and floured 8-inch loaf pans. Bake at 350 degrees for 25 to 40 minutes or until cakes test done. Cool in pans for 10 minutes. Remove to wire rack to cool completely. Combine confectioners' sugar, cream cheese, butter, vanilla, remaining ½ cup pecans and evaporated milk in bowl; mix well. Frost cooled cakes. Yield: 30 servings.

Approx Per Serving: Cal 347; T Fat 20 g; 52% Calories from Fat;
   Prot 3 g; Carbo 41 g; Fiber 1 g; Chol 46 mg; Sod 190 mg.

Donna Farnes, Boise, Idaho

DATE-CARROT CAKE

2 cups sugar
1½ cups oil
4 eggs
2 cups flour
2 teaspoons baking soda
1 teaspoon salt
2 teaspoons cinnamon

1 teaspoon almond extract
1 8-ounce can crushed
   pineapple
3 cups grated carrots
1 cup coconut
1 cup chopped walnuts
1 cup chopped dates

Cream sugar, oil and eggs in mixer bowl until light and fluffy. Add flour, baking soda, salt and cinnamon; mix well. Stir in flavoring, pineapple, carrots, coconut, walnuts and dates. Spoon into greased and floured 11x15-inch cake pan. Bake at 350 degrees for 45 minutes. Spread with favorite cream cheese or buttermilk frosting. Yield: 24 servings.

Approx Per Serving: Cal 316; T Fat 19 g; 52% Calories from Fat;
   Prot 3 g; Carbo 36 g; Fiber 2 g; Chol 36 mg; Sod 176 mg.

Bernice Farner, Meridian, Idaho

CARROT CAKE

2 cups flour
1¹/₂ teaspoons baking soda
¹/₂ teaspoon salt
¹/₂ teaspoon cloves
¹/₂ teaspoon allspice
1 teaspoon cinnamon
1 teaspoon nutmeg

2 cups grated carrots
1¹/₂ cups sugar
¹/₃ cup shortening
1 cup raisins
1¹/₂ cups water
1 teaspoon vanilla extract
¹/₂ cup chopped pecans

Sift flour, baking soda, salt and spices together. Combine carrots, sugar, shortening, raisins and water in saucepan. Boil for 5 minutes, stirring frequently. Cool to room temperature. Stir in flour mixture. Add vanilla and pecans; mix well. Spoon into greased and floured 9x13-inch cake pan. Bake at 350 degrees for 35 to 45 minutes or until cake tests done. Spread with favorite cream cheese frosting. Yield: 16 servings.

Approx Per Serving: Cal 229; T Fat 7 g; 27% Calories from Fat;
   Prot 2 g; Carbo 41 g; Fiber 2 g; Chol 0 mg; Sod 150 mg.

LaRae Bateman, Idaho Falls, Idaho

OLNA'S CHOCOLATE CAKE

2¹/₂ cups cake flour
1 teaspoon baking powder
¹/₂ teaspoon baking soda
¹/₂ teaspoon salt
2 ounces melted
   unsweetened chocolate
1 teaspoon baking soda

¹/₂ cup hot water
2 cups sugar
1 cup shortening
5 eggs
1 cup buttermilk
1 teaspoon vanilla extract
¹/₂ teaspoon red food coloring

Sift cake flour, baking powder, ¹/₂ teaspoon baking soda and salt together. Combine melted chocolate and remaining 1 teaspoon baking soda in large bowl; mix well. Stir in hot water. Cream sugar and shortening in mixer bowl until light and fluffy. Beat in eggs 1 at a time. Add flour mixture and buttermilk alternately to creamed mixture ¹/₃ at a time, beating well after each addition. Stir in chocolate mixture. Add vanilla and food coloring; mix well. Pour into greased and floured 9x13-inch cake pan. Bake at 350 degrees for 30 minutes. Spread with favorite frosting. Yield: 20 servings.

Approx Per Serving: Cal 257; T Fat 13 g; 46% Calories from Fat;
   Prot 3 g; Carbo 32 g; Fiber 1 g; Chol 54 mg; Sod 162 mg.

Olna C. Rantz, Lindon, Utah

CHOCOLATE CAKE IN SAUCE

In this recipe, the sauce goes to the bottom and the cake to the top.
My family always wanted it served with half and half.

2/3 cup shortening
1 3/4 cups sugar
1 1/2 ounces melted
  unsweetened chocolate
1 1/2 teaspoons vanilla extract
1 teaspoon salt
2 1/2 cups flour

1 1/4 cups milk
1 cup chopped pecans
1 cup packed brown sugar
1 cup sugar
1/4 cup baking cocoa
1/4 teaspoon salt
2 3/4 cups boiling water

Cream shortening and 1 3/4 cups sugar in mixer bowl until light and fluffy. Stir in chocolate, vanilla and 1 teaspoon salt. Add flour and milk alternately, mixing well after each addition. Stir in pecans. Spoon into 9x13-inch cake pan. Combine brown sugar, 1 cup sugar, cocoa and 1/4 teaspoon salt in bowl; mix well. Sprinkle over cake batter. Pour boiling water over all. Bake at 350 degrees for 1 hour. Yield: 12 servings.

Approx Per Serving: Cal 546; T Fat 21 g; 34% Calories from Fat;
  Prot 5 g; Carbo 88 g; Fiber 2 g; Chol 3 mg; Sod 243 mg.

Arline Brown, Missoula, Montana

HEAVENLY HASH CAKE

4 eggs
2 cups sugar
1 cup margarine
1 1/2 cups flour
1/4 cup baking cocoa
1/2 teaspoon baking powder
2 teaspoons vanilla extract

1 1/2 cups chopped pecans
1 16-ounce package
  marshmallows
2 cups confectioners' sugar
1/2 cup evaporated milk
1/4 cup melted margarine
1/4 cup baking cocoa

Beat eggs, sugar and 1 cup margarine in bowl. Add flour, 1/4 cup cocoa, baking powder, vanilla and pecans; mix well. Spoon into greased and floured 9x13-inch cake pan. Bake at 325 degrees for 40 minutes. Cover top of cake with marshmallows. Bake for 3 minutes longer. Combine confectioners' sugar, evaporated milk, melted margarine and remaining 1/4 cup cocoa in bowl; mix well. Spread over marshmallows. Yield: 12 servings.

Approx Per Serving: Cal 839; T Fat 48 g; 50% Calories from Fat;
  Prot 7 g; Carbo 102 g; Fiber 2 g; Chol 74 mg; Sod 485 mg.

Linda P. Olsen, Logan, Utah

SOURDOUGH CHOCOLATE CAKE

½ cup thick Sourdough
  Starter (page 92)
1 cup water
1½ cups flour
¼ cup nonfat dry milk
½ cup shortening
1 cup sugar

½ teaspoon salt
1 teaspoon vanilla extract
1 teaspoon cinnamon
1½ teaspoons baking soda
3 ounces melted chocolate
2 eggs

Combine Sourdough Starter, water, flour and dry milk in glass bowl; mix well. Let stand in warm place for 2 to 3 hours or until mixture is bubbly and has a strong sour milk odor. Combine shortening, sugar, salt, vanilla, cinnamon, baking soda and melted chocolate in mixer bowl; beat well. Add eggs 1 at a time, beating well after each addition. Combine with sourdough mixture; beat well. Spoon into greased and floured 9x13-inch cake pan. Bake at 350 degrees for 25 to 30 minutes or until cake tests done. Yield: 20 servings.

Approx Per Serving: Cal 159; T Fat 8 g; 44% Calories from Fat;
  Prot 3 g; Carbo 21 g; Fiber 1 g; Chol 21 mg; Sod 143 mg.

Irene Crane, Boise, Idaho

TURTLE CAKE

1 2-layer package German
  chocolate cake mix
1 14-ounce package caramel
  candies

½ cup evaporated milk
¾ cup butter
2 cups chopped pecans
1 cup chocolate chips

Prepare cake mix using package directions. Pour half the batter into 9x13-inch cake pan. Bake at 350 degrees for 15 minutes. Combine candy, evaporated milk and butter in saucepan. Cook over low heat until candy is melted, stirring frequently. Pour over cake. Sprinkle with pecans and chocolate chips. Top with remaining batter. Bake for 20 minutes longer. Yield: 16 servings.

Approx Per Serving: Cal 477; T Fat 28 g; 51% Calories from Fat;
  Prot 4 g; Carbo 56 g; Fiber 2 g; Chol 27 mg; Sod 335 mg.

Florence L. Chamberlain, Caldwell, Idaho

MOIST COCONUT CAKE

1 2-layer package pudding-
recipe yellow cake mix
1 8-ounce can cream of
coconut

1 14-ounce can sweetened
condensed milk
8 ounces whipped topping
1 cup coconut

Prepare and bake cake mix using package directions for 9x13-inch cake pan. Pierce warm cake with toothpick several times. Spread cream of coconut over cake. Pour condensed milk over all. Chill overnight. Spread with whipped topping. Sprinkle with coconut. Yield: 15 servings.

Approx Per Serving: Cal 312; T Fat 17 g; 47% Calories from Fat;
Prot 4 g; Carbo 38 g; Fiber 1 g; Chol 8 mg; Sod 246 mg.

Imogene Sweeney, Boise, Idaho

LIGHT FRUITCAKE

2 cups sifted flour
3/4 teaspoon baking powder
4 cups pecan halves
2 cups walnut halves
2 cups whole candied
cherries
2 cups chopped candied
pineapple

1 1/2 cups golden raisins
1 cup sifted flour
1 1/2 cups butter, softened
1 1/2 cups sugar
3 eggs
7 teaspoons lemon extract
1/4 cup light corn syrup
1/4 cup candied cherries

Sift 2 cups flour and baking powder together. Combine pecans, walnuts, 2 cups candied cherries, candied pineapple and raisins in large bowl. Toss with remaining 1 cup flour. Cream butter and sugar in mixer bowl until light and fluffy. Beat in eggs 1 at a time. Stir in lemon extract. Beat in baking powder mixture 1/3 at a time to creamed mixture. Stir into fruit mixture, coating fruit and nuts well. Spoon into well greased 10-inch tube pan. Cover tightly with aluminum foil. Place pan of hot water on bottom rack of oven. Place cake on shelf above water. Bake at 300 degrees for 2 1/2 hours. Remove foil. Bake for 3 to 5 minutes longer or until top is slightly dry. Cool thoroughly in pan. Invert onto serving plate. Brush with corn syrup. Garnish with remaining 1/4 cup candied cherries. Store in tightly covered container. Yield: 15 servings.

Approx Per Serving: Cal 831; T Fat 50 g; 52% Calories from Fat;
Prot 9 g; Carbo 95 g; Fiber 4 g; Chol 43 mg; Sod 251 mg.

Shirley Allen, Boise, Idaho

MEXICAN FRUITCAKE

1 20-ounce can crushed
   pineapple
2 cups flour
2 cups sugar
2 teaspoons baking soda
2 eggs, beaten

1 cup chopped walnuts
4 ounces cream cheese,
   softened
1/4 cup margarine, softened
2 cups confectioners' sugar
1 teaspoon vanilla extract

Combine pineapple with juice, flour, sugar, baking soda, eggs and walnuts in bowl; mix well. Spoon into lightly greased 9x13-inch cake pan. Bake at 350 degrees for 40 minutes. Combine cream cheese, margarine, confectioners' sugar and vanilla in bowl; mix well. Spread over warm cake. Yield: 12 servings.

Approx Per Serving: Cal 491; T Fat 19 g; 34% Calories from Fat;
   Prot 5 g; Carbo 79 g; Fiber 2 g; Chol 46 mg; Sod 268 mg.

Jackie Seamons, Paradise, Utah

HEAVENLY CAKE

1 2-layer package lemon
   cake mix
4 eggs
1/2 cup oil
1 11-ounce can mandarin
   oranges

1 6-ounce package vanilla
   instant pudding mix
1 8-ounce can crushed
   pineapple
8 ounces whipped topping

Combine cake mix, eggs, oil and oranges with juice in bowl; mix well. Spoon into greased and floured 9x13-inch cake pan. Bake at 350 degrees for 30 minutes or until cake tests done. Combine pudding mix, pineapple with juice and whipped topping in bowl; mix well. Spread over cooled cake. Yield: 12 servings.

Approx Per Serving: Cal 447; T Fat 19 g; 38% Calories from Fat;
   Prot 4 g; Carbo 66 g; Fiber 1 g; Chol 71 mg; Sod 387 mg.

Dena E. Hale, New Plymouth, Idaho

*Because things go wrong is no reason
you must go with them.*

OATMEAL CAKE

1½ cups boiling water
1 cup quick-cooking oats
1½ cups flour
1 teaspoon baking soda
1 teaspoon cinnamon
½ teaspoon salt
½ cup butter, softened
1 cup sugar
1 cup packed brown sugar
2 eggs
½ cup butter
1 cup packed brown sugar
¼ cup evaporated milk
1 cup coconut
1 cup chopped pecans

Mix water and oats in bowl; set aside. Sift flour, baking soda, cinnamon and salt together. Cream next 4 ingredients in mixer bowl until light and fluffy. Add flour mixture and oatmeal; mix well. Spoon into greased and floured 9x13-inch cake pan. Bake at 350 degrees for 35 minutes. Bring ½ cup butter, 1 cup brown sugar and evaporated milk to a boil in saucepan. Boil for 1 minute, stirring frequently. Stir in coconut and pecans. Spread over cake. Broil until coconut is browned and frosting is bubbly. Yield: 12 servings.

Approx Per Serving: Cal 579; T Fat 27 g; 40% Calories from Fat;
Prot 5 g; Carbo 83 g; Fiber 3 g; Chol 79 mg; Sod 345 mg.

Sandy Kiser, Twin Falls, Idaho

ORANGE PUDDING CAKE

½ cup shortening
1½ cups sugar
3 eggs
1 cup buttermilk
1 teaspoon vanilla extract
2¼ cups flour
1½ teaspoons baking soda
1 teaspoon salt
1 cup water
1   12-ounce can frozen
    orange juice concentrate
¼ cup butter
1½ cups sugar

Combine first 8 ingredients in bowl; mix well. Spoon into greased 9x13-inch cake pan. Bring water to a boil in saucepan. Remove from heat. Stir in concentrate, remaining ¼ cup butter and 1½ cups sugar. Pour over cake batter. Bake at 350 degrees for 25 minutes. Cut into squares and invert onto serving plates. Yield: 12 servings.

Approx Per Serving: Cal 460; T Fat 14 g; 27% Calories from Fat;
Prot 5 g; Carbo 80 g; Fiber 1 g; Chol 64 mg; Sod 354 mg.

Deloris Marking, Billings, Montana

PISTACHIO CAKE

1 2-layer package yellow
  cake mix
1 cup oil
3 eggs
1 4-ounce package pistachio
  instant pudding mix

1 cup club soda
1 4-ounce package pistachio
  instant pudding mix
1 cup milk
8 ounces whipped topping

Combine cake mix, oil, eggs, 1 package pudding mix and club soda in bowl; mix well. Spoon into greased and floured 9x13-inch cake pan. Bake at 350 degrees for 35 minutes. Dissolve remaining 1 package pudding mix in milk. Stir in whipped topping. Spread over cooled cake. Yield: 12 servings.

Approx Per Serving: Cal 488 ; T Fat 29 g; 52% Calories from Fat; Prot 4 g; Carbo 55 g; Fiber <1 g; Chol 56 mg; Sod 391 mg.

Peggy Shepherd, Helena, Montana

PISTACHIO POPPY SEED CAKE

1 2-layer package yellow
  cake mix
1/2 cup warm water
1/2 cup milk
5 eggs

2 4-ounce packages
  pistachio instant pudding
  mix
2 tablespoons flour
1/2 cup poppy seed

Combine cake mix, warm water, milk, eggs, pudding mix, flour and poppy seed in bowl; mix well. Spoon into greased and floured bundt pan. Bake at 375 degrees for 40 to 45 minutes or until cake tests done. Cool in pan for 10 minutes. Invert onto serving plate. Yield: 15 servings.

Approx Per Serving: Cal 237; T Fat 5 g; 19% Calories from Fat; Prot 4 g; Carbo 44 g; Fiber <1 g; Chol 72 mg; Sod 337 mg.

Laurel A. Wadley, Sandy, Utah

*Life was a lot simpler when what we honored was
Father and Mother rather than all major credit cards.*

POUND CAKE

3 cups sugar
1 cup butter, softened
1 teaspoon vanilla extract
1 teaspoon lemon extract

1 teaspoon almond extract
1 cup whipping cream
6 eggs
3 cups sifted flour

Cream sugar and butter in mixer bowl until light and fluffy. Stir in flavorings. Add whipping cream, eggs and flour alternately, beating well after each addition. Spoon into greased and floured 10-inch tube pan. Bake at 350 degrees for 1½ hours. Cool in pan on wire rack for 15 minutes. Invert onto wire rack to cool completely. Yield: 16 servings.

Approx Per Serving: Cal 405; T Fat 19 g; 42% Calories from Fat;
Prot 5 g; Carbo 54 g; Fiber 1 g; Chol 131 mg; Sod 130 mg.

Bertha Bateman, Logan, Utah

PUMPKIN CAKE ROLL

¾ cup flour
1 teaspoon baking powder
2 teaspoons cinnamon
1 teaspoon ginger
½ teaspoon nutmeg
½ teaspoon salt
3 eggs
1 cup sugar

⅔ cup pumpkin
1 teaspoon lemon juice
1 cup finely chopped walnuts
1¼ cups confectioners' sugar
6 ounces cream cheese,
   softened
¼ cup butter, softened
½ teaspoon vanilla extract

Sift first 6 ingredients together. Beat eggs at high speed in mixer bowl for 5 minutes. Beat in sugar gradually. Stir in pumpkin and lemon juice. Add flour mixture; mix well. Spread in greased and floured 10x15-inch cake pan. Sprinkle with walnuts. Bake at 375 degrees for 15 minutes. Turn onto towel sprinkled with ¼ cup confectioners' sugar. Roll up in towel as for jelly roll. Cool. Unroll. Combine remaining 1 cup confectioners' sugar, cream cheese, butter and vanilla in bowl; mix well. Spread over cake. Re-roll. Chill until serving time. Yield: 8 servings.

Approx Per Serving: Cal 452; T Fat 25 g; 49% Calories from Fat;
Prot 6 g; Carbo 53 g; Fiber 1 g; Chol 119 mg; Sod 313 mg.

Hope Reiste, Great Falls, Montana

PUMPKIN CAKE

1 2-layer package yellow
  cake mix
1 4-ounce package vanilla
  pudding and pie filling
  mix
2 cups pumpkin
3/4 cup water
2 eggs

1 teaspoon cinnamon
1/4 teaspoon baking soda
1/2 teaspoon nutmeg
1/8 teaspoon ginger
1/8 teaspoon cloves
1 cup whipped cream
8 ounces whipped topping
1/2 cup packed brown sugar

Combine first 10 ingredients in bowl; mix well. Spread in greased and floured 9x13-inch cake pan. Bake at 350 degrees for 30 minutes. Combine whipped cream, whipped topping and brown sugar in bowl; mix well. Spread over cooled cake. Yield: 12 servings.

Approx Per Serving: Cal 382; T Fat 13 g; 30% Calories from Fat;
   Prot 4 g; Carbo 64 g; Fiber 1 g; Chol 49 mg; Sod 354 mg.

RaNee Taggart, Smithfield, Utah

ROYAL RASPBERRY CAKE

2 cups flour
1/2 teaspoon salt
1 tablespoon baking powder
1/3 cup butter, softened
1 cup sugar
1 egg, at room temperature
1 cup milk, at room
  temperature

1 teaspoon vanilla extract
3 1/2 cups raspberries
1 1/2 cups confectioners' sugar
2 tablespoons whipping
  cream
1 teaspoon vanilla extract

Sift flour, salt and baking powder together. Cream butter and sugar in mixer bowl until light and fluffy. Add egg; beat for 1 minute. Add flour mixture and mixture of milk and 1 teaspoon vanilla alternately to creamed mixture. Spread in greased and floured 9x13-inch cake pan. Top with raspberries. Bake at 350 degrees for 30 to 35 minutes or until cake springs back when lightly touched. Cool for 5 minutes. Combine confectioners' sugar, cream and remaining 1 teaspoon vanilla in bowl; mix well. Spread over cake. May serve warm with ice cream. Yield: 15 servings.

Approx Per Serving: Cal 232; T Fat 6 g; 23% Calories from Fat;
   Prot 3 g; Carbo 42 g; Fiber 2 g; Chol 30 mg; Sod 184 mg.

Emil and Doris Nygard, Great Falls, Montana

RHUBARB CAKE

2 cups flour
1/4 teaspoon salt
1 1/2 cups packed brown sugar
1/2 cup margarine, softened
1 egg
1 teaspoon vanilla extract

1 cup buttermilk
2 cups sliced rhubarb
1/2 cup sugar
1 teaspoon cinnamon
1 tablespoon margarine
1 cup chopped pecans

Sift flour and salt together. Cream brown sugar and 1/2 cup margarine in mixer bowl until light and fluffy. Add egg and vanilla; beat well. Add flour mixture and buttermilk alternately to creamed mixture, beating well after each addition. Fold in rhubarb. Spoon into greased 9x13-inch cake pan. Combine sugar, cinnamon, remaining 1 tablespoon margarine and pecans in bowl; mix well. Sprinkle over batter. Bake at 350 degrees for 35 to 45 minutes or until cake tests done. Yield: 15 servings.

Approx Per Serving: Cal 298; T Fat 13 g; 38% Calories from Fat;
Prot 4 g; Carbo 44 g; Fiber 1 g; Chol 15 mg; Sod 148 mg.

Colleen Rogan, Helena, Montana

RHUBARB PUDDING CAKE

5 to 6 cups rhubarb, cut into
small pieces
1 1/2 cups sugar
1 3-ounce package
raspberry gelatin

2 cups miniature
marshmallows
1 2-layer package yellow
cake mix

Place rhubarb in 9x13-inch cake pan. Sprinkle with sugar and gelatin. Top with marshmallows. Prepare cake mix using package directions. Pour batter over marshmallows. Bake at 350 degrees for 1 hour. Serve warm or cold with vanilla ice cream or whipped topping. Yield: 15 servings.

Approx Per Serving: Cal 279; T Fat 3 g; 9% Calories from Fat;
Prot 3 g; Carbo 62 g; Fiber 1 g; Chol 0 mg; Sod 237 mg.

Hulda Larsen, Logan, Utah

*Some people think they're generous because they
give away free advice.*

RUM CAKE

1 cup chopped pecans
1 2-layer package yellow
cake mix
1 4-ounce package vanilla
instant pudding mix
4 eggs
1/2 cup cold water

1/2 cup oil
1/2 cup 80 proof dark rum
1/2 cup butter
1/4 cup water
1 cup sugar
1/2 cup 80 proof dark rum

Grease and flour 10-inch tube pan. Sprinkle with pecans. Combine cake mix, pudding mix, eggs, cold water, oil and 1/2 cup rum in bowl; mix well. Spoon into prepared pan. Bake at 325 degrees for 1 hour. Cool in pan for 10 minutes. Invert onto serving plate. Prick top of cake. Melt butter in saucepan. Add water and sugar. Boil for 5 minutes, stirring constantly. Remove from heat. Stir in remaining 1/2 cup rum. Spoon and brush 1/3 of the glaze over top and side of cake. Let stand for several minutes. Repeat applications of glaze. Yield: 16 servings.

Approx Per Serving: Cal 426; T Fat 22 g; 49% Calories from Fat;
Prot 4 g; Carbo 48 g; Fiber 1 g; Chol 69 mg; Sod 312 mg.

Ann Morrell, Sandy, Utah

WAFER CAKE

1 cup sugar
1/2 cup shortening
2 eggs
1 16-ounce package vanilla
wafers, crushed
1/2 teaspoon baking powder
1/3 cup milk

1 7-ounce can coconut
1 cup chopped pecans
1/2 cup margarine
1 cup packed brown sugar
1/4 cup milk
1 cup confectioners' sugar

Cream sugar and shortening in mixer bowl until light and fluffy. Add eggs; beat well. Add mixture of wafer crumbs, baking powder and 1/3 cup milk; mix well. Stir in coconut and pecans. Spoon into greased 9x13-inch cake pan. Bake at 350 degrees for 50 minutes or until cake tests done. Melt margarine in saucepan. Stir in brown sugar. Bring to a boil; reduce heat. Stir in remaining 1/4 cup milk and confectioners' sugar until of spreading consistency. Spread over cooled cake. Yield: 15 servings.

Approx Per Serving: Cal 583; T Fat 28 g; 42% Calories from Fat;
Prot 4 g; Carbo 83 g; Fiber 2 g; Chol 49 mg; Sod 243 mg.

Kitty D. Lightfoot, Boise, Idaho

PINEAPPLE-ZUCCHINI CAKE

3 eggs
2 cups sugar
2 teaspoons vanilla extract
1 cup oil
2 cups grated peeled zucchini
3 cups flour
1 teaspoon baking powder

1 teaspoon baking soda
1 teaspoon salt
1 cup drained crushed
  pineapple
1/2 cup raisins
1 cup chopped pecans

Combine eggs, sugar, vanilla and oil in mixer bowl; beat until light and fluffy. Add zucchini, flour, baking powder, baking soda and salt; beat well. Stir in pineapple, raisins and pecans. Spoon into greased and floured 9x13-inch cake pan. Bake at 325 degrees for 1 hour. Yield: 20 servings.

Approx Per Serving: Cal 314; T Fat 16 g; 45% Calories from Fat;
  Prot 4 g; Carbo 41 g; Fiber 1 g; Chol 32 mg; Sod 176 mg.

Jean Edwards, Clancy, Montana

BLACK BOTTOM CUPCAKES

1 egg
1/8 teaspoon salt
8 ounces cream cheese,
  softened
1/3 cup sugar
2 cups chocolate chips
1 1/2 cups flour
1 cup sugar

1/4 cup baking cocoa
1 teaspoon salt
1 teaspoon baking soda
1 cup water
1 tablespoon vinegar
1/3 cup oil
1 teaspoon vanilla extract

Combine egg, 1/8 teaspoon salt, cream cheese and 1/3 cup sugar in small bowl; mix well. Stir in chocolate chips. Set aside. Combine flour, remaining 1 cup sugar, cocoa, salt and baking soda in large bowl; mix well. Add water, vinegar, oil and vanilla; beat until smooth. Spoon into 24 paper-lined muffin cups, filling 1/3 full. Top each with spoonful of cream cheese mixture. Bake at 350 degrees for 20 to 25 minutes or until cupcakes test done. Yield: 24 servings.

Approx Per Serving: Cal 208; T Fat 12 g; 49% Calories from Fat;
  Prot 3 g; Carbo 26 g; Fiber 1 g; Chol 19 mg; Sod 168 mg.

Evelyn Cameron, Blackfoot, Idaho

Golden Nuggets

Cookies

'89 H. CREEKMORE

YELLOWSTONE VALLEY COUNCIL

Billings, Montana

The Council's largest yearly project is the Special Children's Christmas Party. Over 100 volunteers have been involved each year for about 10 years in this heart-warming holiday event. Funds are raised by a fruitcake fund raiser and by the raffle of gifts donated by U S West Communications and AT&T. The School District provides a list of the physically challenged youth in the district, as well as their ages and what they want from Santa. Everyone helps put on the party, provide presents and make refreshments. Special thanks go to United Properties in Billings, which handles the management of the First Interstate Bank where the party is held. They stop elevators for children, hold doors open and clean up afterwards. Cafe Express in the lower level provides dishes, silverware, punch and coffee.

The Council has many other projects including selling lilac seedlings, collecting canned goods for local food banks and bedding and coats for the homeless. New projects at the nursing home include Bingo, aerobic workouts and nationality months featuring videos of cultures and food of different nationalities.

APPLESAUCE COOKIES

½ cup shortening
1 cup sugar
2 eggs
1 cup unsweetened
  applesauce
½ teaspoon cinnamon
½ teaspoon cloves

½ teaspoon nutmeg
2 cups flour
1 teaspoon baking soda
½ teaspoon salt
1½ cups quick-cooking oats
1 cup raisins
1 cup chocolate chips

Cream shortening and sugar in mixer bowl until light and fluffy. Beat in eggs. Add applesauce, cinnamon, cloves and nutmeg; mix well. Add flour, baking soda and salt; mix well. Stir in oats, raisins and chocolate chips. Drop by teaspoonfuls 2 inches apart onto nonstick cookie sheet. Bake at 400 degrees for 6 to 8 minutes or until brown. Cool on wire rack. Yield: 36 servings.

Approx Per Serving: Cal 130; T Fat 5 g; 34% Calories from Fat;
  Prot 2 g; Carbo 20 g; Fiber 1 g; Chol 12 mg; Sod 58 mg.

Darla Wheeler, Brigham City, Utah

BUTTERSCOTCH CHEESECAKE BARS

8 ounces cream cheese,
  softened
1 14-ounce can sweetened
  condensed milk
1 teaspoon vanilla extract
1 egg

2 cups butterscotch chips
½ cup butter
2 cups graham cracker
  crumbs
1 cup chopped walnuts

Beat cream cheese in mixer bowl until fluffy. Add condensed milk, vanilla and egg; mix well. Melt butterscotch chips and butter in saucepan. Stir in graham cracker crumbs and walnuts. Pat half the mixture into bottom of greased 9x13-inch baking dish. Spread cream cheese mixture evenly over crumb layer. Top with remaining crumb mixture. Bake at 350 degrees for 25 to 30 minutes or until toothpick inserted near center comes out clean. Let stand until completely cooled. Cut into bars. May substitute margarine for butter. Yield: 24 servings.

Approx Per Serving: Cal 270; T Fat 18 g; 57% Calories from Fat;
  Prot 4 g; Carbo 26 g; Fiber 1 g; Chol 35 mg; Sod 148 mg.

Dorris Calton, Ogden, Utah

CHERRY CHEW BARS

1½ cups margarine, softened
3 cups sugar
6 eggs
2¾ cups flour
2 teaspoons vanilla extract
1 teaspoon almond extract

1 8-ounce jar maraschino
  cherries, drained, chopped
1 cup coconut
1 cup chopped walnuts
¼ cup confectioners' sugar

Cream margarine and sugar in mixer bowl until light and fluffy. Beat in eggs. Stir in flour and flavorings. Fold in cherries, coconut and walnuts. Spread in greased 9x13-inch baking pan. Bake at 350 degrees for 25 to 30 minutes or until lightly browned. Let stand until slightly cooled. Cut into bars. Sprinkle with confectioners' sugar. May substitute pecans for walnuts if desired. Yield: 30 servings.

Approx Per Serving: Cal 267; T Fat 14 g; 45% Calories from Fat;
  Prot 3 g; Carbo 34 g; Fiber 1 g; Chol 43 mg; Sod 123 mg.

Hazel M. Johnson, Murray, Utah

BLONDE BROWNIES

1 cup butter, softened
2 cups packed brown sugar
2 eggs, beaten
2 cups flour
2 teaspoons baking powder

1 teaspoon baking soda
1 teaspoon salt
½ cup chopped pecans
1 cup chocolate chips

Cream butter and brown sugar in mixer bowl until light and fluffy. Add eggs; mix well. Add flour, baking powder, baking soda and salt; mix well. Stir in pecans and chocolate chips. May add a small amount of milk if necessary. Spread evenly in greased 9x13-inch baking pan. Bake at 350 degrees for 20 minutes or until edges pull from sides of pan. Let stand until cool. Cut into squares. Yield: 24 servings.

Approx Per Serving: Cal 250; T Fat 13 g; 43% Calories from Fat;
  Prot 2 g; Carbo 35 g; Fiber 1 g; Chol 39 mg; Sod 232 mg.

Dorothy Peterson, Logan, Utah

ZUCCHINI BROWNIES

2 cups flour
1½ teaspoons baking soda
1 teaspoon salt
¼ cup baking cocoa
1¼ cups sugar

2 cups grated zucchini
½ cup oil
2 teaspoons vanilla extract
½ cup chopped pecans

Sift flour, baking soda, salt, baking cocoa and sugar together. Combine zucchini and oil in mixer bowl. Add sifted dry ingredients; mix well. Stir in vanilla and pecans. Spread batter in greased and floured 10x15-inch baking pan. Bake at 350 degrees for 18 to 20 minutes or until edges pull from sides of pan. Let stand until cool. Cut into bars. Yield: 25 servings.

Approx Per Serving: Cal 134; T Fat 6 g; 41% Calories from Fat; Prot 2 g; Carbo 19 g; Fiber 1 g; Chol 0 mg; Sod 135 mg.

EvaLue Bowen, Hyrum, Utah

CHOCOLATE MERINGUES

2 egg whites
⅛ teaspoon salt
⅛ teaspoon cream of tartar

¾ cup sugar
1 cup chocolate chips
1 teaspoon vanilla extract

Beat egg whites in mixer bowl until foamy. Add salt and cream of tartar. Beat until soft peaks form. Add sugar gradually, beating until stiff peaks form. Fold in chocolate chips and vanilla gently. Drop by small spoonfuls onto greased cookie sheet. Bake at 300 degrees for 25 to 30 minutes. Yield: 30 servings.

Approx Per Serving: Cal 50; T Fat 2 g; 34% Calories from Fat; Prot <1 g; Carbo 8 g; Fiber <1 g; Chol 0 mg; Sod 13 mg.

Luella Merriman, Great Falls, Montana

It is better to pay the baker than the doctor.
French Proverb

CHOCOLATE CHIP COOKIES

½ cup margarine, softened
1 cup packed brown sugar
½ cup sugar
1 teaspoon vanilla extract
2 eggs
¼ cup applesauce

3 cups flour
1 teaspoon salt
1 teaspoon baking soda
1 cup chocolate chips
1 cup chopped pecans

Cream margarine, brown sugar, sugar and vanilla in mixer bowl until light and fluffy. Add eggs and applesauce; mix well. Add flour, salt and baking soda; mix well. Stir in chocolate chips and pecans. Drop by teaspoonfuls 2 inches apart onto nonstick cookie sheet. Bake at 350 degrees for 15 minutes or until golden brown. Cook on wire rack. Yield: 42 servings.

Approx Per Serving: Cal 125; T Fat 6 g; 41% Calories from Fat; Prot 2 g; Carbo 17 g; Fiber 1 g; Chol 10 mg; Sod 102 mg.

Ione Raymond, Logan, Utah

CHOCO-CHIP OATMEAL COOKIES

1¼ cups margarine, softened
½ cup sugar
¾ cup packed brown sugar
1 egg
1 teaspoon vanilla extract
1½ cups flour

1 teaspoon baking soda
1 teaspoon salt
3 cups oats
2 cups chocolate chips
¾ cup pecans

Cream margarine, sugar and brown sugar in mixer bowl until light and fluffy. Beat in egg and vanilla. Add mixture of flour, baking soda and salt; mix well. Stir in oats, chocolate chips and pecans. Drop by teaspoonfuls onto nonstick cookie sheet. Bake at 375 degrees for 9 to 11 minutes or until golden brown. Cool on wire rack. Yield: 72 servings.

Approx Per Serving: Cal 101; T Fat 6 g; 51% Calories from Fat; Prot 1 g; Carbo 12 g; Fiber 1 g; Chol 3 mg; Sod 81 mg.

Jean Edwards, Clancy, Montana

CARAMEL CRACKERS

40 saltine crackers
1/2 cup butter
1 cup packed brown sugar

1 cup chocolate chips
1/2 cup chopped pecans

Arrange crackers in 10x15-inch baking pan. Melt butter in saucepan. Stir in brown sugar. Bring to a boil, stirring constantly. Pour over crackers. Bake at 350 degrees for 5 to 10 minutes or until crackers rise to top. Sprinkle with chocolate chips. Bake for 1 minute longer. Spread melted chocolate over top. Sprinkle with pecans. Cut around outline of crackers to serve. May substitute margarine for butter. Yield: 40 servings.

Approx Per Serving: Cal 90; T Fat 5 g; 49% Calories from Fat;
Prot <1 g; Carbo 12 g; Fiber <1 g; Chol 7 mg; Sod 62 mg.

Marguerite C. Harper, Great Falls, Montana

FRUITCAKE COOKIES

1/2 cup margarine, softened
1 1/2 cups packed brown sugar
4 eggs
3 cups sifted flour
1 tablespoon baking soda
1 teaspoon salt
1 teaspoon cloves
1 teaspoon nutmeg
1 pound dark raisins

1 pound glazed cherries,
    finely chopped
1 pound candied pineapple,
    finely chopped
1 pound walnuts, chopped
1 pound pecans, chopped
3 tablespoons milk
1/4 cup whiskey

Cream margarine, brown sugar and eggs in mixer bowl. Add flour, baking soda, salt, cloves and nutmeg; mix well. Stir in raisins, cherries, pineapple, walnuts and pecans. Add milk and whiskey; mix well. Drop by spoonfuls onto greased cookie sheet. Bake at 325 degrees for 15 minutes. Cool on wire rack. Yield: 60 servings.

Approx Per Serving: Cal 237; T Fat 12 g; 43% Calories from Fat;
Prot 3 g; Carbo 32 g; Fiber 2 g; Chol 14 mg; Sod 104 mg.

Virginia Lee, Logan, Utah

LEMON SQUARES

1 cup butter, softened
1/4 teaspoon salt
1/2 cup sugar
2 cups flour
2 cups sugar

1/4 cup flour
1/2 teaspoon baking powder
4 eggs, beaten
1/2 cup lemon juice
1/4 cup confectioners' sugar

Combine butter, salt, 1/2 cup sugar and 2 cups flour in bowl; mix well. Pat into greased 9x13-inch baking pan. Bake at 350 degrees for 15 minutes. Combine 2 cups sugar, 1/4 cup flour and baking powder in mixer bowl. Add eggs and lemon juice; mix well. Pour over baked layer. Bake at 350 degrees for 25 minutes or until set. Edges will brown before center is set. Let stand until cool. Sprinkle with confectioners' sugar. Cut into squares. Yield: 36 servings.

Approx Per Serving: Cal 140; T Fat 6 g; 37% Calories from Fat; Prot 2 g; Carbo 21 g; Fiber <1 g; Chol 38 mg; Sod 71 mg.

Barbara Hayes, Ogden, Utah

PEANUT BUTTER COOKIES

1 2-layer package yellow
   cake mix
1 cup peanut butter

1/2 cup vegetable oil
2 tablespoons water
2 eggs

Combine cake mix, peanut butter, oil, water and eggs in bowl; mix well. Drop by teaspoonfuls 2 inches apart onto ungreased cookie sheet. Dip fork in water; press crisscross on each cookie. Bake at 350 degrees for 10 to 12 minutes. Cool on cookie sheet for 1 minute. Remove to wire rack to cool completely. This recipe is easy for children to make. Yield: 24 servings.

Approx Per Serving: Cal 202; T Fat 12 g; 53% Calories from Fat; Prot 4 g; Carbo 20 g; Fiber 1 g; Chol 18 mg; Sod 180 mg.

Deloris Marking, Billings, Montana

*The best angle from which to approach any
problem is the try-angle.*

PUMPKIN BARS

2 cups sugar
1/2 cup vegetable oil
1 16-ounce can pumpkin
4 eggs, beaten
2 cups baking mix
2 teaspoons cinnamon
1/2 cup raisins

1/3 cup margarine, softened
3 ounces cream cheese,
  softened
1 tablespoon milk
1 teaspoon vanilla extract
2 cups confectioners' sugar

Combine sugar, oil, pumpkin and eggs in large mixer bowl. Beat at medium speed for 1 minute, scraping bowl occasionally. Stir in baking mix, cinnamon and raisins. Pour into greased 10x15-inch baking pan. Bake in preheated 350-degree oven for 25 to 30 minutes or until wooden pick inserted in center comes out clean. Let stand until cool. Cream margarine and cream cheese in mixer bowl. Add milk and vanilla; mix well. Add confectioners' sugar; beat until smooth. Spread frosting over pumpkin layer. Cut into 1x3-inch bars. Store in refrigerator. Yield: 50 servings.

Approx Per Serving: Cal 122; T Fat 5 g; 37% Calories from Fat;
    Prot 1 g; Carbo 18 g; Fiber <1 g; Chol 19 mg; Sod 89 mg.

Terri Rogers, Great Falls, Montana

PINEAPPLE-RAISIN COOKIES

1 cup packed brown sugar
1/2 cup margarine, softened
1 egg
1 teaspoon vanilla extract
3/4 cup drained crushed
  pineapple

1/2 cup raisins
2 cups flour
1 teaspoon baking powder
1/2 teaspoon baking soda
1/2 teaspoon salt
1/2 cup chopped walnuts

Beat brown sugar, margarine, egg and vanilla in mixer bowl until fluffy. Add pineapple and raisins; mix well. Add flour, baking powder, baking soda and salt; mix well. Stir in walnuts. Drop by spoonfuls 2 inches apart on nonstick cookie sheet. Bake at 375 degrees for 12 to 15 minutes or until lightly browned. Cool on wire rack. Yield: 48 servings.

Approx Per Serving: Cal 70; T Fat 3 g; 36% Calories from Fat;
    Prot 1 g; Carbo 11 g; Fiber <1 g; Chol 4 mg; Sod 64 mg.

Norma Harrison, St. George, Utah

RAISIN-CREAM CHEESE COOKIES

1/4 cup butter, softened
8 ounces cream cheese,
  softened
1 egg yolk
1 teaspoon vanilla extract

1 2-layer package yellow
  cake mix
1 1/4 cups raisins
1/4 cup shredded coconut
1/4 cup chopped walnuts

Cream butter, cream cheese, egg yolk and vanilla in mixer bowl. Blend in cake mix 1/3 at a time, mixing the last portion by hand. Stir in raisins, coconut and walnuts. Drop by level tablespoonfuls 2 inches apart onto greased cookie sheet. Bake at 350 degrees for 15 minutes or until lightly browned. Cool on wire rack. May substitute margarine for butter and white cake mix for yellow cake mix. Yield: 48 servings.

Approx Per Serving: Cal 92; T Fat 4 g; 40% Calories from Fat; Prot 1 g; Carbo 13 g; Fiber <1 g; Chol 12 mg; Sod 90 mg.

Ruth Baird, Billings, Montana

OLD-FASHIONED SOFT SUGAR COOKIES

1/2 cup margarine, softened
1 cup sugar
1 egg
1 1/2 teaspoons vanilla extract

1/2 cup sour cream
3 1/4 cups sifted flour
1 teaspoon baking soda
1/2 teaspoon salt

Beat margarine, sugar, egg and vanilla in mixer bowl until light and fluffy. Add sour cream; mix well. Sift flour, baking soda and salt together. Add to sugar mixture gradually, beating well after each addition. Roll 1/4 inch thick on lightly floured surface. Cut with floured cookie cutter. Place on greased cookie sheet. Bake at 350 degrees for 8 minutes. Do not overbake. Cool on wire rack. May frost and decorate as desired. May substitute butter for margarine if desired. Yield: 48 servings.

Approx Per Serving: Cal 69; T Fat 3 g; 34% Calories from Fat; Prot 1 g; Carbo 10 g; Fiber <1 g; Chol 6 mg; Sod 65 mg.

Bernice Farner, Meridian, Idaho

INDEX

Turkey Enchiladas, 77

This Cookbook Is A Perfect Gift For Holidays, Weddings, Anniversaries and Birthdays.

You may order as many of our Cookbooks as you wish for the price of $10.00 each, plus $2.00 postage and handling per cookbook ordered.

CUSTOMER INFORMATION: (Please Print)

Name_____

Address_____

City/State/Zip _____

Phone ___(_____)_____

Please send _____ copies of *Reflections of the West—a Cookbook*

@ $10.00 each copy plus $2.00 shipping and handling (per copy)

TOTAL AMOUNT ($12.00 x #books) = $ _____

Enclosed is my check for $ _____

(Payable to Skyline Chapter)

Mail Order Form To:
Telephone Pioneers
Skyline Chapter
560 North Park Avenue, Room 100
Helena, Montana 59601

(Please Print All Information)

SHIP TO: (Person receiving shipment)

Name_____

Address_____

City/State/Zip _____

Phone ___(_____)_____

Gift Card From _____

SHIP TO: (Person receiving shipment)

Name_____

Address_____

City/State/Zip _____

Phone ___(_____)_____

Gift Card From _____